GOING TO GUIDES

HEY KIDS COLOR ME IN!

GOING TO WALT DISNEY WORLD

A GUIDE FOR KIDS & KIDS AT ♥

by Shannon W. Laskey

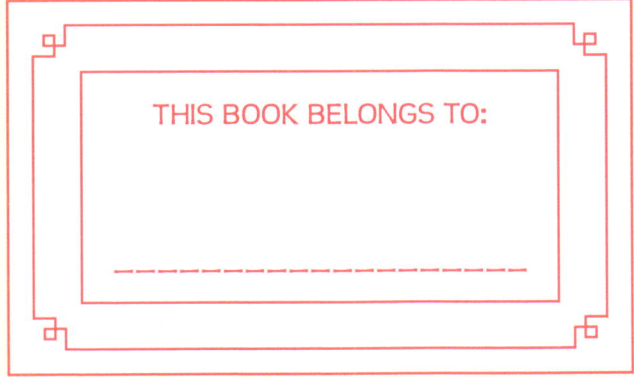

THIS BOOK BELONGS TO:

_____

Orchard Hill Press

This book is dedicated to the memory of brothers Walt & Roy Disney!

GOING TO GUIDES

A NOTE FROM THE AUTHOR

Back when I lived in Los Angeles, an airline messed up my flight and, to make it up to me, they gave me a free round-trip ticket to anywhere they flew to in the United States. Can you guess what I said to that? "I'M GOING TO WALT DISNEY WORLD!" It was my first time to ever go there and, of course, it was fabulous!

Fast-forward many years to the launch of my Going To Guides series in 2015 with the first edition of "Going To Disneyland" and later "Going To Disney California Adventure." The number one question people asked me was, "Are you going to create a book for Florida?" My answer was "YES!!!" and "Going To Magic Kingdom" became the third book in the series.

In 2024 I made a BIG decision to upgrade that Florida book to cover not just Magic Kingdom but the other three theme parks too—and "Going To Walt Disney World" was born.

I hope this guide helps kids and kids at heart like YOU to better understand and appreciate the magic of this extraordinary place. Thanks for joining in the fun!

xoxo,
Shannon

ABOUT THE AUTHOR
Shannon lives outside of San Francisco, California. She is a freelance graphic artist, author, wife, and mom of two darling lads.

Hello from above Walt Disney World in the Skyliner!

©2024 Shannon W. Laskey • First edition • All rights reserved
Edited, proofread, factchecked, fine-tooth combed and contributed to by Hugh Allison
Front cover and spine illustrations and photographs by Shannon W. Laskey
Back cover hot air balloon illustration by Kirsten Ulve

LEGAL JARGON	WHAT IT MEANS
No part of this publication may be reproduced, distributed or transmitted in any form or by any means, including photocopying, recording or other electronic or mechanical methods, without the prior written consent of the author, except in the case of brief quotations in critical reviews and certain other non-commercial uses permitted by copyright law.	Don't copy this book, okay?
This book is neither authorized nor sponsored nor endorsed by The Walt Disney Company or its subsidiaries. It is an unofficial and unauthorized book, and not a product of The Walt Disney Company.	This book is NOT made by Disney!
All images and mentions of names, places, products and services associated with The Walt Disney Company, its businesses and other companies independent of The Walt Disney Company are not intended to infringe on any existing copyrights or registered trademarks of their respective companies, but are used in context for educational purposes.	The stuff talked about in this book is owned by other people. We're just telling you about it.
The opinions and statements expressed in the quotations are the opinions of those people who are quoted and do not necessarily reflect the opinions and policies of The Walt Disney Company and its subsidiaries nor the author or the publisher.	The quotes in this book are what the person who said it thought and might not be what Disney, the author or the publisher thinks.
While every precaution has been taken in the preparation of this book, no responsibility is taken by the author or the publisher for unintentional errors or omissions. Neither is any liability assumed for damages resulting, or alleged to result, directly or indirectly from the use of the information contained herein.	We tried not to make any mistakes while writing this book but if we did, well, these things happen. (But if we did, we're sorry!) (And if you notice something that's a mistake, will you let us know?)

Printed in the United States of America
ISBN #978-0-9995721-5-3
Orchard Hill Press
Visit www.OrchardHillPress.com for more information

Table of Contents

SECTION	PAGE
Dictionary of Words & Phrases	6
Special Stuff in This Book	7
My Trip Planner	9
Walt Disney's World	15
Planning to Have Fun	25
Magic Kingdom	37
EPCOT	95
Disney's Hollywood Studios	133
Disney's Animal Kingdom	165
My Trip Journal	193
Game Answers	202
Index	204
Contributor Credits	207
Heartfelt Thanks	207
Waiting Games	208

How did it all come to be? → (Walt Disney's World)

Write your plans here! → (My Trip Planner)

The 4 theme parks → (Magic Kingdom / Disney's Animal Kingdom)

Info for planning your visit → (Planning to Have Fun)

One last page of games! → (Waiting Games)

Detailed list of what's in this book → (Index)

Illustration by Kirsten Ulve • www.kirstenulve.com

Dictionary of Words & Phrases

A **ATTRACTION**—Anything from a stunt show you watch, to a roller coaster you ride on, to a treehouse you walk through is called an attraction.
AUDIO-ANIMATRONICS—Mechanical figures of bears, birds, droids, humans and more that make sounds and are programmed to move or be animated.

C **CAST MEMBER**—In a play or movie, the performers are called the cast. The people who work in Walt Disney World are performing their jobs for the visitors, so they are called Cast Members.
CHARACTERS—The friendly mice, dashing princes, kind princesses, funny monsters, sassy villains and brave Jedi in movies and TV shows are called characters. In Walt Disney World you'll find them appearing at Meet n' Greet locations, in restaurants with Character Meals, and in parades and shows.

D **DISNEY LEGEND**—People who have made an extraordinary contribution to the company are named Disney Legends—a sort of Hall of Fame for Disney employees which launched in 1987. Today there are over 300 recipients.

G **GUESTS**—Disney doesn't call their visitors customers, they call them Guests. You probably won't hear a Cast Member call you a Guest but you may hear them address you as "friend."

H **HIDDEN MICKEY**—Images of Mickey Mouse are hidden in attractions, shops, restaurants and other places around the parks. These Hidden Mickeys are sometimes made in the shape of Mickey's whole body but are usually the simple three-circle symbol that looks like his head. You'll also find Hidden Mickeys on clothing, mugs, toys and other souvenirs.

I **IMAGINEER**—This term is a combination of the words "imagination" and "engineer." It describes the talented people who create the magic in Disney parks. They design and oversee every detail, from the machinery that makes the rides work right down to the wallpaper patterns inside of the restaurants.

R **RIDE CAR**—The vehicle you board to go on a ride is called a ride car. It might be shaped like a boat, an elephant, a rat or even an actual car! Some attractions have a ride car outside so you can test them out or take a photo.
RESORT—A resort is a place you go on vacation for recreation. Walt Disney World (or WDW) is a resort with theme parks, water parks, hotels, boating, golf courses and more. Disney uses "Resort" in their hotel names but, in this book, that word is left out of hotel names.

Special Stuff in This Book

Look out for these handy-dandy symbols and features!

 Hot Tip symbols are found next to insider info that not just everyone knows about.

 **Eye Spy** symbols let you know about special things to spy with your little eye.

 Smiley **Fun Fact** symbols are near tidbits of fascinating info and trivia.

So You Know areas define words and phrases you might not know—like commissary, figment of imagination, and lappet.

Attraction pages (like page 42) have **gold star** outlines on them, so you can color in your rating for each attraction.

These symbols are near **black-and-white images** that are designed for you to add color to. **HEY KIDS COLOR ME IN!**

Some info is **color coded** to show you which land or theme park it relates to.

These **stamps** tells you the type of attraction and the year it opened. Write what YOU think along the bottom.

Interactive activities like fill-in-the-blank questions, games, mini quizzes and scavenger hunts are fun to do before you leave home, during your trip and after you get back.

A **Trip Planner** in the front of this book and a **Trip Journal** in back have places for you to write about your plans, record how it all went, collect character autographs and create a scrapbook.

MAY BE SCARY These **caution** symbols are near attractions that some people find scary. If you're unsure about any experience, ask a Cast Member for more info about what it's like. If you're in line and change your mind, speak to a Cast Member for help.

WORD TO THE WISE: This book has areas for you to color, draw and write. Ballpoint pens, crayons, colored pencils or regular pencils will work best. Be careful if you use markers as the ink may bleed through to the other side of the page.

Illustration by Fiona Dulieu • www.fionadulieu.com

Inspired by faraway locales like Indonesia and Nepal, Drinkwallah in Disney's Animal Kingdom has endless details to drink in—and a waterside seating nook.

My Trip Planner

Use this Trip Planner to get ready for your visit to Walt Disney World (WDW)!

PACKING LIST
This book

MY TRIP PLANNER–ITINERARY

How **excited** are you about visiting **Walt Disney World?** Draw an **arrow** from the **black circle** below to the word that best describes how you feel:

SO YOU KNOW... itinerary = detailed plan for a trip

EXCITED-O-METER

FAIRLY · PRETTY · VERY · BEYOND

Date(s) of your visit to Walt Disney World: ....

How many **days** will you be there? ....

Who will you be going with? ....
....

Will you be going to any **other places** near Walt Disney World? ☐ Yes ☐ No

If yes, **where?** ....
....
....
....

How **far away** from Walt Disney World do you live? ....

Will you be staying in a **hotel?** ☐ Yes ☐ No

If yes, what's it **called?** ....

10

MY TRIP PLANNER—ABOUT MY PLANS

Which **attractions** do you want to do?

You may want to read this book & THEN fill out the trip planner!

....
....
....
....
....
....
....
....

Which **characters** do you want to see?

....
....
....
....
....
....

Do you want to meet Alice? Put a ✓ in the box next to your answer to this question.
☐ Indeed I do! ☐ No, thank you!

MY TRIP PLANNER—ABOUT MY PLANS

Which **entertainment** do you want to see?

....

....

....

....

....

....

....

Which spots for **food and drinks** do you want to visit?

....

....

....

....

....

....

....

Upstairs seating at Magic Kingdom's Columbia Harbour House

MY TRIP PLANNER—COUNTDOWN

How many days until you go to **Walt Disney World?** ....

When it's exactly **10 days** before your visit, start this **countdown** by coloring in the **10 circle**. Each day, fill in the **next** shape in the countdown until it's time for your trip. For days **10** through **2** use a **black** crayon or colored pencil. For the **last day,** color in the bowtie with **red** to complete the picture.

wahoo!
You're going to Walt Disney World!

Walt Disney's World

Maps in this book are simplified and not to scale!

- LOS ANGELES CALIFORNIA
- ANAHEIM CALIFORNIA
- KANSAS CITY MISSOURI
- MARCELINE MISSOURI
- CHICAGO ILLINOIS
- NEW YORK CITY NEW YORK
- ORLANDO FLORIDA

In Walt's Footsteps!

Which of the above **cities** have **you** been to?
Put a ✓ in the box next to the ones you've visited.

☐ Los Angeles, CA ☐ Kansas City, MO ☐ Orlando, FL
☐ Anaheim, CA ☐ Marceline, MO ☐ New York City, NY
☐ Chicago, IL

Walt illustration by Mariana Koontz • www.landandworld.com

Meet Walt Disney

"It's kind of fun to do the impossible."
—WALT DISNEY

You're going to Walt Disney World? Yay! So, how did this place come to be? It all began with a fellow named Walter Elias Disney. Walt was born in Chicago, Illinois on Dec. 5, 1901 and grew up in the Midwest—including in Marceline, Missouri which he would later think of as his hometown. He loved to draw and was a cartoonist for his high school paper. His career began in Kansas City, Missouri where he worked at an art studio, an advertising agency and his own **animation** studio before moving to Los Angeles, California to start a new animation studio in 1923 with his big brother Roy. The first major success for Walt Disney Studios was an animated black-and-white cartoon called *Steamboat Willie* which debuted in 1928. It was shown before the main movie at New York City's Colony Theater. This 8-minute short starred Mickey and Minnie Mouse and used an amazing brand-new type of sound that went along with the action!

SO YOU KNOW...
animation = made with drawn images
live-action = made by filming real animals, people and places

HEY KIDS COLOR ME IN!

Tough question...which Disney movie do you think is the best one ever?
_____

Making Magic

After creating many more black-and-white shorts, the studio released their first one in color in 1932 called *Flowers and Trees*. When Walt wanted to make one of the world's first full-length animated movies, people said he was crazy. They thought that audiences wouldn't sit through a cartoon with such a long running time. But 1937's *Snow White and the Seven Dwarfs* was almost an hour and a half long—and it was a huge hit! Many more animated movies followed like *Pinocchio*, *Dumbo* and *Bambi* and then a non-animated nature documentary series in 1948 called *True-Life Adventures*. The studio's first **live-action** movie was the 1950 pirate drama *Treasure Island*. When the popularity of television swept the nation in the 1950s, Walt and his team launched their first TV show in 1954. It was called *Disneyland* and it was about a new place that was being built in California.

 FUN FACT

The *Snow White and the Seven Dwarfs* record of 1938 was the **first movie soundtrack** sold to the public.

The Happiest Places

Disneyland in 1962

As Walt's career grew, so did his family. He and his wife Lillian had two children, Diane and Sharon. The legend goes that one day, as Walt was sitting on a bench watching his daughters enjoy the merry-go-round in Griffith Park in Los Angeles, he had an idea for a different kind of place where kids and parents could have fun together. He had visited many amusement parks, carnivals and circuses but he felt like most of them were kind of rundown. He imagined a clean, beautiful park divided into different areas that each had a unique theme. Walt's vision came to life when the Disneyland theme park opened on July 17, 1955 thirty miles south of L.A. in Anaheim, California. About a decade later, The Walt Disney Company created all-new attractions for the New York World's Fair which later made their way into Disneyland. As the 1970s approached, the West Coast park was getting plenty of visitors but not many people came from the eastern part of America. That gave Walt a new idea—to create a vacation kingdom on the East Coast!

Vintage photograph from the collection of Dave DeCaro • www.davelandweb.com

 SPY If you visit the **New York World's Fair** site today you'll see its **140-foot-tall Unisphere** globe sculpture is still there. Replicas of that globe were used in the 2010 *Iron Man 2* movie and *Captain America: The First Avenger* from 2011.

Fun at the WORLD'S FAIR

Starting in the mid-1800s, **enormous expos** that showcased the latest ideas and inventions from different nations began to take place. People traveled from **all over the globe** to be dazzled by special exhibits created especially for these World's Fairs. In 1964-1965, America hosted the **New York World's Fair** in a park in New York City, NY and these four **Disney attractions** made their debut:

Magic Skyway

In this attraction, Guests traveled back to the days of the dinosaur in convertible cars on a fixed track. Technology developed for this ride was used to create PeopleMovers for Disneyland (since closed) and Walt Disney World *(see page 68).*

Carousel of Progress
After a run in Disneyland, this attraction moved to Walt Disney World *(see page 70).*

Great Moments with Mr. Lincoln
Abraham Lincoln Audio-Animatronics are in Disneyland & Walt Disney World *(see page 74).*

It's a Small World
Versions of this ride can be found in most Disney resorts worldwide including Walt Disney World *(see page 52).*

The Florida Project

Walt wanted to create something even bigger than Disneyland. As that park got more and more popular, lots of other businesses crowded in on it so the main goal was to get plenty of land. Orlando, Florida's affordable swampland, warm climate and access to roads and an airport made it the perfect location! Walt's original plan was to create a theme park like Disneyland but with its own airport, a business center and a new type of planned city called the Experimental **Prototype** Community of Tomorrow (or EPCOT). This futuristic metropolis was going to be an always-changing place where new technologies would be tested including:

- A giant climate-controlled dome
- A no-cars-allowed downtown
- Multiple levels of underground roads
- PeopleMover & monorail transportation

> SO YOU KNOW... prototype = original model that other versions copy

Brotherly Love

"We're going to finish the Florida park, and we're going to do it just the way Walt wanted it."
–ROY DISNEY

Sadly, in the middle of working on all of this, Walt passed away on December 15, 1966. His brother Roy O. Disney delayed retiring so he could make sure Disney World would still be created without Walt. The two had worked together for most of their lives. Walt dreamed up the creative ideas and Roy made sure the company could afford them! When it came to the Florida Project, Roy said the new resort needed to be called <u>Walt</u> Disney World as a tribute to his brother so that people would always remember the man behind the magic.

 Roy Disney stood with Mickey Mouse to deliver a **dedication speech** at WDW's Grand Opening Ceremony. In Magic Kingdom's **Town Square** you can find his words on a **plaque**—and a **statue** of him with Minnie called **Sharing the Magic**. This was sculpted by Disney Legend **Blaine Gibson** who also created the Partners statue and Cinderella Fountain *(see pages 45 and 46)*.

WEST COAST VS. EAST COAST

Disneyland Resort today:	Walt Disney World Resort today:
★ Located in Anaheim, California	★ Located in Orlando, Florida
★ About 500 acres in size	★ About 27,500 acres in size
★ About 35,000 Cast Members	★ About 77,000 Cast Members
★ 2 theme parks	★ 4 theme parks
★ 3 Disney hotels	★ 20+ Disney hotels
★ No water parks	★ 2 water parks
★ No golf courses	★ Several golf courses
★ 1 shopping & dining area outside of the theme parks	★ 2 shopping & dining areas outside of the theme parks

Magic Kingdom on Opening Day

Opening New Doors

WDW opened on Friday October 1, 1971 with the Magic Kingdom theme park, the Contemporary and Polynesian Village hotels and two golf courses. At the Grand Opening Ceremony later in the month, about 10,000 Guests enjoyed a parade with marching bands and characters, and a chorus singing as thousands of balloons filled the sky. Since then, many more hotels and golf courses—including mini golf—have been added. There are now three more theme parks too: EPCOT (first called EPCOT Center), Disney's Hollywood Studios (first called Disney-MGM Studios) and Disney's Animal Kingdom!

Vintage photograph from the collection of George Miranda

Mini Quiz!

Can you guess which of these songs was sung at Walt Disney World's Grand Opening Ceremony? *Answer on page 202.*
- ☐ "Once Upon a Dream"
- ☐ "With a Smile and a Song"
- ☐ "When You Wish Upon a Star"

 **HOT TIP** Today **Walt Disney World** also has bike and boat rentals, fishing, horse riding **and** the **ESPN Wide World of Sports Complex** with playing fields, sports courts and a stadium. See even **more activities** on page 22!

Happiness Worldwide!

There are now **SIX** Disney Resorts around the world.
Put a ✓ in the box next to the parks that **you've** visited—**so far!**

NORTH AMERICA
Disneyland Resort:
- ☐ Disneyland Park, 1955
- ☐ Disney California Adventure Park, 2001

Walt Disney World Resort:
- ☐ Magic Kingdom, 1971
- ☐ EPCOT, 1982
- ☐ Disney's Hollywood Studios, 1989
- ☐ Disney's Animal Kingdom, 1998
- ☐ Disney's Typhoon Lagoon, 1989*
- ☐ Disney's Blizzard Beach, 1995*

* Water park

ASIA
Tokyo Disney Resort:
- ☐ Tokyo Disneyland, 1983
- ☐ Tokyo DisneySea, 2001

Hong Kong Disneyland Resort:
- ☐ Hong Kong Disneyland Park, 2005

Shanghai Disney Resort:
- ☐ Shanghai Disneyland, 2016

EUROPE
Disneyland Paris Resort:
- ☐ Disneyland Park, 1992
- ☐ Walt Disney Studios Park, 2002

The Vacation Kingdom

Walt Disney World's theme parks each have their own style and are made up of themed sections called "lands" with attractions, characters, entertainment, restaurants and shops. Below are some basics—but you'll learn much more in the pages ahead!

October 1, **1971**

MAGIC KINGDOM
This park has the same basic layout as California's Disneyland, with an old-fashioned main street that ends at a fairytale castle. Paths that radiate out from that central hub lead to a storybook village, space-age structures, a tropical plaza and settlements inspired by America's early days. Magic Kingdom has 6 lands.

October 1, **1982**

EPCOT
This park has a silver sphere at its Main Entrance. Beyond this are retro-futuristic buildings and pavilions that explore space, imagination, innovation, and the natural world. Pavilions inspired by countries around the globe are near a secondary entrance called International Gateway. EPCOT has 4 lands which are actually called "neighborhoods!"

May 1, **1989**

DISNEY'S HOLLYWOOD STUDIOS
This park has wide boulevards that lead to Hollywood-style landmarks like a grand movie palace and a towering hotel. There's also a pleasant lake, a haven for Muppet fans, an outer space outpost, animated plazas, an oversized world built from toys and more. Disney's Hollywood Studios has 9 lands—though some are tiny!

April 22, **1998**

DISNEY'S ANIMAL KINGDOM
This park has paths that branch out from a one-of-a-kind tree. Hundreds of real animals and thousands of exotic plants live in artfully crafted environments in a lush oasis, a bustling African village, a riverside Asian kingdom, an area dedicated to dinosaurs, and a bizarre—but beautiful—moon. Disney's Animal Kingdom has 6 lands.

Illustrations by Chris Buchholz • www.etsy.com/shop/buchworks

A Home Away from Home!

The **unique styles** of the WDW **hotels** are described below. Look at each photo and write the hotel number **(7, 12, 14, 16, 18** or **20)** in the box that's over that pic. One has been done for you. *Answers on page 202.*

HOTEL NAME:	THEME:
1 All-Star Movies	Animated movies like *Fantasia* & *Toy Story*
2 All-Star Music	Music genres like country, jazz & rock
3 All-Star Sports	Sports like baseball, football & surfing
4 Animal Kingdom Lodge	African lodges & wildlife savannas
5 Art of Animation	Artistry of Disney & Pixar animation
6 Beach Club	Traditional nautical coastal towns
7 BoardWalk Inn	1900s colorful seaside boardwalks
8 Caribbean Beach	Bright, vibrant Caribbean Islands
9 Contemporary	1950s-1970s style retro-modern design
10 Coronado Springs	Spanish, Mexican & Southwest cultures
11 Fort Wilderness	American woodland cabins & camps
12 Grand Floridian	Mid-1800s Victorian-era elegance
13 Old Key West	Palm tree-filled islands of Florida Keys
14 Polynesian Village	Tropical tiki culture & Hawaii
15 Pop Century	Fads from the 1950s through 1990s
16 Port Orleans–French Quarter	Historic New Orleans neighborhood
17 Port Orleans–Riverside	Romance of rural Louisiana
18 Riviera	Elegance of the French & Italian Riviera
19 Saratoga Springs	1800s New York horse racing retreat
20 Wilderness Lodge	1900s National Park lodges
21 Yacht Club	Grand New England yacht clubs

Top Things To Do Beyond the Theme Parks

Walt Disney World is filled with fun activities like the ones listed below! Keep in mind, some of these may cost extra or require a reservation.

• CATCH THE ELECTRICAL WATER PAGEANT—Since 1971, this charmingly simple parade of twinkling lights in the shapes of water-loving creatures (and more) has been tootling across Bay Lake and Seven Seas Lagoon nightly as merry music plays. It starts its loop outside Magic Kingdom's Main Entrance and travels past the shores of the Grand Floridian, Polynesian Village, Contemporary, Wilderness Lodge and Fort Wilderness.

Which activity sounds best?
_____
_____

• CRUISE DISNEY'S BOARDWALK—This promenade along Crescent Lake by BoardWalk Inn was inspired by East Coast seaside promenades. There are shops, restaurants, four-wheeled surrey bike rentals, street performers, and live entertainment for grownups in the lounges.

• FROLIC IN WATER—There are two water parks with slides, splash zones and wave pools. Typhoon Lagoon (which opened in 1989) is a tropical paradise where it seems everything has been tossed around topsy-turvy by a major storm. Blizzard Beach (which opened in 1995) looks like a ski resort with melting snow. Many of the hotels in the area have awesome pools for their guests with lazy rivers, water play areas and over-the-top slides.

Polynesian Village pool

• HOTEL HOP—Many of WDW's hotels are so amazing, they're worth a visit just to see 'em! You can take in incredible sights like African animals roaming the grounds of Animal Kingdom Lodge, and the groovy 90-foot-tall tile mural designed by Disney Legend Mary Blair at the Contemporary. Most hotels have unique lobby shops and restaurants. Fort Wilderness has the rousing Hoop-Dee-Doo Musical Revue dinner show with live entertainment. Also on the grounds of that hotel is the Tri-Circle-D Ranch where you can visit the horses who live and work in Walt Disney World. For more horsey fun, visit Port Orleans for old-fashioned carriage rides. The monorail *(see page 28)* travels to Polynesian Village, and Grand Floridian, and *into* the Contemporary lobby so it's easy to visit those three in one day.

• SHOP AT THE SPRINGS—Disney Springs is an outdoor area with shops, eateries, a bowling alley, live entertainment, a movie theater, and rides like a hot air balloon and an Amphicar—a convertible that goes from land into the water!

Guess the Goner!

Which now-gone attraction pictured here is where Winnie the Pooh's ride is today? *Answer on page 202.*

Rest In Peace

Many things have come and gone in WDW like...

1970s
Bob-A-Round Boats
These groovy, round motorboats with striped roofs, cushioned seats and radios could be rented to bob around Seven Seas Lagoon.

1974–1999
Discovery Island
Guests visited this island to discover the birds, lemurs, monkeys and tortoises that lived there.

1989–2008
Pleasure Island
Named after the wild place in *Pinocchio*, this area had a comedy club, country line dancing, live entertainers and a 1930s-era club for adventurous travelers.

1995–2015
Walt Disney World Speedway
At this outdoor speedway, Guests could ride in—or even actually drive—real race cars around a racing circuit.

1998–2017
DisneyQuest
This indoor location was where Guests could try out motion simulators, virtual reality experiences and video games.

2022–2023
Star Wars: Galactic Starcruiser
This immersive hotel simulated a two-night cruise through a galaxy far, far away.

Wilderness Lodge has comfy chairs, a river running through the lobby, totem poles and Whispering Canyon Café where zany waiters make your meal memorable.

Planning to Have Fun

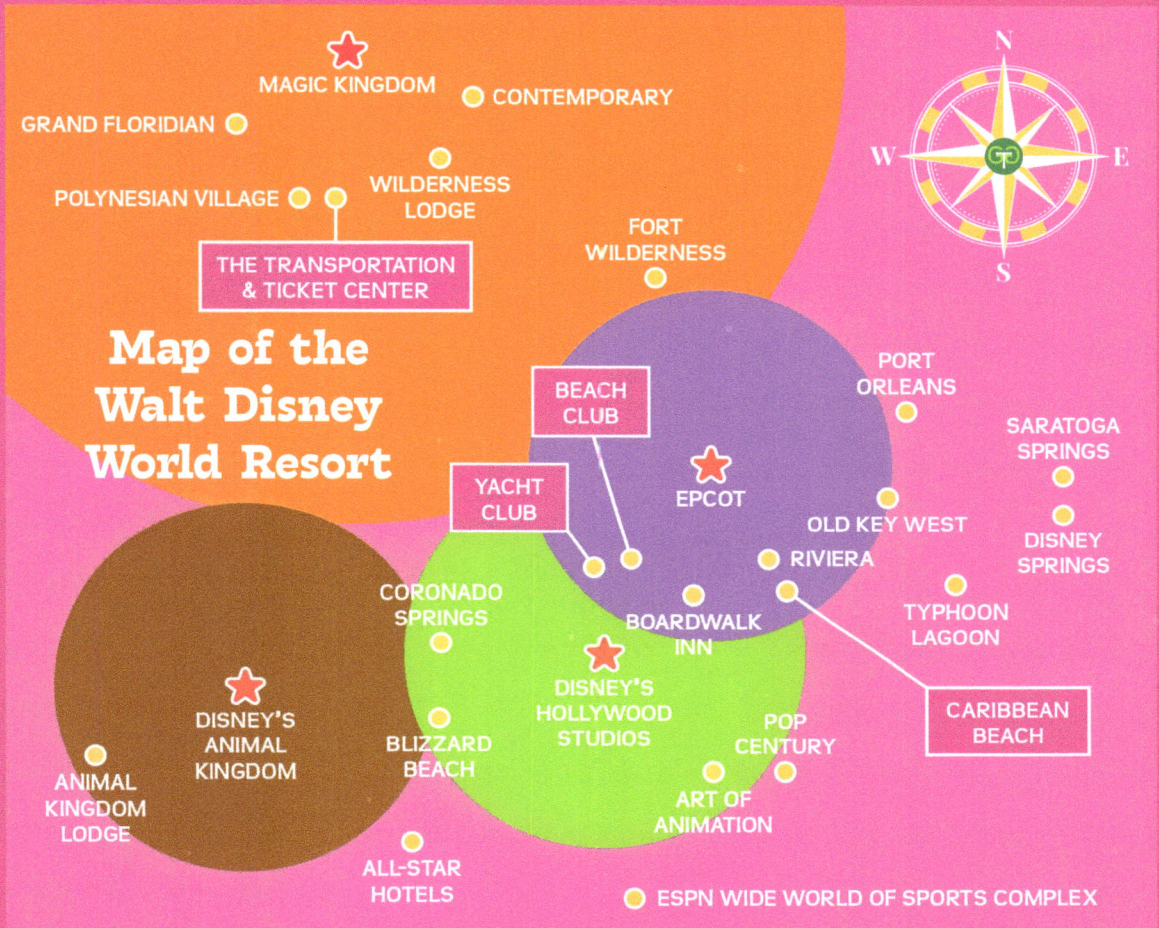

Rank Your Options!

What do you want to do **most** when you're in Walt Disney World? **Number** the activities 1 through **6**, starting with 1 for the one that interests you the **most** and ending with **6** for the one that interests you the **least**. It's okay to leave the "other" one blank if you want!

- ◯ Eat special **food and drinks**
- ◯ Go **shopping**—or window shopping
- ◯ Meet **characters**
- ◯ Ride **rides**
- ◯ See **live entertainment** ♪
- ◯ Other _____

"I'm travel-size for your convenience!"
—MUSHU

A Wondrous Place

Millions of people travel from all over the globe each year to visit Walt Disney World—which is open every day of the year, even on Thanksgiving and Christmas! This popular vacation destination sprawls over a whopping 43 square miles—which is about the size of the city of San Francisco. Because there are so many things to do (and so many ways to do them), planning a visit can feel kind of challenging. The good news is, once you get there you'll see it's really not too hard to have a wonderful time. So, where do you begin? Choosing when and how long you want to visit and buying your ticket is a great place to start!

HEY KIDS COLOR ME IN!

Your Disney Experience

Whoever is in charge of planning your trip will want to sign up for a free "My Disney" account on the Walt Disney World website (www.disneyworld.disney.go.com) and/or on Walt Disney World's "My Disney Experience" app. The site has attraction and park hours, food and drink menus, maps, special event details and **refurbishment** lists. The app has this info too, along with news on wait times, schedules for characters and entertainment, and if anything is temporarily closed because of weather or other issues. Play Disney Parks is another free app that has at-home activities, and interactive games you can only play inside the parks.

 If trip planning is feeling **overwhelming**, a **travel agent** may be the answer. Their services are **free** as they're paid by **Disney**.

*SO YOU KNOW... **refurbishment** = when something is closed to be spruced up or given routine maintenance*

 Each WDW theme park gives out paper **park guidemaps.** These are useful AND they are a great, **free souvenir!**

...MagicBand+ & More

Ah, the wonders of **technology!** You can easily enter the parks, link to **PhotoPass** images *(see page 32),* open your Disney hotel room door and pay for things with a **MagicBand+** wristband *(costs extra),* **Key to the World** card, or **MagicMobile** pass on the WDW app. These are all **free** to use and can be used **separately** or **together** but the Key to the World is **only** for Disney hotel guests. You'll need to link whichever one(s) you'll be using to your **My Disney Experience** account to **hook up** to any credit or debit cards, tickets, and reservations you have there. The **MagicBand+** wristband **glows** and **vibrates** with some shows and is needed to play the **Star Wars: Batuu Bounty Hunter game** on the **Play Disney Parks app.**

Ticket Talk

To enter the parks, each person three years old and over needs a ticket for each day of their visit. The places where Disney sells tickets include:
- Booths by park entrances
- Disney Springs Ticket Center
- Hotel lobbies
- The Transportation & Ticket Center (TTC) — *A hub for transit, ticketing & parking!*
- The WDW website

There are also Annual Passes that grant passholders park entry throughout the year and offer perks like discounts on dining, parking and shopping. Some types of passes and tickets may require a reservation—but most don't!

 HOT TIP: **Multiple** day tickets usually cost less **per day** than single day tix. Companies like AAA and CostCo may have **lower prices**.

STANDARD 1-10 DAY TICKET TYPES

★ **One Park Per Day:**
   Entry into 1 theme park per day

★ **One Park Per Day with Add-on:**
   Same as above, along with entry to water parks or sports venues

★ **Park Hopper:**
   Entry into any of the 4 theme parks in a day (as long as a park has not hit its limit of Guests that day)

★ **Park Hopper Plus:**
   Same as above, along with entry to water parks or sports venues

Checking Inn

Staying at one of the **20+** Disney-owned hotels can have its **perks**—like handy transportation, a prime location, dining plans, and water park entry on check-in day. Hotel guests may also be offered **extra hours** on some days where they can go into the theme parks **earlier** or stay **later** than other visitors. **Activities** that are often available to hotel guests include:
- Arts and craft classes *(may cost extra)*
- Campfire storytimes
- Movies under the stars
- Swimming and lounging by the pool

Over 40 **Good Neighbor hotels** are recommended by Disney on this website: **www.wdwgoodneighborhotels.com** These lodgings are **close to** or **within** the resort and may cost **less** than the Disney-owned hotels.

Getting Around

You can travel between WDW hotels, theme parks, water parks and shopping spots by using the resort's free network of buses, boats, **gondolas** and monorails. Some routes are direct and others have stops along the way or require you to change to another line. There are also Minnie Vans, rideshare services and taxis—but those cost extra!

BUSES

Buses go almost everywhere (and can run during storms unlike boats, gondolas and monorails).

SO YOU KNOW... **gondolas** = enclosed cabins suspended from an overhead cable

BOATS—FERRYBOATS, CRUISERS & WATER TAXIS

Between Magic Kingdom and:
- Fort Wilderness
- Grand Floridian
- Polynesian Village
- Wilderness Lodge
- The Transportation & Ticket Center (TTC)

Between Disney's Hollywood Studios and EPCOT's International Gateway and/or:
- Beach Club
- BoardWalk Inn
- Yacht Club

Between Disney Springs and:
- Old Key West
- Port Orleans (French Quarter and Riverside)
- Saratoga Springs

SKYLINER GONDOLAS

Between Disney's Hollywood Studios and EPCOT's International Gateway and/or:
- Art of Animation and Riviera (shared station)
- Caribbean Beach
- Pop Century

WDW MONORAIL ELECTRIC TRAINS

Between Magic Kingdom and:
- Contemporary
- TTC
- Polynesian Village
- Grand Floridian

Between Magic Kingdom & TTC
Between EPCOT's Main Entrance & TTC

NOTE: Beach Club, BoardWalk and Yacht Club are a short walk from EPCOT's International Gateway and its nearby Skyliner gondola station, and a walking path goes from there to Disney's Hollywood Studios. There's also a walking path from the Contemporary to Magic Kingdom and then on to Grand Floridian, Polynesian Village and TTC.

Park Bag Match-Up!

Fill in the **names** of the character from *Beauty and the Beast, Moana, Tangled* and *Up* who might take each **bag** to the parks. One has been done for you. *Answers on page 202.*

(1) __Moana__

(2) _____

(3) _____

(4) _____

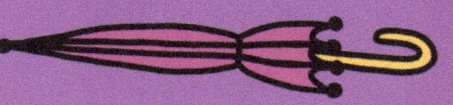

Security Tips

For safety's sake, Guests must go through a quick **security screening** before entering the parks. If you cause the metal detector to **beep**, you'll be sent to a **secondary screening** with an officer who will scan you with a **wand** and check any **bags**. To avoid that—and get to the **fun** faster—have items with **metal** out of your bag (like an umbrella, charger or eyeglass case). Then hold them **straight out** in front of yourself as you go through the **security gate**. If you **do** beep, you can speed things along by opening any **pockets** or **pouches** in your bag. They'll need to look in them **ALL**.

Accessibility For All

Many **services** are available for **Guests with disabilities** who visit WDW. These include:

- Accessible hotel rooms
- American Sign Language interpreters at some shows
- Braille guidebooks and map signs
- Companion restrooms
- Conveniently located parking
- Disability Access Service (DAS) for Guests unable to wait in line
- Electric Conveyance Vehicle (ECV) and wheelchair rentals *(cost extra)*
- Handheld assistive listening, audio and captioning devices
- Service animal relief areas
- Special loading areas and boarding help at attractions
- Wheelchair ramps on transportation

To use some of these support services, **preregistration** may be required. Visit the **WDW app** or **website** and search **"disabilities"** for more info.

The Main Attractions

WDW has all kinds of attractions—fast and slow, short and long, indoors and outdoors—and some are even scented! Though most have the same hours as the park they're in, a few open later or close earlier. Some attractions (like shows) have a schedule with set start times and others (like walk-throughs) can be done at your own pace. The types of attraction lines are:

• STANDBY—This is the regular entrance and line (or "queue") for an attraction. You can enter right up until its closing time and may experience it after the park has closed!

• LIGHTNING LANE—For some experiences, Guests can buy a Lightning Lane pass *(see opposite page)* to skip the standby line.

• SINGLE RIDER—When Cast Members need someone to fill an extra spot in a ride car, they pull people from the Single Rider line—which is often shorter than the standby line. Your whole group can choose to do this but you'll probably be split up for the ride.

• VIRTUAL QUEUE—New and/or popular rides have a Virtual Queue that you wait in within the WDW app instead of in person. If you don't have the app, you'll need to chat with a Cast Member.

 If you want to be **sure** to experience something with a **set start time,** get there **early.** Sometimes locations fill up, so people who get there late are **turned away!**

It's a Small World has a standby line & a Lightning Lane!

Switch It Up with Rider Switch

This service lets part of your group do all the waiting if there's someone with you who won't be riding but can't be left behind alone. To do this, speak with a Cast Member at the ride's entrance. Your group will split into two parties. After the first party is done riding, the ones who stayed behind will board without waiting in the same line. *NOTE: Kids under 7 must be with someone 14 or older on all attractions!*

Which type are you?
☐ Morning person
☐ Night owl

Rise n' Shine For Rope Drop

The entrances of each theme park usually open **before** the official opening times. To be among the first Guests let in, arrive about an **hour** early so you'll be there when the gates open. You'll be able to go into the land that's just inside the entrance but the paths that lead past that point will be **roped off.** At the official opening time, **Cast Members** will let you through to the rest of the park—a moment known as **Rope Drop!** This is a great way to be **first in line**—or experience **no line** at all—at attractions that open at the start of the day. Some **WDW hotel guests** get even earlier entry into **some sections** of a park. If you're **not** in that group, you may find the **shortest lines** at attractions in **other** sections of the park. Visit the **WDW app** or **website** and search **"early entry"** to see the list.

Say What? Attraction Edition!

Guess which **quote** can be heard in which **attraction**. Draw a line from the **attraction's name** to the related **speech bubble**. One has been done for you. *Answers on page 202.*

- Don't tell him, Carlos! Don't be chicken!
- Here, in this hostile world, is where our story begins.
- Excuse me, we are looking for a duck.
- I know you're probably feeling a little nervous right now.

Attractions:
- Festival of the Lion King
- Gran Fiesta Tour
- Mission: SPACE
- Pirates of the Caribbean
- Spaceship Earth
- The Twilight Zone Tower of Terror
- Toy Story Mania!

- Something tells me this ain't the floor show.
- That door's opening once again and, this time, it's opening for you.
- Ready, aim, break those plates!

Illustration by Chris Buchholz • www.etsy.com/shop/buchworks

LEARN ABOUT ...Lightning Lanes

Looking to speed things up? There are two types of **Lightning Lane** pass where Guests pay a **fee** (per person, per day) to join a (usually) shorter line at a **reserved time**. The Lightning Lane **"Multi"** Pass and the Lightning Lane **"Single"** Pass each include different **attractions**. Most of the attractions that have a Lightning Lane are part of the Multi Pass and the more in-demand attractions use the **Single Pass** where **each** pass for **each** experience is a separate purchase. To enter a Lightning Lane when the time window has arrived, whatever was scanned for **park entry** is tapped onto a **touchpoint** near the front of the attraction. *NOTE: A pricey Lightning Lane "**Premier**" Pass may also be available which doesn't require times or attractions to be selected in advance. Pricing and availability may change for all Lightning Lane passes. Check the **WDW app** or **website** to see the latest info.*

Signing Sites

You don't **have** to have an autograph book to collect **signatures**. Characters can sign:

- **A photo frame** or **matte**—which you can put a picture in after your trip
- **This book**—either in the scrapbook or on a page that's related to them
- **Your clothing, hat or shoes**—but you can't be wearing them at the time
- **Your free park guidemap**—which you can display at home, or tuck in the pages of this book

Meet n' Greet Moments

The characters in WDW can't WAIT to visit with you! They can be found at indoor and outdoor Meet n' Greet locations—or sometimes just roaming around. There are also Character Meals where they stop by your table and visit with you while you dine. Some restaurants that offer this are in theme parks and others are in hotels. When you meet characters you can ask for their autograph, take photos and get a handshake, high-five or hug.

Do you like s'mores?
☐ Yes! ☐ No.

FUN FACT: **Chip 'n Dale's Campfire Sing-A-Long** is a unique character experience at **Fort Wilderness** with a guitar player, free **movie** and **s'mores kits** for sale!

Treasured Memories

...PhotoPass

A picture says a thousand words! **PhotoPass** is a service where photos (and sometimes videos) of your group are taken in some scenic locations, at some **Meet n' Greets** and on some rides. The friendly, professional **PhotoPass photographers** take standard **snapshots** and **Magic Shots**—which have surprises added later. They are happy to take pix with **your camera** too! Once your photo shoot is complete, the photographer will link the images to a **free PhotoPass card** or your **My Disney Experience** account. Linked pix and videos can be previewed for **free** on your account where you'll see info on how to **buy** and **download** the ones you want. **ALL** images can be bought together with a **Memory Maker** package—which costs less if pre-purchased before arrival. For help with the PhotoPass service around the resort, visit: **PhotoPass Studio** in Disney Springs; **Box Office Gifts** in Magic Kingdom; **Camera Center** in EPCOT; **Sid Cahuenga's One-of-a-Kind** in Disney's Hollywood Studios; or **Garden Gate Gifts** in Disney's Animal Kingdom. You can buy **photo prints** and **picture frames** in those locations too!

♫ So Entertaining

The resort's live entertainment offerings are popular, so you may want to find a place to watch from before the fun begins. Because these events draw a crowd, some attractions and walkways near them close temporarily. The different types of entertainment include:

- EVENTS WITH CHARACTER—Musical extravaganzas feature characters and dancers performing on stage with peppy music. Cavalcades and parades have characters, dancers and music too but with fancy floats that move along the parade route.
- LIVE PERFORMERS—You can find incredible acrobats, bands, dancers, jugglers, musicians, singers and other entertainers at indoor venues, on outdoor stages and even strolling along the pathways.
- NIGHTTIME SPECTACULARS—These evening events have dazzling details like dramatic lighting, fantastic fireworks, spellbinding narration, stirring music and stunning projections (where characters and movie clips are shown on the front of buildings).

Fun For All Seasons

Throughout the year, WDW has **holiday celebrations** and **short-term events**. These may include special characters, decor, entertainment, food and drinks, photo spots, souvenirs **and** ride overlays! Here are examples of just **some** of these:

MAGIC KINGDOM
- Easter parade
- Fourth of July fireworks
- Mickey's Not-So-Scary Halloween Party*
- Mickey's Very Merry Christmas Party*

EPCOT
- Easter egg hunt *(costs extra)*
- Various festivals *(see page 109)*

DISNEY'S HOLLYWOOD STUDIOS
- Disney Jollywood Nights*

DISNEY'S ANIMAL KINGDOM
- Earth Day celebrations
- Merry Menagerie

* Scheduled, ticketed event, costs extra

Tour Time

Walt Disney World fans can get a look behind the scenes on a **tour** *(costs extra)*. These experiences take Guests into areas they can't normally go—like backstage at EPCOT's **greenhouses** where they test out new ways to grow plants or into the **utilidors,** a network of tunnels under **Magic Kingdom** that were built so that Cast Members could move through the park without being seen by Guests. You can also sign up to have a **private guide** take you through the theme parks. All tours should be reserved **before** your visit but sometimes **same-day** reservations are available to book.

Fab Food & Delish Drinks

The menus change from time to time but one thing that never changes is that you'll have lots of yummy fare to choose from—and many ways and places to enjoy it. It's always a good idea to check the schedule. Some eateries don't open until lunchtime.

 Ask **which** allergy-friendly, kosher, low-fat, low-salt, plant-based, vegan and vegetarian **options** are available—they may not **always** be listed. Plus most restaurants have **kids' menus** and some sit-down locations let children **build their own meal** by choosing their entrée and side dishes.

Sit-Down Meals

Reservations for these types of meals are highly recommended and can be made before your visit. If you don't snag a reservation, you may be able to join a walk-up list in person or on the WDW app on the day you're there. Sit-down meals can be:
- BUFFETS—All-you-care-to-enjoy food stations where you serve yourself
- FAMILY STYLE—Shareable, all-you-care-to-enjoy dishes brought by waiters
- TABLE SERVICE—Waiters take your order and bring it to the table (also called full service)

Grub on the Go

HEY KIDS COLOR ME IN!

No advance planning needed! These more casual places include:
- QUICK SERVICE—Order and take your meal to go or to a nearby table—although some locations have little or no seating (it's okay to sit at a different quick-service spot if it has available seating)
- CARTS—Grab n' go carts are dotted all over with snacks like churros, fruit, ice cream, pickles, popcorn, pretzels (some Mickey-shaped!) and drinks like sodas and bottled water

NOTE: This book doesn't list ALL on-the-go spots.

Food at Your Fingertips

Throughout the resort, you can use the WDW app to buy food and drinks from quick-service eateries, to-go orders from sit-down restaurants, and treats from candy shops without waiting in the usual ordering line. You'll choose from the available locations and times, and what you want to get. The app will alert you when your order is ready for pickup.

Packages & Parties

Buying a Dining Package (with a full meal, including dessert) or a Dessert Party (with drinks and sweets) will get you a reserved spot for select live entertainment like parades, shows and nighttime spectaculars. Both types can be reserved and paid for before your visit.

🛍️ Shop Around

Carts, stands and shops have a variety of souvenirs for sale as well as useful items like medicine, reusable shopping bags, sunscreen, snacks and drinks. Some shops offer Mobile Checkout so Guests can buy wares through the app. Stores near park entrances often open early and stay open late! *NOTE: This book doesn't list ALL shopping spots.*

 Many store display windows are **works of art.** Be sure to stop and notice all the thoughtful **details!**

🎀 Mini Quiz!
Can you guess what the first piece of Mickey Mouse merchandise was? *Answer on page 202.*

☐ Mouse ear hat ☐ Stuffed animal
☐ Pad of paper ☐ Wristwatch

Simple Souvenirs

You can find vending machines in and around shops and in hotel lobbies with personalized luggage tags, pressed coins and collectible medallions *(see page 118)*. There are also many styles of free pin-back buttons with themes like First Visit, Happy Birthday, I'm Celebrating and more! If you don't see them around, ask at a Guest Relations location or inside a shop (they are often kept behind the counter). Cast Members who are out and about may also have some, along with free stickers.

Illustration by Chris Buchholz • www.etsy.com/shop/buchworks

Helpful Spots

- **Baby Care Centers:** Basic baby supplies for sale, fridges, highchairs, kid-sized potties and changing tables

- **Bottle Filler Stations:** Free, filtered water for filling your water bottle
- **Charger Machines:** Vending machines which sell new charging rods and let you swap a used one for a fresh one
- **First Aid Centers:** Bandages for boo-boos, fridges for medicine, hot and cold filtered water and expert nurses
- **Guest Relations:** Lobbies, windows and stands staffed with Cast Members who can help with dining reservations, lost Guests and more
- **Guidemap Racks:** Free park guidemaps are in racks at park entrances
- **Information Boards:** Display boards that show entertainment schedules, park hours and wait times
- **Lockers:** Stash stuff in a rented locker for the day *(costs extra)*
- **Lost and Found:** Get help tracking down lost items (or you can fill out a form on the website)

On your way to board Tiana's Bayou Adventure in Magic Kingdom, you'll get to peek inside this tidy office where she works on her latest projects.

Magic Kingdom

FANTASYLAND

LIBERTY SQUARE

FRONTIERLAND

TOMORROWLAND

ADVENTURELAND

MAIN STREET USA

MAIN ENTRANCE

It may end up being the same land!

Lands in Brief!

Put a **dot** in the circle next to the **land** that you **think** you'll like best. Once you've visited them all, **color in** the circle by your **favorite**.

- ○ **Adventureland:** bold, tropical
- ○ **Fantasyland:** enchanting, quaint
- ○ **Frontierland:** wild, Western
- ○ **Liberty Square:** Colonial, historic
- ○ **Main Street USA:** inviting, old-timey
- ○ **Tomorrowland:** futuristic, sleek

MAGIC KINGDOM AT A GLANCE

MAIN STREET USA ATTRACTIONS	MEET N' GREETS	ENTERTAINMENT
• Main Street Vehicles • Walt Disney World Railroad	• Mickey	• Casey's Corner Pianist • Dapper Dans • Flag Retreat • Happily Ever After • Let the Magic Begin • Main Street Philharmonic • Mickey's Magical Friendship Faire

FANTASYLAND ATTRACTIONS	MEET N' GREETS	
• Dumbo the Flying Elephant • Enchanted Tales with Belle • It's a Small World • Mad Tea Party • Mickey's PhilharMagic • Peter Pan's Flight • Prince Charming Regal Carrousel • Seven Dwarfs Mine Train • The Barnstormer • The Many Adventures of Winnie the Pooh • Under the Sea—Journey of The Little Mermaid	• Ariel • *Cinderella* Characters • Daisy Duck • Donald Duck • Goofy • Minnie • Mirabel • Peter Pan • Tigger • Various Princesses • Winnie the Pooh	**ENTERTAINMENT**

TOMORROWLAND ATTRACTIONS	MEET N' GREETS	ENTERTAINMENT
• Astro Orbiter • Buzz Lightyear's Space Ranger Spin • Monsters, Inc. Laugh Floor • PeopleMover (Tomorrowland Transit Authority) • Space Mountain • Tomorrowland Speedway • TRON Lightcycle Run • Walt Disney's Carousel of Progress	• Buzz Lightyear • Stitch	

LIBERTY SQUARE ATTRACTIONS	MEET N' GREETS	ENTERTAINMENT
• Haunted Mansion • Liberty Square Riverboat • The Hall of Presidents		

ADVENTURELAND ATTRACTIONS	MEET N' GREETS	ENTERTAINMENT
• Jungle Cruise • Pirates of the Caribbean • Swiss Family Treehouse • The Magic Carpets of Aladdin • Walt Disney's Enchanted Tiki Room	• Aladdin • Captain Jack Sparrow • Jasmine	

FRONTIERLAND ATTRACTIONS	MEET N' GREETS	ENTERTAINMENT
• Big Thunder Mountain Railroad • Country Bear Musical Jamboree • Tiana's Bayou Adventure • Tom Sawyer Island	• Chip • Country Bears • Dale	• Adventure Friends Cavalcade • Festival of Fantasy parade • Hoedown Happening • Starlight parade

❖ QUICK-SERVICE EATERY

FOOD & DRINKS

- Casey's Corner ❖
- Main St. Bakery ❖
- Plaza Ice Cream Parlor ❖
- The Crystal Palace
- The Plaza
- Tony's Town Square Restaurant

SHOPS

- Box Office Gifts
- Crystal Arts
- Curtain Call Collectibles
- Emporium
- Main Street Cinema
- Main Street Confectionery
- Uptown Jewelers

FOOD & DRINKS

- Be Our Guest
- Big Top Treats (inside Big Top Souvenirs) ❖
- Cinderella's Royal Table
- Cheshire Café ❖
- Gaston's Tavern ❖
- Pinocchio Village Haus ❖
- Prince Eric's Village Market ❖
- Storybook Treats ❖
- The Friar's Nook ❖

SHOPS

- Bibbidi Bobbidi Boutique
- Big Top Souvenirs
- Bonjour Village Gifts
- Fantasy Faire
- Hundred Acre Goods
- Sir Mickey's

FOOD & DRINKS

- Auntie Gravity's Galactic Goodies ❖
- Cool Ship ❖
- Cosmic Ray's Starlight Café ❖
- Energy Bytes ❖
- The Lunching Pad ❖
- Tomorrowland Terrace

SHOPS

- Buzz Lightyear Space Ranger's Spin Photos
- Star Traders
- Tomorrowland Launch Depot

FOOD & DRINKS

- Columbia Harbour House ❖
- Liberty Square Market ❖
- Liberty Tree Tavern
- Sleepy Hollow ❖
- The Diamond Horseshoe

SHOPS

- Memento Mori
- Ye Olde Christmas Shoppe

FOOD & DRINKS

- Aloha Isle ❖
- Skipper Canteen (Jungle Navigation Co. LTD)
- Sunshine Tree Terrace ❖
- Tortuga Tavern

SHOPS

- Bwana Bob's
- Island Supply
- La Princesa de Cristal
- Plaza del Sol Caribe Bazaar

FOOD & DRINKS

- Golden Oak Outpost ❖
- Pecos Bill Tall Tale Inn and Café ❖
- Westward Ho ❖

SHOPS

- Big Al's
- Critter Co-Op
- Frontier Trading Post
- Tiana's Bayou General

39

Main Street USA

"Come on kids!"
—PONGO

After going through the Main Entrance, you'll go under railroad tracks to a downtown square and beyond in this land that's named for its main street lined with eateries and shops. Here you'll find quaint buildings, flickering gas lamp lights and antique mailboxes that recreate the setting of small town America at the turn of the 20th century!

Town Square

This central square has a flagpole, garden beds and the statue of Roy Disney with Minnie. Around the square are buildings like those of any bustling town including City Hall (the park's main Guest Relations lobby) and a grand "theater" that's actually *not* a theater but has a character Meet n' Greet, an Italian restaurant and two shops!

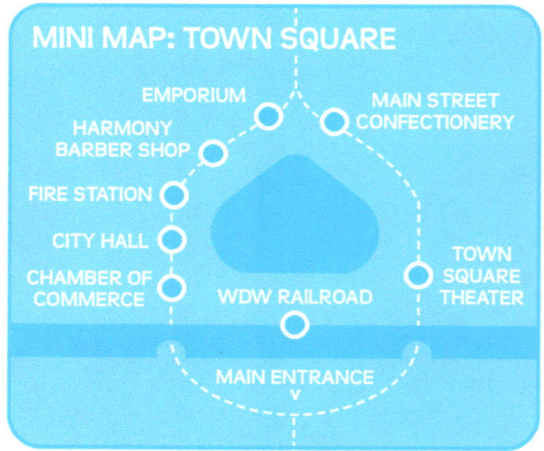

MINI MAP: TOWN SQUARE
- EMPORIUM
- MAIN STREET CONFECTIONERY
- HARMONY BARBER SHOP
- FIRE STATION
- CITY HALL
- CHAMBER OF COMMERCE
- WDW RAILROAD
- TOWN SQUARE THEATER
- MAIN ENTRANCE

 **HOT TIP** You can get an **UH-mazing** view of **Main Street USA** from the upper level of the Main Street **train station.**

Did you visit the Fire Station?
☐ Yes! ☐ Nah.

Hot Times Ahead

The **Fire Station** is the headquarters for **Fire Company 71,** named after the year Magic Kingdom opened (1971). Inside you'll see **tools of the trade** like axes, buckets and hoses, and **patches** from fire departments across America. The traditional firehouse dog is a **dalmatian** and statues of characters from the 1961 animated *101 Dalmatians* movie can be **spotted** here too. You may even find designs with those cute pooches for sale at the Fire Station's unique **pressed coin machine** *(see page 118.)*

♪ Entertainment

The Flag Retreat takes place nightly in Town Square in tribute to all U.S. military branches, with patriotic music played by the Main Street Philharmonic marching band. These musicians also play big band, ragtime and swing-style classics elsewhere in Main Street USA and in Fantasyland's Storybook Circus.

SHOP SPOTLIGHT

The old-fashioned **Emporium** has a prodigious (as in, HUGE) array of wares!

📷 Meet n' Greets

Meet Mickey backstage at the Town Square Theater near props and posters from his magical career.

A Cut Above

Haircuts might be the **last** thing you'd bother with on a vacation but you may want to think again. The cheery stylists working at **Harmony Barber Shop** specialize in making a child's **first haircut** a truly memorable—and fun—experience! Along with the haircut, customers get a mouse ear hat, a souvenir certificate for "**Bravely and Cheerfully submitting to our Clippers and Shears**" and a little pouch to save that first snip of hair. Reservations **are** recommended but **walk-ins**—and older kids and grownups—**are** welcome. If they're not too busy, you can get FREE **pixie dust** sprinkled in your hair here or at Fantasyland's **Bibbidi Bobbidi Boutique**.

🍴 Tony's Town Square Restaurant

Table Service • Indoor & Outdoor Seating

Italian faves like pasta and pizza are the specialties here. A TV in the lobby plays the 1955 animated *Lady and the Tramp* movie where Lady the spaniel and Tramp the mutt dine on spaghetti at Tony's place. Fetching details from the movie in and around this restaurant include a heart with pooch pawprints on the ground out front, Tony on the sign and a fountain inside with the dog duo!

☆ ☆ ☆ ☆ ☆ COLOR IN YOUR RATING!

Walt Disney World Railroad

All aboard for a relaxing ride on a classic steam train! The railroad travels in a *clockwise* circle with stops at *three* stations: Main Street, Frontierland and Fantasyland. You can hop on or off at any station you like, or take the *Grand Circle Tour* to end up back where you started. Each of the trains is pulled by an antique *locomotive engine*. In 1969, Disney Legend Roger E. Broggie led a team to recover the engines in *Mexico*, restore them and create replicas of the original passenger cars for Guests to ride in—in *Style!*

OPEN-AIR TRAINS
EST. 1971

Write what YOU think of each attraction in the bottom part of these stamps!

 SPY — Walt **loved** trains and even had a small one in his own backyard called the **Lilly Belle!** In the **lower level** of **Main Street Station** look for displays related to Walt's train and the trains you can catch on the **upper level.**

Name That Locomotive!

Fill in the **missing letters** of the **names** of the Walt Disney World Railroad **train engines.** One has been done for you. *Answers on page 202.*

| L | I | L | L | y | B | E | L | L | E |

| _ | R | _ | G _ R | _ | B | O | _ | G | E |

| R | _ | Y | _ | D | S | E | _ |

| _ | W | _ L _ E | E | _ | E _ | _ I | N | Y |

TIME MACHINE

1916 — Baldwin Locomotive Works of Philadelphia builds the oldest of the WDW Railroad's engines.

1971 — Main Street Vehicles & the railroad are Opening Day attractions & Main Street USA is the only station.

1972 — Frontierland Station opens & relocates about twenty years later to make more room in that land.

1988 — Happy birthday! What is now Fantasyland Station opens as part of Mickey's 60th anniversary.

⭐⭐⭐⭐⭐

Main Street Vehicles

OPEN-AIR VEHICLES ★ EST. 1971 ★

Ah-ooo-gah! These old-fashioned vehicles were an Opening Day attraction. Each one will take you on a *one-way trip* up or down Main Street USA's main street between *Town Square* and *Central Plaza* in front of Cinderella Castle. They all follow the same route but start and end at *slightly* different points. Look for the signs that mark where these pick-up and drop-off spots are.

 HOT TIP — When they're not out and about, the vehicles and **Belgian** and **Percheron** horses that pull the streetcar go into the **Car Barn** next to Harmony Barber Shop. If the doors are left open, you can **peek inside**.

🎵 Entertainment

The Dapper Dans barbershop quartet sing near the barber shop, from aboard Main Street Vehicles, and in other locations along Main Street whilst wearing dapper bowties and hats.

Vehicle Challenge!

See if you can ride in each type of **Main Street Vehicle!** It may take you **more than one visit** because they may not **ALL** be running on the **same day**. The good news? There's **no deadline**. Put a ✓ in the box next to the ones you've ridden in!

☐ **Horse-drawn Streetcar:** 1800s-style Horse-Powered Trolley

☐ **Horseless Carriage/Jitney:** 1900s-style Car (blue, red or yellow)

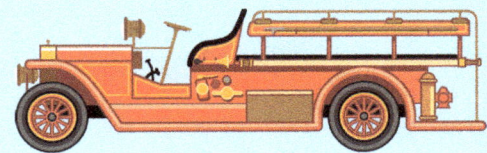

☐ **Fire Engine:** 1910s-style Fire Truck

☐ **Omnibus:** 1920s-style Double-Decker Bus

Main Street Vehicles illustration by Chris Buchholz • www.etsy.com/shop/buchworks

Famous Panes

Signs on the windowpanes in Main Street USA honor **real people** who did exceptional work for **Disney** as animators, artists, carpenters, designers, executives, landscapers, sculptors, writers and more. These **Main Street Window Honors** have people's **names** on them and amusing made-up **jobs** or **company names** related to what they did for the park **or** to their hobby. One example is on a window above **Plaza Ice Cream Parlor** which has a sign for **Sully's Safaris** in honor of Disney Legend **Bill Sullivan.** Bill started out working on Disneyland's Jungle Cruise ride and went on to become the **Vice President** of Magic Kingdom. Look around and you'll see many of these window signs!

SHOP SPOTLIGHT

Watch artisans like glassblowers and engravers inside **Crystal Arts.**

1888

🍴 Casey's Corner

Quick Service • Indoor & Outdoor Seating

Ballpark favorites like corn dog nuggets, hot dogs and french fries are up at bat at this corner spot. Striped wallpaper and baseball memorabilia bring back the days of 1888 when the poem "Casey at the Bat" was written by Ernest Thayer. Part of the 1946 animated movie *Make Mine Music* was about good ole Casey!

PLUS: **Main Street Bakery** with pastries, sandwiches & specialty coffee
Plaza Ice Cream Parlor with ice cream cones, floats & sundaes

🎵 Entertainment

Enjoy dazzling live piano playing by the Casey's Corner Pianist while you dine!

🍴 The Plaza Table Service • Indoor Seating

Dine in fancy **Art Nouveau** splendor at this restaurant! The mirrored walls and swirly whirly light fixtures create a chic setting for you to enjoy sandwiches, soups, salads and milkshakes.

🍴 The Crystal Palace Buffet • Indoor Seating

This is the spot to have a Character Meal with Winnie the Pooh and his friends. This eatery's glass-domed ceilings, dramatic windows and hanging plants are inspired by the elegant greenhouses that were popular in the Victorian era. There's a morning buffet with breakfast options and a lunch and dinner buffet with dishes like fried chicken, pasta and roast beef.

SO YOU KNOW...
Art Nouveau = 1900s-era nature-inspired design style

Casey's Corner illustration by Chris Buchholz • www.etsy.com/shop/buchworks

Central Plaza

At the end of Main Street is this central hub with the Partners statue of Walt and Mickey, grassy lawns, an outdoor stage and pathways leading to the other lands!

 SPY Look **closely** at Walt's **necktie** on the Partners statue and you'll see a **tie pin** that says **STR**. Those letters stand for one of his favorite places to rest and relax—**Smoke Tree Ranch** in Palm Springs, California.

🎵 Entertainment

Mickey Mouse and the gang get the day started with fanfare on Central Plaza's stage in front of Cinderella Castle at a short opening ceremony called Let the Magic Begin. This is also where you can catch Mickey's Magical Friendship Faire, a musical extravaganza where Mickey and other characters dance and sing along to tunes from Disney movies. After dark, the nighttime spectacular Happily Ever After lights up the skies over the park with fireworks, dazzling lights and lasers and projections where moving images are shown on the front of the castle and buildings down Main Street!

Mini Quiz!

Can you guess the name of the first fireworks show at Magic Kingdom?
Answer on page 202.

☐ Enchantment
☐ Fantasy in the Sky
☐ Wishes

Fantasyland

"Well, there's one thing. They can't order me to stop dreaming."
—CINDERELLA

Fairytales come true in this land of fantasy. Here you'll find charming cottages, half-timbered wooden buildings, medieval stone walls, picturesque palaces and striped circus tents that bring scenes from your favorite storybooks to life!

In & Around the Castle

At 189 feet tall, Cinderella Castle is the crown jewel of the park! The graceful palace is like those dating back to the 17th-century in Europe with blue-roofed turrets, fierce gargoyles, golden spires and arched stained glass windows. Along the passage that runs between the forecourt to the back courtyard you'll find five tile murals that tell Cindy's tale. Following designs drawn up by Disney Legend Dorothea Redmond, mosaic artist Hanns-Joachim Scharff and his team spent almost two years putting together these colorful mosaics from over 300,000 pieces of Italian glass, ceramic tile, sterling silver and 14-karat gold! Also on the ground floor is a boutique salon for kids. A restaurant and a luxurious suite are on the floors above.

 FUN FACT **Cinderella Fountain** (behind the castle) was designed so that when you view the statue of the princess from a **lower angle** (like a child would) it looks like the **crown** painted on the wall behind her is **on her head.** Don't miss **Cinderella Wishing Well** on the Tomorrowland side of the castle!

> What would you wish for from a Fairy Godmother?
> _____

Looking Boo-tiful

"Bibbidi-Bobbidi-**Boo**" is the song Cinderella's **Fairy Godmother** sings in the movie. Now her **Apprentices** are standing by at Bibbidi Bobbidi **Boutique** to give children ages 3-12 a **magical makeover!** This **salon service** *(costs extra)* can include makeup, nail polish and **hairstyling**—and **add-ons** like knight or princess costumes, crowns, sashes, shields and more. Reservations are **recommended**—and usually fill up **quickly!**

> SO YOU KNOW...
> **apprentices** = workers that learn a skill from those they work for

Cinderella's Royal Table
Table Service • Indoor Seating

After a warm greeting from your hostess Cinderella, you'll take the red-carpeted stairs (or elevator) to the second floor of the castle for your Character Meal. But before you do, notice how the little statues of mice Jaq and Gus are perched on a wall in the foyer! Upstairs in the dining room, the soaring vaulted ceilings and majestic shields and banners make you feel as though you've stepped into the 1950 animated movie *Cinderella*. As you dine, you'll enjoy visits from an array of other princesses and tasty delights like quiche or waffles for breakfast, and steak or fish for lunch and dinner.

Suite Dreams

On the castle's **third floor** is the lavish **Castle Suite**. Normally closed to the public, there are **contests** from time to time with an **overnight stay** here as their prize. Tours *(cost extra)* that take Guests into **backstage areas** sometimes include visits here. A foyer, sitting room, bedroom and bathroom make up this suite of **regal rooms**. The plush decor includes coffered ceilings, sumptuous fabrics, marble fireplaces and a spa tub set underneath a **painted night sky** that actually twinkles!

☆ ☆ ☆ ☆ ☆

Prince Charming Regal Carrousel

The French spelling of carousel!

Take a joyful jaunt round 'n round on this **charming** carousel in the castle's courtyard! Almost one hundred horses prance beneath a **royal** purple tent and rounding boards decorated with scenes from *Cinderella*. Each **hand-carved** steed is uniquely designed with saddles and bridles **festooned** with fancy feathers, flowers, jewels, shields and tassels. As you ride, cheery organ music plays—and you just **may** hear a song you know!

COVERED SPINNER — EST. 1971

 The horses on the **outer** row are **larger** than those on the **inner** row. Pick the size that fits **you** best—or chill out on a **chariot seat!**

 Cinderella's Golden Carrousel was an Opening Day attraction and got its current name in 2010. The **original name** before Disney bought the **1917** antique was **Liberty Carousel.**

Decorate your own carousel horse! Draw over the grey shape or create one in the blank area.

HEY KIDS COLOR ME IN!

★★★★★
Mickey's PhilharMagic

It's showtime! This magical show is presented on a ginormous 150-foot-wide wraparound screen in Fantasyland Concert Hall. You'll get a pair of 3D "opera" glasses to put on when Minnie Mouse gives the word. Next, the curtain rises to reveal Mickey Mouse who rushes offstage—leaving behind his magical, starry blue sorcerer's hat. With the mouse maestro gone, Donald Duck puts on the hat to work a little magic of his own. As the orchestra's instruments play themselves, things start to spiral out of control and Donald loses the hat! As he hunts it down, the dizzy duck makes his way through a medley of musical numbers and settings from animated classics including *Aladdin, Beauty and the Beast, Coco, Fantasia, Peter Pan, The Lion King* and *The Little Mermaid*. Before the show comes to an end, you may be in for a surprise!

SHOP SPOTLIGHT

Sir Mickey's theme is the 1947 animated short "Mickey and the Beanstalk."

INDOOR 3D CARTOON
EST. 2003

FUN FACT: Until 1980 this theater had an **Opening Day** show called **Mickey Mouse Revue** with a concert put on by Audio-Animatronics. In **2015** its **Donald, José** and **Panchito** characters flew over to join **EPCOT's Gran Fiesta Tour** ride *(see page 128).*

SO YOU KNOW...
PhilharMagic = philharmonic (an orchestra) + magic

Who Plays What?

You'll see **musical instruments** in Mickey's PhilharMagic. Some of the movies featured have scenes with **instruments** too. Put a ✓ in the box next to the correct answers below. One has been done for you. *Answers on page 202.*

(1) In *Aladdin*, **Genie** briefly turns his stomach into a ☑ drum ☐ piano ☐ sax

(2) In *Coco*, **Miguel** plays the ☐ guitar ☐ keytar ☐ sitar

(3) In *The Little Mermaid*, **Sebastian** plays an instrument made of shells that sounds like ☐ castanets ☐ maracas ☐ steel drums

(4) In *Peter Pan*, **Peter** plays a ☐ flute ☐ harp ☐ violin

EXTRA CREDIT: In *The Princess and the Frog*, **Louis** plays the _____.

☆ ☆ ☆ ☆ ☆

Peter Pan's Flight

INDOOR DARK RIDE · EST. 1971

Come on everybody, here we go-o-o-o! With the help of some magical *pixie dust*, you'll fly in a pirate ship from the Darling's house in London to Peter Pan's home, Never Land. Your flight begins in the *nursery* of Wendy, John and little Michael. As Nana barks in her bonnet below, you'll soar out the window and over the rooftops of the sparkling city past the *Big Ben* clocktower and *Tower Bridge*. You may glimpse the *shadows* of Peter, Wendy and her brothers moving across the full moon as they fly to Never Land themselves! You'll have a bird's-eye view of the island's glowing volcanoes, lovely waterfalls, blooming flowers, Mermaid Lagoon, Skull Rock and more. Next you'll sail past the *action* aboard the Jolly Roger. Though Hook, Smee and the other pirates try to make poor Wendy walk the plank, Peter will get the last laugh—and make sure the Darling children get *home* safe and sound!

 SPY — You can play with your **shadow,** see **traces** of **Tinker Bell** and look for a **wall calendar** marked with the exact date the *Peter Pan* play debuted in London in this ride's **standby line!**

📷 **Meet n' Greets**

Kick up your heels with Peter Pan who can sometimes be found by the Never Land Map outside of his ride!

TIME MACHINE

1904
J.M. Barrie's "Peter Pan" play is published after the character is well received in an earlier novel.

1953
You can fly! You can fly! You can fly! The animated movie "Peter Pan" hits theaters.

1971
Peter Pan's Flight opens a couple of days after Magic Kingdom's Opening Day.

2015
Interactive fun is added to Peter Pan Flight's recently refurbished standby line.

The Story of...Peter Pan

While getting ready to go out for the evening, Mr. Darling gets jealous that Mrs. Darling and their children, Wendy, John and Michael are paying more attention to Nana the dog than they are to him. He orders Nana outside and tells Wendy it's time for her to grow up and that this will be her last night with her brothers in the nursery. Wendy tries to tell her mother that Peter Pan has been visiting their house and she's captured his shadow, but Mrs. Darling doesn't listen. After the parents leave, Peter and his fairy friend Tinker Bell fly in through the window in search of Peter's shadow. Peter sprinkles the three children with Tinker Bell's pixie dust, tells them to think happy thoughts and flies with them from London, England to Never Land—a wondrous place where children never grow up. Also living in Never Land are the Lost Boys, beautiful mermaids, Native American Indian princess Tiger Lily, pirates like Captain Hook and his faithful assistant Mr. Smee, and the hungry crocodile Tick-Tock—named for the ticking clock he swallowed. The Darling children and the Lost Boys begin to miss their mothers and want to go back to London—but they're captured by pirates and taken onto Hook's ship, The Jolly Roger. After Hook gets Tinker Bell to reveal Peter's location, he delivers a bomb to Peter, now alone in his secret hideout. Tink saves Peter but almost dies in the explosion. She and Peter defeat the pirates and Hook is chased into the distance by Tick-Tock. Peter takes the children home in Hook's ship—which Tinker Bell has sprinkled with pixie dust so that it can fly.

☆☆☆☆☆

It's a Small World

Set sail for the *happiest* of cruises! You and your fellow world travelers will float in a boat on the *Seven Seaways Waterway* to each of Earth's seven continents: Africa, Antarctica, Asia, Australia, Europe, North America and South America. This color-drenched, whimsical *small world* is filled with dozens of darling dolls, each dressed in the traditional clothing of their homeland. The dolls *dance, play* musical instruments and *sing* along with the ride's catchy song in many languages. Joining them are *fanciful animals* like a hot pink camel, a winking blue hippo and coral giraffes with flower-patterned necks! For the *grand finale,* the cute characters from all the countries join together to frolic and sing in a happy *playland* but now the scenery and outfits are pale blue and white as a symbol of *world peace.*

INDOOR BOAT RIDE * EST. 1971 *

HOT TIP A few tables inside the **Pinocchio Village Haus** restaurant next door have a great view of the **hububb** in It's a Small World's **boarding area.** If you sit there, give the riders a **friendly wave** and see how many wave back!

TIME MACHINE

1964
Disney Legend Mary Blair leads the design of It's a Small World for the New York World's Fair.

1966
The original ride is shipped to Disneyland & Walt Disney hosts the opening ceremony.

1971
It's a Small World is an Opening Day attraction in Magic Kingdom. It's a world of laughter!

2021
Originally white & gold, the boarding area is painted in rainbow colors for the park's 50th anniversary.

Rest Up in Corona

When you've got to go, you've **GOT** to go to the **rest area** by It's a Small World that's inspired by the 2010 animated movie *Tangled*. The main draw here is the **restrooms** but there's also a bubbling **brook, Rapunzel's tower** and a **seating area**—which has tree stumps with **charging plugs** inside. Several pals of **Pascal** the chameleon are hiding in the **greenery,** near **window boxes** and by the **water!**

> How many chameleons did you spot?
> _____

Pinocchio Village Haus

Quick Service • Indoor & Outdoor Seating

Step into the charming world of little Pinocchio! This restaurant's candy-colored stained glass windows and murals feature the puppet and his friends and foes—like Figaro the cat and Monstro the whale. Choose chicken strips, flatbread pizzas or salad. The upstairs balcony seating has views of Cinderella Castle!

Legend Close-Up: Joyce Carlson

Joyce Carlson was born in Wisconsin in 1923. Her family moved to **Southern California** in 1938 where she graduated from high school. A friend who worked at the **Walt Disney Studios** in Burbank said she should get a job there too and Joyce was hired in 1944. She started out **delivering supplies** to animators but once they saw her artistic talent, she was promoted to the **Ink & Paint Department.** Joyce worked on movies like *Cinderella, Lady and the Tramp, Peter Pan* and *Sleeping Beauty.* In the 1960s Joyce moved to **Imagineering** where she built **miniatures** for the upcoming **1964** World's Fair. She even got to go to **New York** as part of the team who set up It's a Small World. Known as the company's resident **"small world expert,"** Joyce also helped bring the attraction to **Walt Disney World** in 1971 and **Tokyo Disneyland** in 1983 for their Opening Days. After her time in Japan she returned to Florida where she maintained **Carousel of Progress, It's a Small World** and other attractions for over **fifteen years.** Joyce was named a Disney Legend in **2000.**

⭐⭐⭐⭐⭐
Enchanted Tales with Belle

Welcome to the cottage **Belle** and her papa called home in the 1991 animated *Beauty and the Beast* movie! Inside the cozy dwelling you'll see stacks of books, rolled-up sketches and Maurice's *clever* inventions. On the wall hangs a gift from the Beast—a *Magic Mirror* which transforms into a doorway to his castle! Once inside the Beast's home, Cast Members will introduce you to chatty Madame Wardrobe and then chose members of the *audience* who'd like to volunteer to act out scenes from the story. When everyone heads into the library, Lumiere calls for Belle who'll be so *delighted* you've come to visit. Now it's time for the princess and her helpers to put on the show!

INDOOR LIVE SHOW — EST. 2012

SHOP SPOTLIGHT

Say hello to **Bonjour Village Gifts,** a darling store that's fit for a princess.

HOT TIP: The **volunteer actors** get to have their photo taken with **Belle** after the performance.

FUN FACT: Before you say **"adieu,"** a Cast Member will hand out free **souvenir bookmarks.**

TIME MACHINE

1740 — "La Belle et la Bête" by French author Gabrielle-Suzanne Barbot de Villeneuve is published.

1991 — Ooh la la! Over in Disney's Hollywood Studios park Beauty & the Beast—Live on Stage debuts.

2012 — Fantasyland's Enchanted Forest opens with eateries & Ariel, Belle & Snow White-themed attractions.

2020 — Beauty & the Beast Sing-Along debuts at Palais du Cinema in EPCOT's France Pavilion.

🍴 Be Our Guest Table Service • Indoor Seating

A stone bridge leads to the entrance of the Beast's elegant castle. This restaurant is named after the showstopping song in *Beauty and the Beast.* The front hall and dining rooms have cloud-painted ceilings, the red rose under a glass dome, snow falling outside the windows and whispering suits of armor. For your three-course French-inspired meal, you'll choose an appetizer, main course and dessert as your gracious host makes his rounds.

🍴 Gaston's Tavern

Quick Service • Indoor Seating

No one serves up yummy warm cinnamon rolls and fruity, foam-topped frozen apple juice like Gaston! Just past the statue of this burly, brawny guy and his pal LeFou, you'll find this antler-filled eatery.

☐ Team Beast
☐ Team Gaston

📖 The Story of...Beauty and the Beast

Belle lives in a French village with her father, the inventor Maurice. She loves to read but does not love stuck-up Gaston, even though he thinks she should. Gaston tells his faithful friend LeFou how he plans to make Belle his wife, never dreaming she'll say no. Maurice gets lost in the woods and looks for shelter in a nearby castle, the home of a cursed prince who has been turned into a hideous beast by an enchantress. The prince must earn someone's love before the last petal falls from an enchanted red rose or he will stay a beast forever. Maurice meets the Beast's servants who have been turned into objects as part of the curse—a candlestick (Lumiere), a clock (Cogsworth), a teapot (Mrs. Potts), a teacup (Chip) and a clothing cabinet (Madame Wardrobe). After tracking down her father, Belle takes his place as the Beast's prisoner. Belle is delighted by the castle's performing dishes and flatware and, as she and the Beast spend more time together, they start to become friends. When she looks in the Beast's enchanted mirror and sees her father is in danger, the Beast lets her go back to her village to help him. Gaston learns about the Beast and leads an angry mob to storm the castle. Belle finds the Beast dying and, as the last petal falls from the rose, tells him "I love you." With those words, the curse is broken and the prince becomes human again. After the happy couple kiss, everyone changes back into their human form to live happily ever after!

★ ★ ★ ★ ★
Under the Sea— Journey of The Little Mermaid

Visit Prince Eric's *castle* to journey through the *tale* of The Little Mermaid. You'll climb into a *clamshell* and pass Scuttle who starts off the story. After you dive under *"da bubbles"* you'll float past Ariel as she sings with friendly Flounder among her treasures. From there it's on to a festive *shindig* with singing Sebastian and other fun-loving *undersea* creatures. Things take a dark turn when you reach Ursula's lair where she *croons* and *conjures* her evil magic. When Ariel gets her legs, you'll follow her to the surface where she *shares a moment* with Eric in an enchanting lagoon. When Ursula's spell is broken at last, King Triton and the sea creatures celebrate Eric and Ariel's *royal wedding!*

INDOOR DARK RIDE ★ EST 2012 ★

 **SPY** — Near this ride, the name **H. Goff** is on a **map shop sign.** This is a tribute to Disney Legend **Harper Goff** who drew one of the **first** maps of Disneyland in California!

 FUN FACT — Ursula's **eels** are named **Flotsam** and **Jetsam.** "**Flotsam**" means loose stuff floating in the sea, like after a shipwreck, and "**Jetsam**" is the term for goods thrown overboard to make a ship **lighter** or more **balanced.**

Illustrations by Mary Pavlou • www.etsy.com/shop/MareBearPress

TIME MACHINE

1837 — Danish author Hans Christian Andersen's book "Den Lille Havfrue" about a little mermaid is published.

1989 — Splash! The animated "The Little Mermaid" movie hits theaters with a live-action version in 2023.

1992 — Disney's Hollywood Studios' live stage show based on Ariel's adventures debuts.

2012 — Under the Sea—Journey of The Little Mermaid opens & Ariel's Grotto moves to its current spot.

🍴 Prince Eric's Village Market Quick Service • No Seating

Named after Ariel's favorite prince, this stand is stacked with wooden crates filled with a variety of yummy grab n' go snacks like fruit, pretzels, turkey legs and frozen slushy drinks.

📷 Meet n' Greets

Swim over to meet Ariel (from the animated movie) perched among seaweed and seashells inside Ariel's Grotto next to her attraction.

📖 The Story of… The Little Mermaid

Ariel the mermaid lives under the sea with her father King Triton and her sisters (Aquata, Andrina, Arista, Attina, Adella and Alana) but she daydreams of living on land. She's friends with Flounder the fish, Sebastian the crab and Scuttle the seagull who she chats with about the objects she collects and her fond feelings for a human prince named Eric. Longing to be where the people are, Ariel trades her voice to Ursula the sea witch in exchange for legs. Ursula traps Ariel's voice in a shell and warns her that she only has three days to kiss Eric or her voice—and soul—will be Ursula's forever. When Eric discovers Ariel on the beach, he welcomes her to stay at his oceanside castle. The two get along swimmingly and are about to smooch during a rowboat ride when Ursula's eels tip over the boat! Disguising herself as a human named Vanessa, Ursula uses her magic and Ariel's voice to trick Eric into agreeing to marry her. But Scuttle and the other animals save the day by causing the shell necklace that holds Ariel's voice to shatter. Ursula's spells are now broken but the sun has set on the third day. Now that Ariel's time is up, she turns back into a mermaid. King Triton confronts Ursula and agrees to become her prisoner so his daughter can go free. At last Eric and Ariel triumph over Ursula, and everyone she ever trapped—including King Triton—is set free. When the king sees how Ariel and Eric feel about each other, he uses his power to turn his daughter into a human forever and the happy couple get married!

Storybook Circus

With its special gateway, this feels like its own land but it's simply a part of Fantasyland. This area opened in 2012 and it has scented elephants to search for, two rides, a splash zone, and striped circus tents that hold a Meet n' Greet, a shop and a rest area with seating and charging plugs. One of Walt Disney World Railroad's stations is here too!

☆ ☆ ☆ ☆ ☆

Dumbo the Flying Elephant

Dressed in his band major uniform, Dumbo's tiny pal Timothy is atop the archway leading to this attraction. There are actually two *matching* rides sitting side by side. One ride spins to the left and the other to the right. There are sparkling *fountains* at the base of the central columns that are decorated with *Mr. Stork* making a special delivery and the smiling face of Dumbo's mother. As you board your color-coordinated *pachyderm,* Timothy's voice welcomes you and cheerful music plays. You'll be able to control your flying height with a lever to skim *down* along the water or soar *up* into the clouds!

OUTDOOR SPINNER * EST. 1971 *

 **HOT TIP** — In between the two rides there's a **Dumbo ride car** near **red-and-gold** swooping **curtains** and a colorful **circus backdrop** that makes an excellent **photo spot.**

 FUN FACT — The standby line here includes an **indoor, air-conditioned playground!** Grownups can sit down and **chill out** while their kids play until it's time for their group to have **their turn** on the ride!

TIME MACHINE

1932 — Goofy makes his debut in a short cartoon called "Mickey's Revue." Gawrsh!

1941 — The animated movie "Dumbo," based on a 1939 story by Helen Aberson, hits theaters.

1996 — The Barnstormer at Goofy's Wiseacre Farm debuts & gets a new theme & a shorter name in 2012.

2012 — An Opening Day attraction, Dumbo's ride moves to its current spot & gets a second ride.

⭐⭐⭐⭐⭐

MAY BE SCARY

HEIGHT: 35"+

The Barnstormer

You can be a daredevil like *The Great Goofini,* the famous barnstormer stunt pilot! Your bright red *stunt plane* will depart from a hangar made from an old barn. As you skyrocket outside around the barnyard, you'll burst through an airfield *tower* with a bold red-and-white checkerboard pattern and a *billboard* with a Goofy-shaped hole before coming in for a smooth landing!

★ ROLLER COASTER ★
EST. 1996

HOT TIP
A trip on The Barnstormer is **short** and **sweet** which makes it a great **first roller coaster** for kids.

SPY
Look around **Fantasyland Station** nearby to find uses of the word **Carolwood.** That was the name of Walt's **backyard railroad!**

Meet n' Greets

At Pete's Silly Sideshow you can visit with Daisy Fortuna the fortune teller (Daisy Duck), The Astounding Donaldo the snake charmer (Donald Duck), The Great Goofini the stuntman (Goofy) and Minnie Magnifique the poodle trainer (Minnie Mouse).

Splash Zone

It's fun to cool off at **Casey Jr. Splash 'n' Soak Station!** Happy animals from the circus in *Dumbo* spray gentle jets of water while the cute train **Casey Junior** shoots a cool, refreshing mist into the sky. Look for **numbers** on the railroad cars that match the **years** Walt Disney World's four theme parks opened!

SHOP SPOTLIGHT

Step right this way to shop n' snack in the circus tent of **Big Top Souvenirs.**

⭐⭐⭐⭐⭐
Mad Tea Party

SO YOU KNOW... **topiaries** = bushes trimmed into shapes

COVERED SPINNER • EST. 1971 •

When **Alice** went down the rabbit hole in the 1951 *Alice in Wonderland* animated movie, she happened upon a wacky tea party hosted by the Mad Hatter. Now **you** are invited to join the party too at this Opening Day attraction! Just beyond a row of flowerbeds and **topiaries**, a canopy hung with colorful lanterns sits over a giant **teapot** and colorful **teacups**. Your group can pick whichever cup they'd like to ride in—so long as no one else gets to it first. As **"The Unbirthday Song"** from the movie plays, the jolly teacups twirl and the teapot lid raises to reveal one of the Hatter's chums, the sleepy **Dormouse,** peeking out! You can choose to spin your ride car even faster by turning the **wheel** in the center of your cup.

FUN FACT "Alice's Adventures in Wonderland" by English author **Lewis Carroll** was published in **1865.** Carroll loved to make up words like **chortle** (a type of laugh), **frabjous** (fabulous/joyous) and **galumph** (move clumsily).

Mirabel Illustration by Melissa Chan Stone • www.amuseboosh.com

🍴 Cheshire Café
Quick Service • Outdoor Seating

The treats at this cute cottage are sure to put a grin on your face. Named after the funny striped feline from Wonderland, this eatery has slushy drinks and baked goods like their yummy Cheshire Cat Tails!

📷 Meet n' Greets

Meet the warmhearted Mirabel of the magical Madrigal family from the 2021 animated *Encanto* movie in the lovely Fairytale Garden.

⭐⭐⭐⭐⭐
The Many Adventures of Winnie the Pooh

"A day without a friend is like a pot without a single drop of honey left inside."
—WINNIE THE POOH

INDOOR DARK RIDE · EST. 1999

To take an adventure with this silly old bear, you'll sit inside a *Hunny Pot*, travel through the pages of a giant storybook and visit Hundred Acre Wood! A storm is causing some *blustery* weather for Pooh and his pals: glum Eeyore, hard-working Gopher, shy Piglet, patient Kanga and curious Roo. The strong winds have even wrecked poor Owl's house! Next, energetic Tigger *bounces* over to visit Pooh just before bedtime. With his head full of the tiger's tales of imaginary creatures called *Heffalumps* and *Woozles,* Pooh has zany dreams that you'll have to see to believe. The next day everyone is almost washed away in a *flood* but, in the end, the *storm* goes away and they all gather together and say "Hooray!"

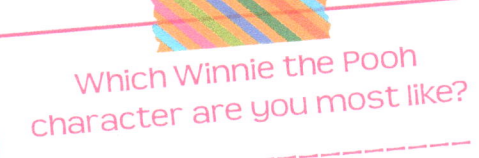

Which Winnie the Pooh character are you most like?
_____

 **SPY** Because **Mr. Toad's Wild Ride** used to be in this spot, you can see ole **Toadie** handing over his home's **ownership papers** as you travel through **Owl's house.**

📷 ## Meet n' Greets

Pop by a giant open storybook at The Thotful Spot next to The Many Adventures of Winnie the Pooh to meet characters like Winnie and Tigger too!

TIME MACHINE

1926 — Englishman A.A. Milne's stories about Pooh are published in the book "Winnie-the-Pooh."

1977 — The animated "The Many Adventures of Winnie the Pooh" movie comes out with Christopher Robin & Pooh.

1999 — How lucky we are! The Many Adventures of Winnie the Pooh ride debuts in Magic Kingdom.

2010 — Pooh's standby line gets interactive fun like gophers that pop up & digital walls of honey.

★ ★ ★ ★ ★
Seven Dwarfs Mine Train

ROLLER COASTER * EST. 2014 *

MAY BE SCARY
HEIGHT: 38"+

Heigh-Ho! Heigh-H-o-o-o! The princess **Snow White** loves to have fun with her seven friends: Bashful, Doc, Dopey, Grumpy, Happy, Sleepy and Sneezy—and now you can too! You'll follow a woodsy path to go inside a **vault** where signs written by **Doc** explain how to play with gemstones and water features in the standby line. Once aboard your train, you'll take a **rollicking ride** outside, smoothly coasting and swaying up, down and all around the mountain. Next, you'll enter the depths of the **mine** where the dwarfs are singing as they work away, collecting glimmering **jewels**. Back outside, you'll dash around twists and turns until you pass the miners and their **princess pal** dancing and playing music inside their cottage. Meanwhile, a certain cloaked, jealous and very **evil lady** lurks outside!

 FUN FACT This ride was the world's **first** coaster with **swinging seats** that rock **side to side** when the track **twists** and **turns**.

TIME MACHINE

1812
"Snow White" by the Brothers Grimm is published in Germany as "Sneewittchen."

1937
The animated "Snow White & the Seven Dwarfs" movie hits theaters.

2012
Opening Day attraction Snow White's Adventures closes to make room for Princess Fairytale Hall.

2014
It's off to ride we go! Seven Dwarfs Mine Train debuts in Magic Kingdom.

Titles of Nobility!

Fill in the missing **royal titles** (King, Prince, Princess or Queen) of the **characters** below. One has been done for you. *Answers on page 202.*

(1) Evil _____ from *Snow White and the Seven Dwarfs*
(2) _____ Naveen from *The Princess and the Frog*
(3) _____ Triton from *The Little Mermaid*
(4) _____ Aurora from *Sleeping Beauty*
(5) _____ Louie from *The Jungle Book*
(6) _____ Charming from *Cinderella*
(7) _____ Rapunzel from *Tangled*
(8) __Prince__ John from *Robin Hood*
(9) _____ Atta from *A Bug's Life*
(10) _____ Elinor from *Brave*

Oo-De-Lally! A crown! How exciting!

Illustration by Christopher Michon • https://failedimagineer.com

🍴 Storybook Treats Quick Service • Outdoor Seating

Once upon a time there was…a sweet, thatched cottage serving treats like soft-serve ice cream cones, floats and sundaes. This stand is right next door to The Friar's Nook and they share an outdoor seating area. …and they all lived happily ever after. The end.

🍴 The Friar's Nook Quick Service • Outdoor Seating

This half-timbered eatery is named after Friar Tuck, a badger in the 1973 animated movie *Robin Hood* about a foxy outlaw who stole from the rich to give to the poor. Nab hearty food here like breakfast sandwiches, hot dogs, potato tots with toppings and specialty drinks.

📷 Meet n' Greets

Princess Fairytale Hall is where various princesses take time to visit with their loyal subjects inside ritzy receiving rooms. The lineup usually includes Cinderella (from *Cinderella* of course), Elena (from *Elena of Avalor*), Rapunzel (from *Tangled*) and Tiana (from *The Princess and the Frog*). Outside you may spot Cindy's sassy stepsisters Anastasia and Drizella or her sweet Fairy Godmother near the Castle Wall or by Cinderella Fountain.

Tomorrowland

"I kept dreaming of a world I thought I'd never see. And then, one day...I got in."
—KEVIN FLYNN

Leave reality behind in this out-of-this-world land that's focused on the future. Here you'll find retro space age and modern buildings lined with vibrant neon lights that play host to your epic intergalactic—and earthbound—odysseys!

☆ ☆ ☆ ☆ ☆

Tomorrowland Speedway

Racers, start your *engines!* Colorful racing flags flutter over the entrance to this Opening Day attraction that automobile fans are sure to enjoy. Hop behind the steering wheel and push *down* on the pedal to go and *release* it to slow down or stop. Your *scenic* drive will take you in a twisty loop around the *Speedway* towards the finish line. The journey ends at *Victory Circle* where you'll stop your car back at the boarding area and let the next driver take a whirl!

 **HOT TIP** To **drive,** you must be at least **54"** tall. Guests **32" and over** may still ride but can't be behind the wheel.

🍴 Cosmic Ray's Starlight Café

Quick Service • Indoor & Outdoor Seating

The most awesome thing here is alien Sonny Eclipse performing on an astro organ while you dine! Swing by for standards like chicken sandwiches, salads and burgers (meat and plant-based).

PLUS: **Energy Bytes** stand with slushies & snacks

★★★★★ TRON Lightcycle Run

In the TRON movies, a video game creator called *Kevin Flynn* and later his son Sam enter a virtual reality called the *Grid* where they battle evil computer-generated characters called *Programs*. To enter the Grid, you'll pass under an arched canopy and go indoors to be *digitized* and join Team Blue. If you have any loose items you can stash them in free lockers (and pick them up after the ride). To travel into this cyber universe, you'll sit atop a glowing motorbike-style *Lightcycle* that's connected to others in a long row. Now it's time to hold on, keep your head up and face forward as you bullet from *zero to 60 MPH* on a high-speed *race* against the Programs on Team Orange. Once you've crossed through the *8 Energy Gates* you'll see which team has won!

ROLLER COASTER EST. 2023

HOT TIP: You can request to ride in a *Lightrover* ride car instead which has a *seat* with a *lap bar*.

SHOP SPOTLIGHT

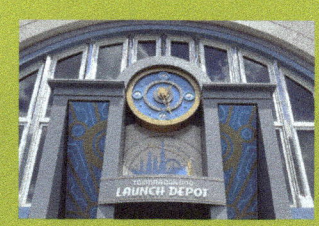

Find fab futuristic gear and gadgets at **Tomorrowland Launch Depot**.

TIME MACHINE

1976 — The 1972 video game Pong & "Alice in Wonderland" inspire animator Steven Lisberger to create "TRON."

1982 — "TRON" hits theaters with groundbreaking visual effects that combine animation & live action.

2010 — "TRON Legacy" is released & music from Daft Punk's soundtrack is later used in the ride.

2023 — Greetings, Programs! Lightcycles come to Magic Kingdom after debuting in Shanghai Disneyland in 2016.

☆ ☆ ☆ ☆ ☆
Space Mountain

ROLLER COASTER EST. 1975

MAY BE SCARY
HEIGHT: 44"+

Rocket through the *universe* on an exciting indoor thrill ride through deepest darkest space! You'll make your way through sleek *Starport 75* to a launchpad where you'll board a rocket-shaped coaster with single file seats. Once all systems are *GO*, you'll zoom into a tunnel *aglow* with pulsing lights towards a mysterious round, glowing orb. After your coaster has *clickclacked* its way uphill, you'll dive and spiral past galaxies of comets, glowing meteors, celestial satellites and shooting stars. *Blasting* through a wormhole, you'll suddenly find yourself back on Planet Earth, safe and sound!

 SPY — As you **exit** the ride you'll pass a futuristic **baggage claim** area, a **command center** run by a robot, a **stylish lounge** with a robotic waiter and scenes from various **outer space** destinations.

TIME MACHINE

1964
Walt Disney approaches Imagineers with an idea for a roller coaster called Space Port or Space Voyage.

1965
Disney Legend John Hench sketches the iconic structure of Space Mountain.

1973
Astronaut Gordon Cooper helps to design Space Mountain to make it as realistic as possible.

1975
Blast off! Magic Kingdom gets its first thrill ride when Space Mountain debuts.

Talk Like an Astronaut!

When astronauts need to make sure they're not misunderstood, they spell out their message using the **Phonetic Alphabet Code** where each **letter** is said as a **word** that starts with that letter.

Hotel India!

DECODER:

A = Alpha	J = Juliet	S = Sierra
B = Bravo	K = Kilo	T = Tango
C = Charlie	L = Lima	U = Uniform
D = Delta	M = Mike	V = Victor
E = Echo	N = November	W = Whiskey
F = Foxtrot	O = Oscar	X = X-ray
G = Golf	P = Papa	Y = Yankee
H = Hotel	Q = Quebec	Z = Zulu
I = India	R = Romeo	

Translate these **phrases** from signs in Space Mountain that have been spelled with the **Phonetic Alphabet** below. One has been done for you.
Answers on page 202.

Golf Romeo Alpha Victor India Tango Yankee • Bravo Alpha Rome
_____Gravity Bar_____

Oscar X-ray Yankee Golf Echo November • Delta Oscar Mike Echo
_____

Romeo Oscar Charlie Kilo Echo Tango • Romeo Echo Alpha Delta Yankee
_____

Now write your **full name** using this code below:
_____
_____

🍴 Auntie Gravity's Galactic Goodies

Quick Service • Indoor & Outdoor Seating

A play on the term "anti-gravity," this is the place for yummy frozen treats like soft-serve ice cream, floats and sundaes. In the indoor area there are posters on the walls promoting things like a rocket show and Astro Orbiter.

PLUS: Cool Ship stand with cotton candy, popcorn & drinks

What's your favorite dessert?
_____

🍴 The Lunching Pad Quick Service • Outdoor Seating

Inspired by a "launching pad" where rockets take off into outer space, this ground floor eatery serves breakfast bowls, hot dogs and pretzels.

☆☆☆☆☆ PeopleMover

OPEN-AIR TRAM RIDE ★ EST. 1975 ★

The full name of this ride is Tomorrowland Transit Authority PeopleMover but, WHEW, that's a mouthful! You can just call it the *PeopleMover* like everyone else. You'll go up a moving ramp to reach the loading platform where you and your group will board your own section of a slowly moving tram. Once you're underway, *magnets* under the vehicle will transfer it over to a slightly faster track. Now you can sit back, relax and enjoy an outdoor and indoor (and sometimes very dark) tour. You'll cross *over* Tomorrowland Speedway and *through* the insides of Space Mountain, Buzz Lightyear's Space Ranger Spin and the Star Traders shop. As you zip about, the voice of a cheerful *robot* called ORAC-5 will narrate where you are and what there is to see. The PeopleMover creates *no* pollution and does indeed *move people* but in the end you'll end up right back where you started. My stars!

SPY — A **model** of Walt Disney's original vision of **EPCOT** is one of the **displays** you'll see when you pass through the tunnels on the PeopleMover.

FUN FACT — The Lunching Pad, PeopleMover's loading platform and Astro Orbiter are all in **Rockettower Plaza**—a play on the name of New York City's **Rockefeller Plaza**. This area also has an **outdoor stage** and a massive **Kugel ball** that's **super heavy** but, because it sits on a thin layer of water, you can turn it pretty easily!

☆ ☆ ☆ ☆ ☆
Astro Orbiter

Pilot your own high-flying, *retro rocket* 'round and 'round the skies of Tomorrowland. Originally called Star Jets, this attraction is actually positioned about *60 feet* off the ground, on top of a raised platform that's reached by an *elevator*. You'll board your ride car to orbit a towering structure that's encircled by a colorful solar system of *planets*. Once the ride begins, the front seat passenger will control how low or high your rocket will fly by *pulling* and *pushing* a lever. Will you hover near the base or reach for the stars?

Illustration by Chris Buchholz • www.etsy.com/shop/buchworks

 **HOT TIP** Because of Astro Orbiter's **height,** you'll have a **fabulous** view—especially at **night.** And if you can ride it during a fireworks show, it's **pure magic!**

 FUN FACT A **gantry** is the name of the structure that surrounds and supports a **rocket** before it takes off. Like **Astro Orbiter,** the gantry has an **elevator** so **astronauts** can reach the top of the rocket to climb in and get ready for **launch.**

OUTDOOR SPINNER EST. 1974

More Missions Nearby

About an hour's drive away from Walt Disney World is the **Kennedy Space Center** in **Cape Canaveral** which is run by the National Aeronautics and Space Administration (or **NASA**). This center has interactive **games** and **simulators,** multimedia **exhibits,** and displays of **rockets** and the **Space Shuttle Atlantis.** You can also experience a recreation of the 1968 launch of **Apollo 8,** the first crewed NASA mission to orbit the moon. If there's a **live** rocket launch happening at Cape Canaveral, this Center has the **closest viewing location** that's open to the public. Other destinations you may want to explore near Walt Disney World include **Blue Spring State Park** (manatees!), **Leu Gardens** (botanical gardens!), **St. Augustine** (history!) and theme parks like **Busch Gardens Tampa Bay, LEGOLAND Florida, SeaWorld Orlando** and **Universal Orlando Resort!**

☆ ☆ ☆ ☆ ☆
Walt Disney's Carousel of Progress

This unique rotating theater circles back to *recap* some of the innovations and inventions developed in recent history. Starting on Valentine's Day around *1900*, you'll visit the home of a folksy father who'll tell you about the handy-dandy new *gizmos* and *modernizations* that are making life *easier* for him and his family—even Uncle Orville! Moving forward in time, you'll visit them on Independence Day in the *1920s*, Halloween in the *1940s* and Christmastime in the *present* day. After each scene, the section you're sitting in will slowly rotate to reveal the next part of the stage as everyone joins together to sing "There's a Great Big Beautiful Tomorrow."

TV screens outside of the theater show recordings of **Walt** giving a behind-the-scenes look at the **Audio-Animatronic technology** used to create the **family**—and **animals**—for this attraction.

The theme song for this show was written by Disney Legends the **Sherman Brothers.** Richard and Robert Sherman also wrote songs that are played in **It's a Small World** and **Enchanted Tiki Room!**

Antiquated Lingo!

The **family** from the Carousel of Progress uses some **words** that you don't hear too often these days! Put a ✓ in the box next to the **meaning** you **think** may be correct below. One has been done for you. *Answers on page 202.*

(1) **Canning** = Preserving food by sealing it in: ☐ a cellar ☑ cans or jars
(2) **Cistern** = Reservoir or tank for holding: ☐ gas ☐ water
(3) **Clodhopper** = Someone who is: ☐ clumsy ☐ good at jumping
(4) **Hoochie Coochie** = An exotic: ☐ dance ☐ spice
(5) **Lumbago** = Pain in the: ☐ feet ☐ lower back
(6) **Rumpus Room** = A room for: ☐ clowns ☐ recreation
(7) **Stereoscope** = Viewing device that make an image seem: ☐ 3D ☐ loud

My lumbago isn't acting up.

☆ ☆ ☆ ☆ ☆
Buzz Lightyear's Space Ranger Spin

Buzz illustration by Kristen O'Dell

Take a *spin* through Buzz's world! Before you begin, Space Ranger Lightyear will brief you on your mission. You need to stop his enemy, the evil *Emperor Zurg* and his army of robots from stealing batteries called *crystallic fusion cells* that would power their weapons! Next, it's time for Junior Space Rangers like you to report to your battle station, an *XP-37 Star Cruiser* ride car. You'll use a joystick to spin into position and rack up points by zapping as many *"Z" targets* as you can with your laser cannon. At the end of the mission, check your score on the dashboard of your cruiser and compare it to the rankings on the status board on the wall. Will you be a *Star Cadet* or rule the galaxy as a *Galactic Hero?*

HOT TIP: To score big, **never stop firing**—even if the ride stops. Targets that are **further** away from you are usually worth **more** points. And when you find a good target, **fire again**—you get points **each time** you hit it!

📷 Meet n' Greets

Buzz Lightyear meets fans outside in the Buzz Lightyear Exit Courtyard by his ride, though you may encounter Experiment 626—also known as Stitch from the 2002 animated movie *Lilo and Stitch*—hanging around here instead.

TIME MACHINE

1972 — If You Had Wings & then Delta Dreamflight (both later renamed) are where Buzz's ride is until 1998.

1995 — The animated "Toy Story" movie hits theaters—the first of many films to feature Buzz Lightyear.

1998 — Buzz Lightyear's Space Ranger Spin debuts in Magic Kingdom & exits through a toy shop.

2022 — Buzz battles Zurg when the animated movie "Lightyear" is released. To infinity & beyond!

⭐⭐⭐⭐⭐ *That's short for Incorporated!*

Monsters, Inc. Laugh Floor

INTERACTIVE SHOW • EST. 2007

Thank goodness the citizens of **Monstropolis** have figured out that human **laughs** create more of the energy they need to power their city than **screams!** You'll go through a portal to Monstropolis and be treated to hilarious jokes inside the **Laugh Floor** comedy club. The more you **giggle,** the more energy will be collected in the giant yellow canister to the right of the stage. Your host is the wonderfully funny Mike Wazowski. This one-eyed, green-skinned guy is the club's **Monster of Ceremonies.** He'll introduce the various acts like his little nephew Marty and a purple, mind-reading monster. Through it all, Mike's **"tender, oozing blossom"** of a boss Roz tunes in on a large screen. She wants to make sure he's meeting his **quota** of chuckles. No two shows are exactly alike and the clever comedians even include the **audience** in their act—so don't be surprised if you see yourself or someone near you caught on camera!

 HOT TIP: While waiting to go in to the Laugh Floor, you'll find out how to **text a joke** to the comedians. Mike's nephew **Marty** will tell some of the Guests' jokes during the show!

FUN FACT: A **theater-in-the-round building** across the walkway from here had an attraction inside called **Stitch's Great Escape** (2004 until 2018). Something **new** will surely be added to that spot **someday...**

 **Mini Quiz!** Can you guess what a giant mythological one-eyed monster is called? *Answer on page 202.*
☐ Cyclops ☐ Gorgon ☐ Hydra

TIME MACHINE

1971 — A theater opens with films like "American Journeys" & "The Timekeeper" shown in Circle-Vision 360.

2001 — We scare because we care! Mike & Sulley star in the animated movie "Monsters, Inc."

2007 — Monsters, Inc. Laugh Floor debuts in Magic Kingdom where the Circle-Vision 360 films used to be.

2013 — The animated "Monsters University" prequel about Mike & Sulley's college days hits theaters.

Illustrations by Fiona Dulieu • www.fionadulieu.com

Say What? Laughs Edition!

Guess which **character** said which funny **quote**. Draw a line from their **name** to their **speech bubble**. One has been done for you. *Answers on page 202.*

Speech bubbles:
- The poison. The poison for Kuzco. The poison chosen especially to kill Kuzco. Kuzco's poison. That poison?
- Not in front of the kids!
- Wow, is my hair out?
- I don't have a skull. Or bones.
- I worship furs!
- My eyeballs could have been sucked from their sockets!
- I don't believe I ordered a wake-up call, Mikey.
- Whatever just happened...blame it on the pig.
- I'm sorry I bit you. And pulled your hair. And punched you in the face.

Characters:
- Buzz Lightyear
- Cruella de Vil
- Gramma Tala
- Hades
- Kronk
- Lilo
- Olaf
- Sulley
- Timon

 Tomorrowland Terrace

Quick Service • Outdoor Seating

This futuristic spot has a prime location on the water with grand views of Cinderella Castle. Lately this terrace has been used as a location for special events like Dessert Parties *(cost extra)*. Psst! If the pathway that goes through this area is open, it's a great way to get from Main Street USA to Tomorrowland.

Liberty Square

"Odds bodkins, gadzooks! Look at that old spook of spooks."
—BROM BONES

Experience America's early days in this sweet land of liberty. Here you'll find the Liberty Tree hung with lanterns for the original 13 states, brick buildings with window shutters, horse hitching posts and a bell made from the same mold as the actual Liberty Bell!

🍴 Sleepy Hollow Quick Service • Outdoor Seating

The 1949 animated *The Adventures of Ichabod and Mr. Toad* movie retold "The Legend of Sleepy Hollow," a story from 1820 about the Headless Horseman. Stop by this brick cottage for legendary funnel cakes and waffles.

☆★★★★ The Hall of Presidents

SO YOU KNOW... *rotunda* = round room, usually with a dome

INDOOR SHOW — EST. 1971

How would you like to hang out with every U.S. President? This Audio-Animatronic Opening Day show featuring American leaders from George Washington onward is as close as you can get! Before the show begins you can see real presidential possessions on display in the **rotunda.** Once inside the theater you'll view a film about America's history. Next, the screen rises and the Commanders in Chiefs are introduced in the order they served the country. When the most recent Prez speaks, you'll be hearing a recording of their actual voice!

 **SPY** Look for **two lanterns** in an outside window. They represent the signal Americans used for warning each other that the British soldiers were coming. *"One if by land, two if by sea."*

Try to spot the tree's 13 lanterns when you're in Liberty Square!

74

☆☆☆☆☆ Ride it while you can! See page 87.

Liberty Square Riverboat

OUTDOOR BOAT RIDE • EST. 1971

Tour the Rivers of America aboard the *Liberty Belle!* This working replica of a 19th-century paddle wheeler uses *steam power* to travel to and from Liberty Square in a loop around *Tom Sawyer Island.* As you enjoy your ride aboard this beauty, listen as *Mark Twain,* the author of the classic American book "The Adventures of Tom Sawyer," shares his *Mississippi memories.* During your journey, you can explore the four decks or find a spot to relax and take in the sights, though seating is limited. This was almost an *Opening Day* attraction—it was ready for Guests on day two!

FUN FACT: Near the dock is a **pillory** (for hands and **heads**) and **stocks** (for hands and **feet**). Devices like these were for **punishing** naughty people in front of other townsfolk.

Riverboat photograph by Dave DeCaro • www.daveland.web.com

Liberty Square Market

Quick Service • Outdoor Seating

Hear ye, hear ye! Here ye can find an open-air Colonial market with wagons and barrels filled with snacks like cheese, fruit, pickles and pretzels, and heartier fare like hot dogs and turkey legs.

Liberty Tree Tavern

Family Style • Indoor Seating

It's easy to imagine it's the 1700s inside this quaint tavern where Thanksgiving meals are served daily. The dining rooms are each related to a different historical figure (like Betsy Ross or Paul Revere) and have wood paneling, brick fireplaces and brass candelabras.

The Diamond Horseshoe **Family Style • Indoor Seating**

This music hall looks like the Old West saloon that Imagineer Harper Goff created for the 1953 Warner Bros. live-action movie *Calamity Jane.* You'll find the same menu here as at Liberty Tree Tavern. While you feast, a Wurlitzer player piano on stage plays merry music!

★★★★★

Haunted Mansion

INDOOR DARK RIDE · EST. 1971

MAY BE SCARY

Inside this home of 999 happy haunts is a mysterious chamber where the *disembodied* voice of your Ghost Host fills the air and eerie portraits stretch before your eyes. Once you find your way out, you'll board a *Doom Buggy* to glide through a library and on past *curious* statues and strange staircases that seem to defy gravity. Winding further into the dark mansion, you'll witness a piano playing itself, a creaking coffin and an odd gent clutching a *hatbox.* After traveling down a long hallway with demon-eye wallpaper, your buggy visits a seance room where the floating head of *Madame Leota* summons spirits to appear. And appear they do! You'll see them dance, dine and duel in a *ballroom* before you move on to a musty *attic* where a ghostly bride pledges her *undying* devotion to a *string* of unlucky husbands. As you near the final scene, you'll descend upon a graveyard that's alive with gleeful ghouls but—*beware*—one of them just might try to follow you home!

HOT TIP: The standby line here is **to die for!** You may be a **muse** to a dead poet, figure out whodunit from **clues** on five statues, play **music** on a creepy crypt and solve a **puzzle** on a haunted bookcase using the **decoder** below.

SHOP SPOTLIGHT

Rap on the portrait of Madame Leota in **Memento Mori** and she may respond.

Silhouette Decoder

13	♥	🍍	🍴	🪓	👤	👤
A	C	D	E	F	G	H

🗡	🐓	🔑	🎷	🪦	🏺	🏺	🐍	🗝	🏺	🕯	🗡
I	K	L	M	N	O	P	R	S	T	U	W	Y

TIME MACHINE

1971 — Welcome, foolish mortals... kindly step all the way in! Haunted Mansion is an Opening Day attraction.

2007 — The ghosts do a bit of remodeling including adding a strange staircase with glowing footprints.

2011 — The standby line is revamped with activities & tributes to Disney Legends like Collin Campbell.

2023 — The live-action "Haunted Mansion" movie hits theaters, 20 years after "The Haunted Mansion."

Do you believe in ghosts?
☐ Yes! ☐ No. ☐ Maybe?

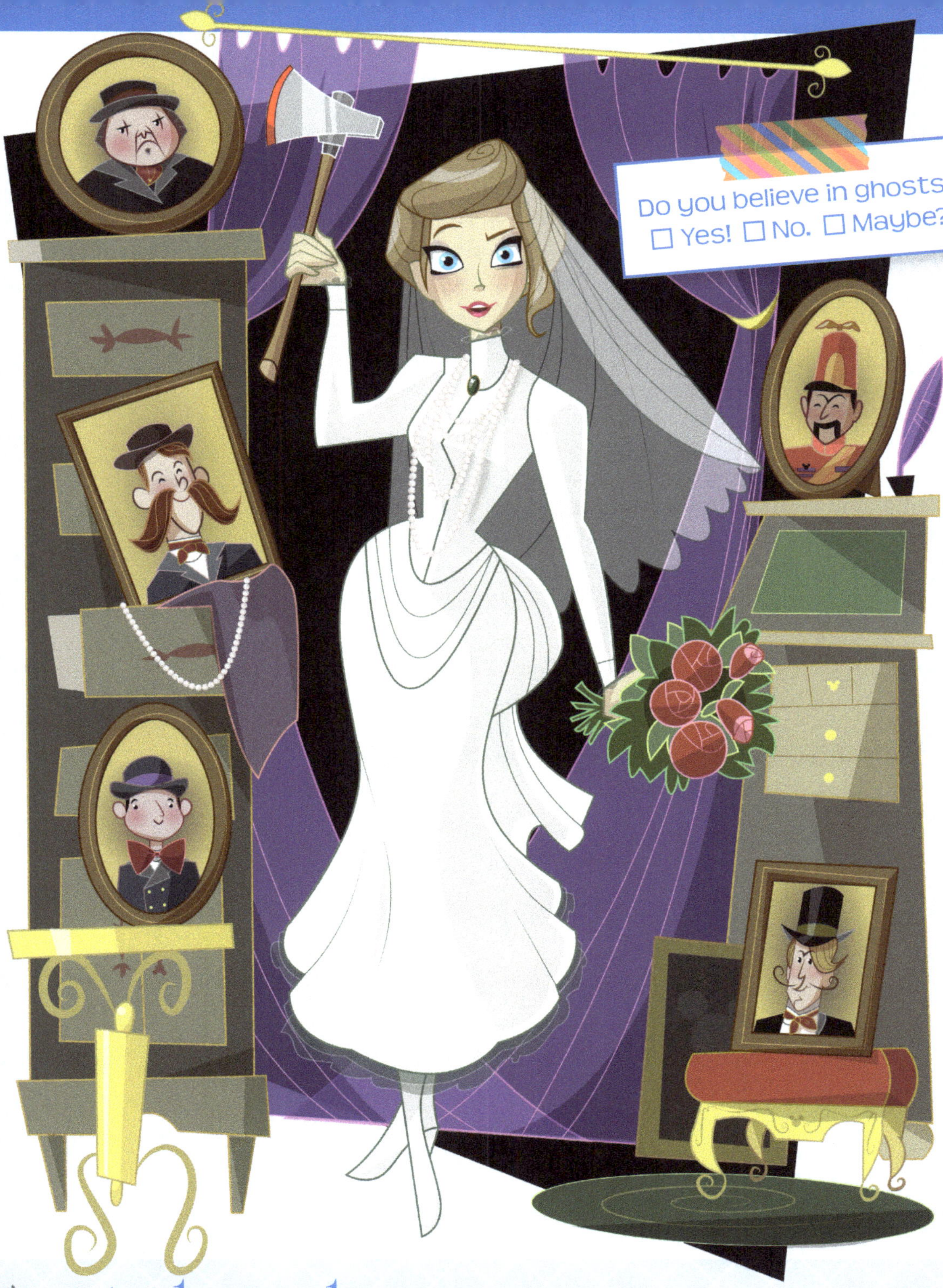

🍴 Columbia Harbour House Quick Service • Indoor Seating

Your hunger doesn't stand a ghost of a chance at this nautical eatery named after the first American ship to circle the globe. Carved wooden figureheads and paneling, braided ropes, and ship's wheels decorate the cozy dining rooms where you can enjoy your seafood selections like clam chowder soup, lobster rolls, and fish or shrimp platters. Don't miss the seating upstairs too!

Adventureland

> "Everything we need—everything—right here, right at our fingertips."
> —FATHER ROBINSON

Find adventure all around you in this land. Here you'll find elements of African, Asian, Caribbean, Middle Eastern and Polynesian cultures blended in a joyful mix of brightly colored buildings, silken canopies, thatched tiki rooftops and sun-bleached stucco!

🍴 Sunshine Tree Terrace

Quick Service • Outdoor Seating

This baby blue building with breezy fans has cool treats like the Citrus Swirl made with frozen orange juice and vanilla soft-serve. This eatery is home to Orange Bird, a character from the 1970s who speaks in orange-colored thought bubbles and started his career promoting Florida citrus and Walt Disney World!

HEY KIDS COLOR ME IN!

🍴 Skipper Canteen *Table Service • Indoor Seating*

The Jungle Navigation Co. runs this establishment which has the large open Mess Hall, the jewel-toned Jungle Room and the cozy S.E.A. (Society of Explorers and Adventurers) Room which you enter through a "secret" passageway. Explore world-famous jungle cuisine like curry, noodles, salads and soups.

☆☆☆☆☆

Swiss Family Treehouse

WALK-THROUGH • EST. 1971

This Opening Day attraction lets you climb your way through the home of the **Robinsons**, the family of five from Switzerland who survived a shipwreck. This **crafty** crew adapted to life on a **deserted island** by salvaging items from their ship and building an incredible treehouse! To tour their abode, you'll **traverse** over 100 stairs to see clever **innovations** like a bamboo water wheel and a giant clamshell sink. Peek into the living room, sleeping quarters, library and kitchen as you make your way up to the **tippity top** of the tree and back down again.

SPY — Look for an organ playing a **merry tune** in the treehouse. It's the **"Swisskapolka,"** the same song Mother Robinson plays in the movie.

☆ ☆ ☆ ☆ ☆
The Magic Carpets of Aladdin

OUTDOOR SPINNER · EST. 2001

Aladdin and Princess Jasmine left from Agrabah to see a **whole new world** on a magic carpet in the 1992 animated movie. Now you can enjoy your own high-flying jaunt! You'll twirl around a column topped by the **magic lamp** and decorated with images of Aladdin's pals, Abu the monkey and Genie. Each carpet has two rows of pillow-shaped seats and each row has **different** controls. If you're up front, you can move a lever to go up and down. If you're in back, you can press a golden scarab beetle to tilt forward or backward. As you sail through the skies, look out to enjoy your **new fantastic point of view!**

HOT TIP **Beware**—the **camel statues** around this ride have been known to **spit**. Real camels tend to do this too!

Meet n' Greets
Visit with Aladdin and Jasmine when they pop by the Agrabah Bazaar market area.

Did you see the live-action *Aladdin* movie from 2012?
☐ Yes, I did! ☐ No, not yet…

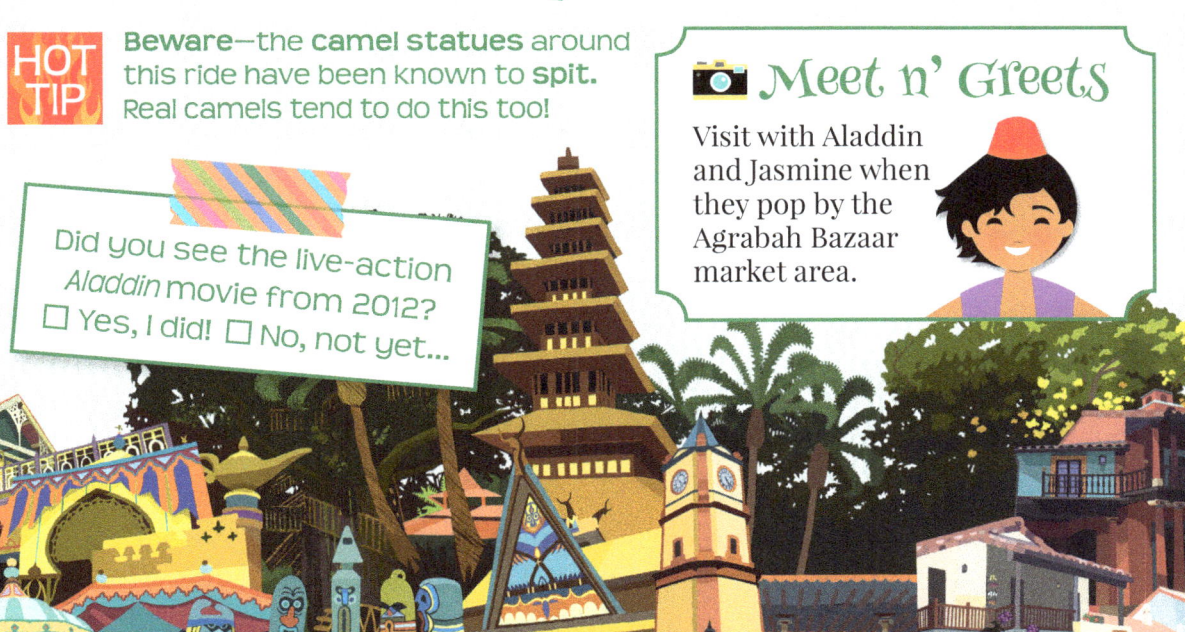

TIME MACHINE

1812 — Let us be content! Swiss author Johann David Wyss's book "Swiss Family Robinson" is published.

1960 — The live-action movie "Swiss Family Robinson" about Fritz, Ernst, Francis & their folks hits theaters.

2001 — The Magic Carpets of Aladdin debuts with camels that came from a Disney's Hollywood Studios parade.

2012 — An Orange Bird statue that was removed in the 1980s flies back to Sunshine Tree Terrace.

Scene illustration by danamarie hosler • www.danamariehosler.com

⭐⭐⭐⭐⭐ Jungle Cruise

It's a jungle out there! But fear not—a daring skipper from the *Jungle Navigation Co.* will guide you safely through the murky waters with an endless supply of *knee-slapping* jokes. To begin your globe-trotting journey, you'll pass trunks, crates and other expedition supplies to catch a *tramp steamer* with your fellow passengers. Rooftop signs on the boats show their names, which are inspired by real rivers. Once aboard, you'll *explore* South America's Amazon rainforest, Africa's Congo and Nile rivers, and Asia's Mekong river and see amusing animals like elephants, hippos and monkeys. You'll *cruise* by a crashed plane, into the dark ruins of an ancient temple and even past the *Backside of Water* before heading back to the dangers of civilization!

Which boats have you ridden in?
_____
_____
_____
_____

OUTDOOR BOAT RIDE — EST. 1971

 **SPY** Look near Jungle Cruise for a row of colorful, carved *Liki Tikis*. These tiki totems stand ready to **surprise you** with sprays and spritzes of water!

TIME MACHINE

1951 — The live-action United Artists movie "The African Queen" premieres & later influences Jungle Cruise.

1971 — Jungle Cruise is an Opening Day attraction & it's later "operated by" Jungle Navigation Co.

2013 — An annual tradition begins when Jungle Cruise becomes Jingle Cruise during the holiday season.

2021 — Kungaloosh! The live-action "Jungle Cruise" movie hits theaters.

Tiki photograph by Dave DeCaro • www.davelandweb.com

☆ ☆ ☆ ☆ ☆

Walt Disney's Enchanted Tiki Room

The birds sing words and the flowers **croon** in the Tiki Room! You can't miss the towering grass-roofed *pagoda* that houses this Opening Day attraction. Before your *tropical serenade* begins, enjoy the playful antics of two talking toucans on the outside patio. As jungle drums play, you'll head indoors to be whisked away to the South Seas by a musical *menagerie*. Around you are over *225* colorful birds, totem poles, tiki sculptures and tropical flowers. Comical parrots José, Michael, Pierre and Fritz are your hosts as the *enchanted* room comes alive with songs, a dazzling fountain and even a loud, thundering storm!

SO YOU KNOW... croon = hum or sing softly

INDOOR SHOW * EST. 1971 *

 FUN FACT — When **Walt Disney's Enchanted Tiki Room** opened in Disneyland in **1963**, it was one of the first attractions **ever** to use Audio-Animatronics.

Mini Quiz!

Can you guess which of these birds appeared in Magic Kingdom's Tiki Room between 1998 and 2011?
Answer on page 202.

☐ Daisy and Donald
☐ Heihei and Scuttle
☐ Huey, Dewey and Louie
☐ Iago and Zazu

🍴 Aloha Isle Quick Service • Outdoor Seating

Topped by a tiki-riffic zigzag roof, this refreshment stand serves a famously delicious frozen treat—the pineapple soft-serve Dole Whip. Tucked right next to Enchanted Tiki Room, you can take your treat to a nearby table or bring it inside with you to enjoy during the show!

☆☆☆☆☆

Pirates of the Caribbean

INDOOR BOAT RIDE — EST. 1973

MAY BE SCARY

If ye be brave, or fool enough, proceed! Pass by a tall clocktower to enter a *fortress* to travel back to the Golden Age of Piracy. You and your fellow *shipmates* will board a boat and sail past the

skeletal remains of unlucky pirates as the wind roars and an *eerie* voice chants "Dead men tell no tales…" After you *plummet* down a waterfall in the darkness, you'll round a bend to witness a fierce battle between Captain Barbossa's *galleon* and a Caribbean fort. Heading into port, the town is abuzz with a lively auction and talk of the *whereabouts* of Captain Jack Sparrow and some missing *treasure*. As the town burns around them, the buccanneers sing about their way of life while Sparrow sits back and enjoys his loot. *Yo ho, yo ho!*

 FUN FACT Pirates of the Caribbean's **Castillo del Morro Fortress** is inspired by a beautiful 16th-century fortress called **Castillo San Felipe del Morro** in Puerto Rico, a U.S. territory southeast of Florida.

🍴 Tortuga Tavern

Quick Service • Indoor & Outdoor Seating

This restaurant named after a Caribbean island (and the Spanish word for turtle) has bright tropical colors, tile floors and a rough-hewn fireplace. During some Adventureland construction *(see opposite page)*, this was set up as a temporary shop!

TIME MACHINE

1973
Pirates of the Caribbean fans who were sad this park didn't have a Pirates ride rejoice when the ride opens.

2003
The first live-action "Pirates of the Caribbean" movie (inspired by the attraction) hits theaters.

2006
Characters from the smash hit "Pirates of the Caribbean" movie series are added to the ride.

2013
Avast, mateys! A Pirate's Adventure— Treasures of the Seven Seas debuts.

Which Pirates flicks have you seen?

- ☐ The Curse of the Black Pearl, 2003
- ☐ Dead Man's Chest, 2006
- ☐ At World's End, 2007
- ☐ On Stranger Tides, 2011
- ☐ Dead Men Tell No Tales, 2017

A Pirate's Life for You

The Crow's Nest near Tortuga Tavern is where you can set sail for **A Pirate's Adventure—Treasures of the Seven Seas**. In this free, interactive activity, you'll look for **treasure** and help Captain Jack defeat foes like **Blackbeard the pirate**. You'll get a special map, a magic **talisman** and training from a Cast Member on how to unlock **cool secrets** all around Adventureland. Finish all five missions to earn a **collectible card** signed by Jack himself!

Meet n' Greets

See if you can catch that scallywag Captain Jack Sparrow gallivanting about outside near the Pirates of the Caribbean.

Imagineers at Play

Plans may change!

Disney announced in **2023** that **Adventureland** would be getting a new **pirate tavern**. **2024** concept art of this **watering hole** showed wood beams, an anchor covered in candles hung from the ceiling and swooping red drapes.

Well, **whaddya think,** matey? Will **you** frequent this spot for **grub n' grog?**
- ☐ Aye, you best believe it!
- ☐ Only time will tell!
- ☐ Gar, I be passing on that!

Frontierland

"I say, y'all come back, ya hear?"
—SAMMY THE RACOON

This rustic frontier town has one of Walt Disney World Railroad's three stations. Here you'll find log cabins, pioneer town buildings with wooden boardwalks, rugged rocks and rollicking rivers, and even a bit of backwoods bayou!

♫ Entertainment

If yer lucky, ya might catch a Hoedown Happening where Cast Members and characters kick up their heels, dance and sing in the open area in front of Grizzly Hall. This shindig isn't on the schedule but usually happens in the late afternoon.

SHOP SPOTLIGHT

Saunter in for your Old West wares (and pins!) at **Frontier Trading Post**.

Do you collect anything?
☐ Nah. ☐ Yes! If yes, what?
_____

The Joys of Pin Trading

Collectible **metal Disney pins** can be bought all over the resort and traded with Cast Members and other Guests. There are **thousands** of designs featuring attractions, characters, events, landmarks, movies, snacks and other themes. Cast Members can help you trade pins from **Pin Trading boards** in and around shops like **Frontier Trading Post** or from **Pin Trading lanyards** around their necks. If you ask to trade with a Cast Member or a Guest, it's up to them whether they want to make the trade or not, just like it's up to **YOU** when you're trading **YOUR** pins.

⭐⭐⭐⭐⭐
Country Bear Musical Jamboree

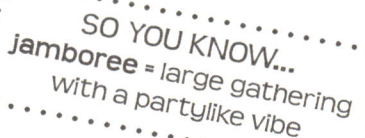
SO YOU KNOW...
jamboree = large gathering with a partylike vibe

INDOOR SHOW EST. 1971

Head on into **Grizzly Hall** for a wild n' woolly musical **jamboree** put on by a pack of funny, furry—and talented—bears. A trio of mounted **trophy heads** named Melvin, Buff and Max join in the fun too. Your host **Henry** will introduce the acts who play instruments and sing **country-western** versions of Disney songs on five stages. Feel free to clap your **claws** and tap your **paws** along with catchy ditties like "Try Everything" from *Zootopia* sung by Trixie and company. You'll hear slow **ballads** too like "A Whole New World" from *Aladdin* crooned by Wendell, Gomer and Teddi Barra—who sits on rose-covered swing. The **loveable** fan-favorite **Big Al** makes a **memorable** appearance too!

Grizzly Hall's **lobby displays** include memorabilia like Romeo's **belt buckle,** Shaker's **guitar strap** and a **concert poster** for The Five Bear Rugs.

📷 Meet n' Greets

The Country Bears visit with folks here and there in Frontierland. You might also run into the chipmunks Chip 'n Dale by the River Walk along the water.

Illustrations by Mariana Koontz • www.landandworld.com

TIME MACHINE

1960s
Imagineers work on a bear-themed show for a Disney ski resort but plans are scrapped.

1971
🎵 Blood on the Saddle? Opening Day attraction Country Bear Jamboree debuts at Grizzly Hall.

1984
The bears get a seasonal Christmas version & it's the first holiday overlay for a Disney attraction.

2024
The show is revamped with new costumes, new songs & a new name: Country Bear *Musical* Jamboree.

🍴 Westward Ho Quick Service • No Seating

The name of this woodsy settler's cabin comes from the 1956 live-action movie *Westward Ho, the Wagons!* Hitch your wagon here for grab n' go vittles like breakfast biscuit sandwiches and frozen lemonade.

🍴 Pecos Bill Tall Tale Inn and Café
Quick Service • Indoor & Outdoor Seating

Mexican tile floors, stone fireplaces and lanterns strung overhead transport you west of the Rio Grande river at this eatery. Dig in to foods with a Southwestern flair like chili con queso burgers, nacho bowls, or rice and bean bowls. Memorabilia around the café showcases the cowboy folk hero Pecos Bill, his daredevil girlfriend and his horse.

🍴 Golden Oak Outpost Quick Service • Outdoor Seating

The menu here is inspired by dishes that Chef Tiana might cook up like gumbo and deep-fried, sugar-dusted beignets. This outpost is tucked along a back path near Pecos Bill's café (where you'll find lots of indoor seating if you want to take your meal there).

Melody Time!

In the **1940s**, Disney released many musical **anthologies.** These were movies made up of collections of several **short** films. Put a ✓ in the box next to which of these sentences about these movies are **TRUE** and which are **FALSE**. One has been done for you. *Answers on page 202.*

(1) **"The Sorcerer's Apprentice"** is one of the films in *Fantasia* from 1940.
☑ TRUE ☐ FALSE

(2) **Donald Duck** appears in both *Saludos Amigos* from 1943 and *The Three Caballeros* from 1945. ☐ TRUE ☐ FALSE

(3) **"Casey at the Bat"** in *Make Mine Music* from 1946 is about a **tennis player.**
☐ TRUE ☐ FALSE

(4) In *Fun and Fancy Free* from 1947, Mickey trades a **cow** for **beans.**
☐ TRUE ☐ FALSE

(5) In *Melody Time* from 1948, Pecos Bill's **horse** is called **Slue-Foot Sue.**
☐ TRUE ☐ FALSE

(6) The anthology from 1949 had films about **Mr. Toad** and **Obadiah Crane.**
☐ TRUE ☐ FALSE

☆ ☆ ☆ ☆ ☆
Tom Sawyer Island

OUTDOOR PLAY AREA • EST. 1973

This island was created as a place to **scramble, ramble** and **amble** in any direction to enjoy freewheeling fun inspired by Tom Sawyer's adventures. Located in the middle of the **Rivers of America,** you can only get here by taking a **log raft** that ferries passengers back and forth between the shore and Tom's Landing. Special spots to discover include a **mine** where water flows uphill, a **cave** with a bottomless pit and a wobbly **bridge** made of barrels. A rustic, wooden **fort** is the largest structure on the island and has a blacksmith forge, rifle roosts and an escape tunnel. When you're ready for a break, relax on a **rocking chair,** play a quiet game of checkers or just enjoy the peaceful scenery.

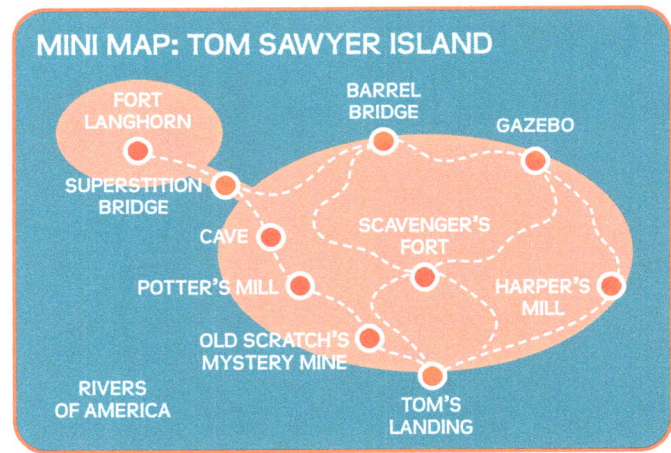

MINI MAP: TOM SAWYER ISLAND — FORT LANGHORN, BARREL BRIDGE, GAZEBO, SUPERSTITION BRIDGE, CAVE, SCAVENGER'S FORT, POTTER'S MILL, HARPER'S MILL, OLD SCRATCH'S MYSTERY MINE, TOM'S LANDING, RIVERS OF AMERICA

 FUN FACT — When the first **Tom Sawyer Island** was being worked on for Disneyland, **Walt Disney** wasn't happy with the way the plans were looking so he took them home and **designed the island himself!**

Imagineers at Play

Plans may change!

In **2024 Disney** announced they were going to permanently **remove** the Rivers of America, Tom Sawyer Island and Liberty Square Riverboat! The plan is to fill in the waterway with a rugged landscape and build two new **Cars** attractions there. Construction is due to begin in **2025.**

What's your **gut reaction?** Which would **you** rather have in Frontierland?
☐ The original stuff! ☐ Uh, I don't know... ☐ The new stuff!

⭐⭐⭐⭐⭐

Tiana's Bayou Adventure

LOG FLUME RIDE EST. 2024

MAY BE SCARY

HEIGHT: 40"+

This ride **whisks** you away to New Orleans to catch up with Tiana. The skillful chef has started up a new business called **Tiana's Foods** with help from her community. Now, to say thanks, she's throwing a big **Mardi Gras** party! To join the fun, you and the other party guests will board a hollowed-out log. As your **adventure** begins, Tiana will greet you and fill you in on how she and **Louis** are searching for the perfect band to jam at the event. You'll float past a vegetable patch outside and then **go on down the bayou** where fireflies dance and light up the night sky—and Tiana and Louis enjoy tunes by two bands of musical critters. Next you'll see Mama Odie who wants you to think **big** and get **tiny**. After a zip down a small hill in the dark, you'll find yourself shrunk to the size of a toadstool as a quartet of frogs play a lively version of "Dig a Little Deeper." Now it's time to make a big **splash** at the party. Your log will take a shortcut and drop an eye-popping **five** stories into the water below. This joyful celebration has all the **ingredients** for a good time!

SO YOU KNOW...
Mardi Gras = the last day of the Carnival festival which is celebrated with feasts, balls and parades

SHOP SPOTLIGHT

Musicians Rufus and Apollo grace the sign for the charming **Critter Co-Op**.

Lari!

HOT TIP
You **might** get wet but just **how** wet you get may depend on **where** you sit. If you'd rather stay as **dry** as possible, ask to sit in the **back** of the log.

SPY
At the **party,** see if you can spot Big Daddy, Eudora, Lottie, Naveen, Ralphie, the **musical critters** and an **armadillo** named **Lari** who you may have first noticed in the vegetable patch. You can see **Lari's house** near **Critter Co-Op**!

TIME MACHINE

1812 — Ribbit! The German fairytale "The Frog Prince" by the Brothers Grimm is published.

1992 — Splash Mountain opens & closes in 2023 to be reimagined with a Tiana theme.

2009 — The animated "The Princess & the Frog" movie hits theaters, taking place from 1912 to the 1920s.

2024 — Tiana's Bayou Adventure opens, along with the shops Critter Co-Op & Tiana's Bayou General.

Parade Illustration by Mary Paviou • www.etsy.com/shop/MareBearPress

🎵 Entertainment

The Adventure Friends Cavalcade is a great way to see lots of characters at once like Bruno, Moana and Woody. The Festival of Fantasy Parade has fancy floats with themes like *Peter Pan, Sleeping Beauty* and *Tangled*. The nighttime Starlight Parade (due to launch in 2025) is led by the Blue Fairy from *Pinocchio*. These all usually start near Tiana's Bayou Adventure, go through Liberty Square, into Central Plaza and on through Main Street USA!

📖 The Story of... The Princess and the Frog

Little Tiana lives in New Orleans with her daddy James and mama Eudora who are big fans of their daughter's cooking—especially her gumbo! Eudora does sewing work for a bigwig named Eli "Big Daddy" La Bouff, and Tiana and his ditzy daughter Charlotte ("Lottie") are friends. James and Tiana plan to open a restaurant together but after he passes away in the war, she works two waitress jobs to save money to make that dream come true. A visiting prince named Naveen runs into trouble with villainous Dr. Facilier who turns him into a frog. At a masquerade ball, Naveen mistakes Tiana for a princess and convinces her to kiss him to break the spell—but that turns her into a frog too! After being chased into the bayou, they befriend a jazz-loving alligator named Louis and a Cajun firefly named Ray who's smitten with a firefly he calls Evangeline, but who everyone else calls the Evening Star. Tiana and Naveen fall in love and try to get help breaking the spell from Mama Odie, a wise old blind woman with magic powers and a snake named Juju. When all of their efforts fail, the frogs have Mama Odie marry them. As they kiss they become human because Tiana is now a princess! The happy couple open a restaurant called Tiana's Palace—and Big Daddy, Lottie, Eudora, Naveen's folks and his little brother Ralphie dine and dance the night away.

⭐⭐⭐⭐⭐

Big Thunder Mountain Railroad

This ride closed most of 2025 for refurbishment!

MAY BE SCARY

HEIGHT: 40"+

This here's the wildest ride in the wilderness! The story goes that *gold* was discovered here back in the *1850s* but members of the Big Thunder Mining Company were frightened away by ghostly happenings and *skeedaddled* out of here quickly. You'll venture inside an abandoned mine shaft to board a rickety mining train. The journey begins in a dark *cavern* filled with screeching bats. Once outside, your coaster *hurtles* through what's left of the rusty, dusty town of *Tumbleweed* and its mining operation. As you dip and dive over hills and through tunnels you'll see spouting water, curious critters and even *dinosaur* bones!

 SPY — The standby line has a portrait of the Big Thunder Mining Company's founder **Barnabas T. Bullion** who looks an awful lot like Disney Legend **Tony Baxter**.

 FUN FACT — Big Thunder's **towering rocks** look like the sandstone **buttes** and **towers** in Arizona's **Monument Valley**—an iconic symbol of the American Wild West!

Canary in a Gold Mine

Big Thunder Mountain Railroad's standby line has comical **AutoCanary** machines to test the air in the mine. Long ago, real **coal miners** would take **canaries** into mines with them. Mining is dangerous work and one of its deadliest hazards is poisonous **carbon monoxide gas.** If there was any of this invisible gas in the air, the little birds would show signs of **distress** long before the workers could tell anything was wrong. This **early warning system** gave people time to get to safety. The use of canaries in mines ended in the **1980s** when **carbon monoxide detectors** were invented.

TIME MACHINE

1849 — The Gold Rush is in full swing as people head west to try & strike it rich in the mines.

1970s — Ideas for a Western pavilion in Magic Kingdom morph into a mine train attraction.

1980 — Hang on to them hats n' glasses! Big Thunder Mountain Railroad opens in Magic Kingdom.

2013 — Interactive fun is added to the standby line for Big Thunder Mountain Railroad.

Coin a Phrase!

Fill in the missing **vowels** from these **Gold Rush-type terms.** One has been done for you. *Answers on page 202.*

B_NANZ_
F_RTY NIN_R
G_LD F_VER
G_LD N_GGET
HIT P_Y D_RT
MOTH_R L_DE
PANN_D O_T
P_TERED _UT
PR_SP_CTOR
SHEN_N_GANS
UNION SUIT

You can see the funny Big Thunder train names on the side of the engine cabs. Put a ✓ in the box next to the trains you've ridden on:
- ☐ I.B. Hearty
- ☐ I.M. Brave
- ☐ I.M. Fearless
- ☐ U.B. Bold
- ☐ U.R. Courageous
- ☐ U.B. Daring

Imagineers at Play

Plans may change!

In **2024** Disney confirmed that in the years ahead they're planning to **expand** past the **current borders** of Frontierland to create a **villain-themed land** beyond Big Thunder Mountain Railroad—which is currently a **dead end.**

Which **villains** do you hope they include in the land? _____
_____

📚 Sample Souvenirs

"Will this about cover it?"
—CHARLOTTE LA BOUFF

Embroidered Ears

Main Street USA's Box Office Gifts is one of many shops where you can buy a classic mouse ear hat. There are mouse ear headbands too but only the hats can be embroidered with your name. First made only in basic black, they now come in a wide variety of colors and styles—though not all of them can be customized. Chat with a Cast Member about your options, including the types of lettering and thread colors you can choose from!

Grid Gear

Tomorrowland Launch Depot in Tomorrowland is the place for all things TRON, like light-up helmets, identity discs, lightcycle handlebars, toy vehicles, light suits and high-end action figures that are customized with your face and voice.

Personal Effects

Amazingly skilled artists create drawn caricatures, cut paper silhouettes and painted umbrellas at carts outside of Liberty Square's Ye Olde Christmas Shoppe. Inside this shop you can buy an ornament and have it painted with your name, a special date or a meaningful message. The in-store artists also paint on the free Disney buttons. All painting costs extra! Days of Christmas in Disney Springs also has customized ornaments and you'll find another silhouette cart in Main Street USA. Caricature artists can be found throughout the resort.

Firefly Friend

Critter Co-Op in Frontierland sells all kinds of Tiana's Bayou Adventure merch like cooking supplies, critter band member plush animals and a tin can bank like Tiana's where you can save up for your dream. There are also light-up fireflies that come in a little jar and interact with other firefly toys that are near them!

Illustration by Melissa Chan Stone • www.amuseboosh.com

M-I-C-K-E-Y M-O-U-S-E

In the **1929** animated short *The Karnival Kid*, Mickey **tips his ears** at Minnie as if they were a hat. That gave Disney Legend **Roy Williams** an idea! He created **black mouse ear hats** for the stars of *The Mickey Mouse Club*. That live-action show debuted in **1955**—the **same year** Disneyland opened—and the hats were first sold there as a unique **souvenir**!

This Land is That Land!

Draw a line connecting the number of the photo on the **left** to the letter of the photo on the **right** that was taken in the **same land** in Magic Kingdom. One has been done for you. *Answers on page 202.*

 1

 A

 2

 B

 3

 C

 4

 D

Riders hold on and get ready for a speedy launch on TRON Lightcycle Run in Tomorrowland.

EPCOT

WORLD SHOWCASE

< INTERNATIONAL GATEWAY

The park's secondary entrance

WORLD DISCOVERY

WORLD NATURE

WORLD CELEBRATION

^ MAIN ENTRANCE

Lands in Brief!

Put a **dot** in the circle next to the **land** that you **think** you'll like best. Once you've visited them all, **color in** the circle by your **favorite**.

○ **World Celebration:** imaginative, modern
○ **World Discovery:** high-speed, visionary
○ **World Nature:** eco-friendly, natural
○ **World Showcase:** cross-cultural, global

EPCOT AT A GLANCE

WORLD CELEBRATION ATTRACTIONS	MEET N' GREETS	ENTERTAINMENT
• Disney & Pixar Short Film Festival • Journey Into Imagination With Figment • Spaceship Earth	• Figment • Mickey	• Celebración Encanto • Forces of Nature • JAMMitors

WORLD NATURE ATTRACTIONS	MEET N' GREETS	ENTERTAINMENT
• Awesome Planet • Journey of Water • Living with the Land • Soarin' Around the World • The Seas with Nemo & Friends • Turtle Talk with Crush	• Moana	

WORLD DISCOVERY ATTRACTIONS	MEET N' GREETS	ENTERTAINMENT
• Guardians of the Galaxy: Cosmic Rewind • Mission: SPACE • Test Track		

WORLD SHOWCASE ATTRACTIONS	MEET N' GREETS	ENTERTAINMENT
CANADA: • Canada Far and Wide FRANCE: • Palais du Cinema • Remy's Ratatouille Adventure AMERICA: • The American Adventure CHINA: • Reflections of China NORWAY: • Frozen Ever After MEXICO: • Gran Fiesta Tour	WORLD SHOWCASE PLAZA: • Asha UNITED KINGDOM: • Alice in Wonderland • Winnie the Pooh FRANCE: • Belle • Princess Aurora MOROCCO: • Princess Jasmine GERMANY: • Snow White CHINA: • Mulan NORWAY: • Anna • Elsa MEXICO: • Donald Duck	THROUGHOUT WORLD SHOWCASE: • Luminous: The Symphony of Us UNITED KINGDOM: • Rose & Crown Pub Musician JAPAN: • Matsuriza AMERICA: • Voices of Liberty ITALY: • Sergio PLUS: Live entertainment in the Canada, UK, Morocco, America, Germany and Mexico pavilions

WORLD SHOWCASE SHOPS

CANADA: Northwest Mercantile
UNITED KINGDOM: Lords and Ladies, Sportsman's Shoppe, The Crown & Crest, The Queen's Table, The Tea Caddy and The Toy Soldier

FRANCE: La Signature, L'Esprit de la Provence, Plume et Palette and Souvenirs de France
MOROCCO: Marketplace in the Medina

JAPAN: Mitsukoshi Department Store
AMERICA: Art of Disney
ITALY: Il Bel Cristalo, La Bottega Italiana and La Gemma Elegante

❖ QUICK-SERVICE EATERY

FOOD & DRINKS

- Connections Café ❖
- Connections Eatery ❖
- Festival Favorites ❖

SHOPS

- Camera Center
- Club Cool
- Creations Shop
- ImageWorks

FOOD & DRINKS

- Coral Reef
- Garden Grill
- Sunshine Seasons ❖

SHOPS

- SeaBase Gift Shop

FOOD & DRINKS

- Refreshment Station ❖
- Space 220
- The Odyssey ❖

SHOPS

- Mission: SPACE Cargo Bay
- Test Track SIMporium
- Treasures of Xandar

FOOD & DRINK

CANADA:
- Le Cellier Steakhouse
- Refreshment Port ❖

UNITED KINGDOM:
- Rose & Crown Dining Room
- Rose & Crown Pub
- Yorkshire County Fish Shop ❖

FRANCE: Chefs de France
- Crêpes À Emporter ❖
- L'Artisan des Glaces ❖
- La Crêperie de Paris
- Les Halles Boulangerie & Patisserie ❖
- Les Vins de Chefs de France
- Monsieur Paul

MOROCCO:
- Oasis Sweets & Sips ❖
- Spice Road Table
- Spice Road Table Bar ❖
- Tangierine Café ❖

JAPAN:
- Kabuki Café ❖
- Katsura Grill ❖
- Shiki-Sai: Sushi Izakaya
- Takumi-Tei
- Teppan Edo

AMERICA:
- Block & Hans ❖
- Fife & Drum Tavern ❖
- Funnel Cake ❖
- Regal Eagle Smokehouse ❖

ITALY:
- Gelateria Toscana ❖
- Pizza al Taglio ❖
- Tutto Gusto
- Tutto Italia
- Via Napoli

GERMANY:
- Biergarten
- Karamell-Küche ❖
- Sommerfest

THE OUTPOST:
- Refreshment Outpost ❖

CHINA:
- Lotus Blossom Café ❖
- Nine Dragons

NORWAY:
- Akershus Royal Banquet Hall
- Kringla Bakeri Og Kafe ❖

MEXICO:
- Choza de Margarita ❖
- La Cantina de San Angel ❖
- La Cava del Tequila
- La Hacienda de San Angel
- San Angel Inn

SHOPS

GERMANY: Das Kaufhaus, Der Teddybear, Die Weihnachts Ecke, Glaskunst, Kunstarbeit in Kristall, Stein Haus, Volkskunst and Weinkeller

THE OUTPOST: Village Traders
CHINA: Good Fortune Gifts and House of Good Fortune
NORWAY: The Fjording and The Puffin's Roost

MEXICO: El Ranchito del Norte, La Princesa de Cristal, La Tienda Encantada, Plaza de los Amigos and Ring Carvers

World Celebration

"See ya real soon!"
—MICKEY MOUSE

Through the Main Entrance is this first land that celebrates human achievement and creativity. Here you'll find the park's iconic globe surrounded by modern buildings with angled surfaces, landscaped plazas and an imaginative pavilion with glass pyramids!

The Entrance Plaza

Fluttering flags with the bold logos of some of the park's attractions flank a fountain with clear, curved columns that reach towards the sky. Beyond this is Spaceship Earth, a ride inside a 180-foot-tall geodesic sphere made of thousands of interlocking metal triangles. Starting at dusk, the fountain projects a color-changing beam, and light patterns flow over the sphere in time to music throughout the evening.

☆☆☆☆☆

Spaceship Earth

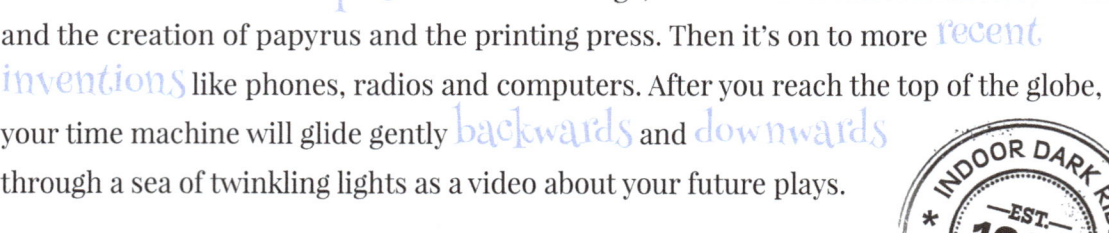

Embark on a trip that begins 30,000 years ago to see how human communication has changed! After you board a *time machine* tram, you'll input some info on its touchscreen. As you slowly spiral up into the sphere, you'll see people of the *past* and witness their *triumphs* like cave drawings, and the creation of papyrus and the printing press. Then it's on to more *recent inventions* like phones, radios and computers. After you reach the top of the globe, your time machine will glide gently *backwards* and *downwards* through a sea of twinkling lights as a video about your future plays.

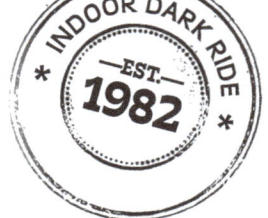
INDOOR DARK RIDE ★ EST. 1982 ★

 **HOT TIP** After your ride, you'll pass through **Project Tomorrow,** an area with **activities, games** and **computers** where you can **email** a pal the image of you on the ride!

TIME MACHINE

1982
Thank the Phoenicians! Opening Day attraction Spaceship Earth debuts & fans call it "the golf ball."

1999
For the new millennium, a giant Mickey hand with a magic wand sits next to Spaceship Earth until 2007.

2007
The fourth & current version of the ride launches with actress Judi Dench as the new narrator.

2021
Future World (EPCOT's front section) splits into World Celebration, World Nature & World Discovery.

Behind the Spaceship

World Celebration Gardens has peaceful green spaces, a statue called Walt the Dreamer at Dreamers Point and tables and chairs where you can recharge yourself—as well any devices! Bordering that is CommuniCore Hall and CommuniCore Plaza which are named after the park's now-gone science and tech pavilion. The indoor hall has an art gallery, character Meet n' Greets, performance areas and a show kitchen for cooking demos, and the outdoor plaza has a stage that hosts live entertainment.

 The **Club Cool** shop has **free samples** of sodas from around the world and the one from **Italy** called **Beverly** is famous for tasting totally **icky**!

🍴 Connections Café & Connections Eatery

Quick Service • Indoor Seating

These two places are connected inside and have fresh, stylish settings. Chefs behind glass create foods with international flair like Asian chicken salads and French bistro burgers for the eatery, and Belgian Liège waffles and German baumkuchen cakes for the café. The oven which makes these layered, ring-shaped "tree cakes" is one of only a handful in the United States! A huge mural that shows people around the globe growing ingredients for food and drinks covers the back wall and the café has a diagram on the floor that's based on Walt's early plans for EPCOT.

PLUS: Festival Favorites stand with dishes from past festivals & specialty drinks

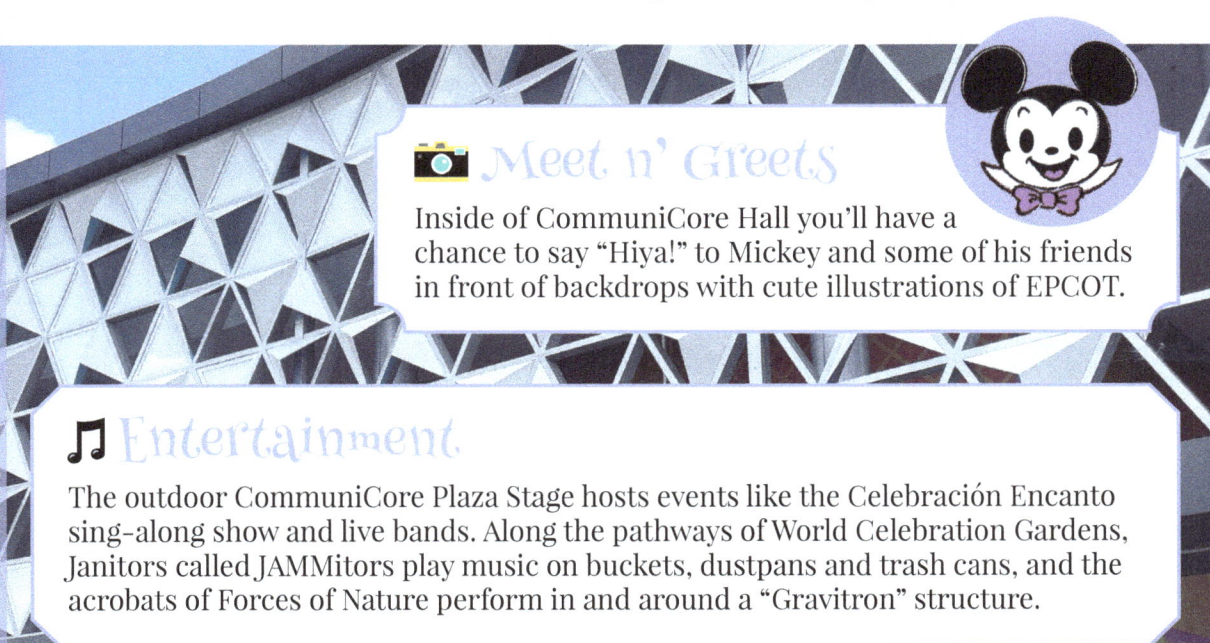

📷 Meet n' Greets

Inside of CommuniCore Hall you'll have a chance to say "Hiya!" to Mickey and some of his friends in front of backdrops with cute illustrations of EPCOT.

🎵 Entertainment

The outdoor CommuniCore Plaza Stage hosts events like the Celebración Encanto sing-along show and live bands. Along the pathways of World Celebration Gardens, Janitors called JAMMitors play music on buckets, dustpans and trash cans, and the acrobats of Forces of Nature perform in and around a "Gravitron" structure.

Imagination Pavilion

Pyramids made of steel and mirrored glass are home to a ride, a play area, a Meet n' Greet, a shop and a theater. The outdoor plaza has playful, jumping fountains where water hops over your head from one pad to the next and a waterfall that flows upside down—if you can believe that!

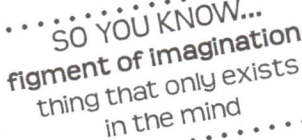

SO YOU KNOW... **figment of imagination** = thing that only exists in the mind

☆☆☆☆☆ Journey Into Imagination With Figment

The Imagination Institute has labs dedicated to the human senses of sound, sight, smell, touch, and taste. Now it's having an Open House and you're invited to take a tour! The Institute's chairman, Dr. Nigel Channing, tunes in to try to give a serious presentation but an impish dragon named Figment has other ideas. This **"figment of imagination"** is one of the Institute's discoveries. Dr. Channing plans to give you visitors hearing and vision tests and a demo about scents. But, at every turn, Figment causes chaos—and breaks into song—because he wants everyone to set their imaginations free. Finally the poor Doctor gives up and sings along with Figment!

INDOOR DARK RIDE — EST. 1983

 After your **journey,** you'll enter **ImageWorks—The "What If" Labs** which has a photo studio, a shop, and an area where you can play with **interactive exhibits** about color, music and sound.

 When this ride debuted, it included an **original song** called "One Little Spark" which was written by Disney Legends the **Sherman Brothers.** After being removed in **1999**, it returned—with new verses—in **2002.**

TIME MACHINE

1982 — The Imagination Pavilion's ImageWorks & Magic Eye Theater welcome Guests on Opening Day.

1983 — Journey Into Imagination debuts with a blimp pilot called Dreamfinder & Figment. It closes in 1998.

1999 — A new version of the ride called Journey Into _Your_ Imagination opens & operates until 2001.

2002 — Needs more Figment! The current version of the ride opens with more scenes of the playful scamp.

Meet n' Greets

You don't have to imagine meeting Figment—he can often be found inside ImageWorks near artwork with the Dreamfinder's blimp, and rainbow-colored neon lights.

Disney & Pixar Short Film Festival

☆☆☆☆☆

INDOOR 3D CARTOON — EST. 2015

A film festival is an event where a group of movies are shown and sometimes a prize is awarded to the best one. Inside the Magic Eye Theater, three animated films are presented—each with their own cute characters and original storylines. Once it's showtime, you'll get a pair of 3D glasses and head in for the show—which has some surprising special effects in store! Since 2017, the festival lineup has included *Get a Horse!* where Mickey and Minnie take a hayride, *Piper* starring a sandpiper bird who overcomes her fear of water and *Feast* about a dog that eats junk food.

 FUN FACT: When EPCOT opened, Guests could "soar on the wings of imagination" at *Magic Journeys* in this theater. From 1987-1993 that film was in Magic Kingdom.

Color Connections!

Fill in the **name** of the **main color** of the **characters** below. One has been done for you.
Answers on page 203.

(1) Anger, Lightning McQueen, Mushu and Sebastian are __red__.

(2) Bing Bong, Hamm, Lotso and Piglet are _____.

(3) Envy, Jiminy Cricket, Kermit and Pascal are _____.

(4) Flounder, Lumiere, Pluto and Pooh are _____.

(5) Genie, Monstro, Stitch and Sulley are _____.

(6) Nemo, Nick Wilde, Rajah and Tigger are _____.

And the award goes to... _____

World Nature

"Conservation isn't just the business of a few people. It's a matter that concerns all of us."
—WALT DISNEY

Dive into the wonders of nature's air, land and sea inside two enormous pavilions. Here you'll find a bubbling brook, stone mosaics and rockscapes, as well as one of the world's largest aquariums, and a trail that invites you explore the wonders of water!

The Land Pavilion

A building that echoes the shape of a volcano has two levels inside with a theater, a simulator, a boat ride and eateries. To enter this pavilion, you'll pass mosaic murals on either side of the walkway that are made to look like cross sections of the Earth.

Awesome Planet

Prepare to be *awed* by the scenic splendor of Earth! This live-action film is shown in the *Harvest Theater* which has effects like **wind, water** and *scents.* From the comfort of your chair you'll travel around the globe to see our planet's *stunning* deserts, forests, grasslands, oceans and treeless tundras. Actor Ty Burrell narrates and explains how people can *protect* the planet by working together!

 **FUN FACT:** Since Opening Day films shown here have had an environmental message, starting with *Symbiosis* and then *Circle of Life: An Environmental Fable.*

SO YOU KNOW...
symbiosis = different species living together

A Commitment to the Planet

Ever since Walt's day, the Disney company has worked to support **a healthy world.** To be an **environmental hero** during your visit to WDW, bring reusable **cutlery** and **straws,** don't waste **water, recycle** empty bottles and cans in the provided bins, and reuse **towels** and turn off **lights** in your **hotel room!**

🍴 Garden Grill Family Style • Indoor Seating

This restaurant on the building's upper level puts a unique spin on things—the dining room actually rotates and you'll go (oh so slowly) past scenes in the Living with the Land ride below. At this Character Meal, pals like Chip 'n Dale—and others—pop by your table as you dine on a farm-fresh "harvest feast" of cinnamon bread, waffles or eggs for breakfast and cornbread, garden salad or roasted turkey later in the day.

☆☆☆☆☆ Soarin' Around the World

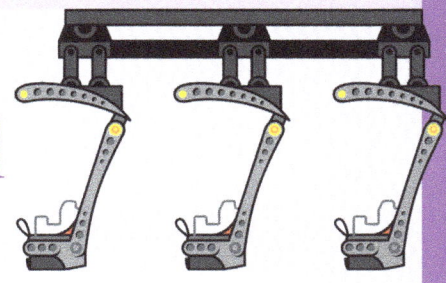

Take a seat on an awaiting row of hang gliders to *soar* through the skies of over a dozen locations! As your feet dangle in a gentle breeze, you'll fly over astounding *natural wonders* like North America's Monument Valley, South America's Iguazu waterfalls and Europe's Matterhorn mountain. Your *flight* will also take you past human-made *landmarks* that include Sydney Opera House in Australia, India's Taj Mahal and the Eiffel Tower in Paris. What do you think you'll *fly* over last?!

FLIGHT SIMULATOR • EST. 2005 •

 MAY BE SCARY

 HEIGHT: 40"+

 **HOT TIP:** Though the **back** rows shift into position when the ride starts, the **front** row still has the **best** view. You can politely **request** to wait for the seat you'd prefer on an attraction but keep in mind it may not **always** be possible for you to sit there.

 **SPY:** During the **Monument Valley** scene, watch for the moment when **hot air balloons** form a **Hidden Mickey!**

Mini Quiz!
Can you guess which of these scents is not used on Soarin' Around the World? *Answer on page 203.*
☐ French bread ☐ Grass
☐ Roses ☐ Sea breeze

TIME MACHINE

1982 — Kitchen Kabaret is a funny Opening Day musical show with singing foods & drinks.

1994 — Rapper Tone Loc adds his voice to a new musical when Food Rocks replaces Kitchen Kabaret.

2005 — Food Rocks closes in 2004 & Soarin' opens where it was with scenes of the state of California only. Eureka!

2016 — Soarin' Around the World takes flight—though the California version is shown instead sometimes.

Illustration by Chris Buchholz • www.etsy.com/shop/buchworks

🍴 Sunshine Seasons   Quick Service • Indoor Seating

Ribbons of fabric and balloons that represent the four seasons hang over the seating area for this lower level restaurant. You'll find fresh fare like baked goods, fruit or yogurt parfait for breakfast, and things like pizza rolls, grilled fish or sandwiches later in the day. In the afternoon, grab n' go snacks like salads and wraps are available.

☆☆☆☆☆

Living with the Land

INDOOR BOAT RIDE • EST. 1982 •

Think a ride about *farming* sounds about as boring as watching grass grow? Think again! This relaxing boat cruise will teach you and your fellow riders *fascinating* facts about how plants grow, the ways people have harvested food in the past and the cool, new methods being developed for *future* generations. Things start off with a *bang* as you travel through a thunderstorm in a *rainforest* and on to other environments like a *desert* and a wind-swept *prairie*. After you see a short video about how humans are learning to help keep the natural world in balance, your boat will enter the *Living Laboratory* where real-life scientists grow plants in greenhouses in all kinds of *unusual* ways—and even raise fish!

 **SPY** Look at the signs in the **Living Laboratory** to see which types of foods are being grown. These **ingredients** are used in some of the resort's restaurants including **Garden Grill** and **Sunshine Seasons** in this pavilion!

TIME MACHINE

1982
Opening Day attraction Listen to the Land debuts with a theme song of the same name.

1993
The opening Symphony of the Seed scene changes to a storm & the attraction is given its current name.

2006
A recording that explains what you see on the ride replaces live narration from Cast Members.

2019
Dazzling! The ride's annual holiday overlay debuts & is renamed Glimmering Greenhouses in 2022.

⭐⭐⭐⭐⭐

Journey of Water

OUTDOOR TRAIL EST. 2023

This lush outdoor trail is **inspired by Moana** and her love of the ocean! In this beautiful tropical oasis, you'll **journey** at your own pace to **play** with fountains, streams and curtains of water. Signs along the pathways explain the many forms that water can take and the **wonderful** way it **cycles** from the sky to the sea and back again!

 **HOT TIP** Will you get **wet?** That's up to you! You can easily **stay dry** if you'd rather and still enjoy this attraction by taking the **dry path**.

📷 **Meet n' Greets**
Find your way to meet plucky Moana outside of Journey of Water under a sail-shaped awning.

Rock On!

Journey of Water's **rocky walls** have the shapes of **Maui, Moana, Te Fiti**, the coconut-shaped **Kakamora** pirates and more. Who **else** did you spot?

TIME MACHINE

1982 — C-shaped buildings house an Opening Day attraction called CommuniCore (later changes to Innoventions).

2016 — Open your eyes, let's begin! Set in Polynesia, the animated movie "Moana" hits theaters.

2023 — Journey of Water, Inspired by Moana debuts where one of the Innoventions buildings used to be.

2024 — Moana's wayfinding ancestors call her to a new adventure with demigod Maui in "Moana 2."

The Seas Pavilion

A trio of seagulls you may recognize perch on rocks near crashing waves outside of this pavilion. Its curved walls have wave shapes and sea creatures who swim towards the entrance. Inside are two levels with an aquarium, a restaurant, a ride, a shop and a show!

🍴 Coral Reef Table Service • Indoor Seating

Panoramic windows at this restaurant face inwards to the pavilion's 5.7-million-gallon aquarium—and you never know who might swim by as you dine! Some seating isn't near the windows but you may request to wait for a closer table. The menu has seafood like fried shrimp and mahi-mahi, along with other options like chicken and steak.

⭐⭐⭐⭐⭐

The Seas with Nemo & Friends

INDOOR DARK RIDE • EST. 2007

Where in the **big blue world** is Nemo? The little fish is lost again! You'll clambor into a shell-shaped **clamobile** to join the search with **Marlin** and **Dory** though of course she keeps forgetting the task at hand. You'll also get to see **Mr. Ray** and his students in a coral reef, **Bruce** and **Chum** inside a wrecked sub, and **Crush** and **Squirt** splish-splashing in the bubbly waters of the East Australian Current. In the end, **Nemo** is reunited with his father **and friends** again!

 HOT TIP: After finding Nemo, explore more of **SeaBase.** Ask a Cast Member for a free **Scavenger Hunt** activity booklet!

 FUN FACT: The **manatee** "sea cows" in SeaBase eat almost **100 heads of lettuce** a day!

Which of these other parts of SeaBase did you sea—er, see?
☐ Aquarium undersea viewing area
☐ Bruce's Shark World exhibit
☐ Manatee Rehabilitation Center

TIME MACHINE

1986 — The Living Seas Pavilion debuts & is rethemed to Nemo & his friends in 2006.

2003 — You guys made me ink! The animated movie "Finding Nemo" hits theaters.

2004 — Turtle Talk with Crush debuts & The Seas with Nemo & Friends opens in 2007 after previews in 2006.

2022 — The indoor live show Finding Nemo: The Big Blue...and Beyond opens in Disney's Animal Kingdom.

☆ ☆ ☆ ☆ ☆

Turtle Talk with Crush

At this indoor show in SeaBase's Turtle Talk Theater you can get up close and personal with quick-witted Crush and some of his pals. The surfer dude sea turtle will swim into view behind the Window to the Pacific and chat with the audience with the help of a hydrophone and a Cast Member. Crush will ask and answer questions, and teach human friends like you how to talk turtle. No two shows are the same so you might want to pop by more than once. Totally tubular!

INTERACTIVE SHOW * EST. 2004 *

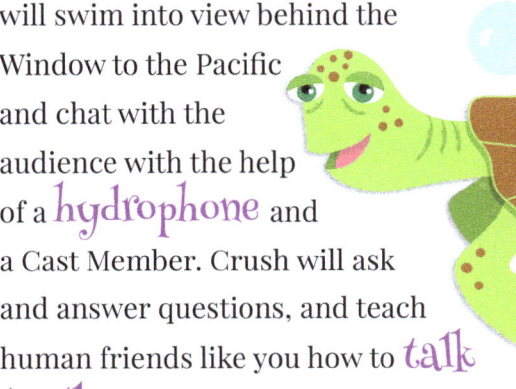

Your show may include characters like **Bailey** the whale and **Destiny** the shark from the 2016 sequel *Finding Dory*.

Marine Life Roll Call!

Using a **light color** like yellow, highlight the **types** of the **sea creatures** you spotted when you were in SeaBase. Then draw one in the **box** below!

CLOWNFISH
DOLPHIN
MANATEE
SEA TURTLE
SHARK
STINGRAY
TANG FISH

The Story of...Finding Nemo

Australia's Great Barrier Reef is home to a cautious clownfish named Marlin who is overly protective of his son Nemo. An eagle ray fish named Mr. Ray teaches Nemo and other students like Pearl the octopus, Sheldon the seahorse and Tad the butterfly fish about their underwater world. Nemo is caught by a scuba-diving dentist whose daughter Darla once killed a fish by shaking the bag it was in. As Marlin searches for Nemo he's joined by a forgetful tang fish named Dory. Marlin and Dory meet wannabe vegetarian sharks named Anchor, Bruce and Chum, and a sea turtle named Crush and his son Squirt who show Marlin and Dory how to ride the East Australian Current—or EAC. Nemo makes friends with the gang who live in the dentist's fish tank but he manages to escape and make his way back to the ocean where he's finally reunited with his dad.

World Discovery

"I think we jumped back."
—GAMORA

Discover a world where time and space travel is within your reach. Here you'll find wide, open walkways and plazas with futuristic structures built with swooshing curves of glass and metal, clusters of planets and even a Xandarian Star Blaster!

☆☆☆☆☆

Guardians of the Galaxy: Cosmic Rewind

MAY BE SCARY

HEIGHT: 42"+

Welcome inside the Wonders of Xandar Pavilion, Terrans! Two commanders from *Nova Corps*, Irani Rael and Tal Marik, appear on screen and prepare to demonstrate their powerful *Cosmic Generator*. Suddenly the device is stolen by a thief who plans to use it to travel to the dawn of time and *erase* humankind! Star-Lord and the rest of the Guardians tune in to help and Rocket hatches a plan to *reprogram* the evacuation shuttles so that you and the other Earthlings can save the day. You'll board a *Starjumper* to go all the way back to the *Big Bang* and follow the bad guy through the darkness and into jump points across time. When the Guardians arrive in their spaceship, one of several possible hit songs will *blast* through the universe!

★ ROLLER COASTER ★
EST. 2022

FUN FACT: The **Big Bang** is the scientific theory that the **universe** began as a single dense **point** that expanded to create all the stars and planets in the **cosmos** today!

TIME MACHINE

1982 — Universe of Energy is an Opening Day attraction with Audio-Animatronic dinos & films about energy.

1996 — Ellen's Energy Adventure with Ellen DeGeneres opens where Universe of Energy was & closes in 2017.

2014 — The live-action "Guardians of the Galaxy" movie series debuts & their ride in Ellen's spot is announced in 2017.

2022 — Cosmic Rewind debuts & gets its first seasonal overlay with holiday music the same year. Ho ho ho!

SHOP SPOTLIGHT

The Broker is pleased to have you explore the many **Treasures of Xandar**.

Fun & Feasting

EPCOT is **known** for its annual **festivals** which have live entertainment, scavenger hunts, special exhibits and outdoor **booths** with unique food and drink menus! Buildings like **Wonders of Life** (near the Guardians of the Galaxy ride), **The Odyssey** and **World ShowPlace** are used as event spaces during these short-term festivals.

Write which song played on your first Cosmic Rewind on the cassette tape!

Which of these have you been to?
- ☐ Festival of the Arts
- ☐ Flower & Garden Festival
- ☐ Food & Wine Festival
- ☐ Festival of the Holidays

 The Story of... Guardians of the Galaxy

Peter Quill is taken from Earth by alien outlaws called Ravagers after his mother's death. Growing up mostly in outer space, Peter listens to classic songs on an "Awesome Mix" cassette tape that his mom made him. Now a grownup, Peter has fancy gadgets and a superhero outfit, and calls himself Star-Lord. He plans to sell a stolen orb to The Broker on the planet Xandar, the capital of the Nova Empire, but he's attacked by three strangers. Green-skinned Gamora wants the orb, and a genetically modified raccoon-ish creature named Rocket and his sidekick Groot want the bounty for capturing Peter. This treelike being only says "I am Groot"—though it can mean many things. Officers from Nova Corps throw the four of them in prison where they meet tattooed Drax. Peter, Gamora, Rocket, Groot and Drax team up to form what becomes known as the Guardians of the Galaxy. They escape together—with the orb—and learn that inside it is an Infinity Stone. This Power Stone is the same one a Celestial villain called Eson the Searcher used to destroy a planet! Peter decides its safest to give the stone to the Nova Corps peacekeepers. Now heroes, the Guardians head off to their next adventure!

☆ ☆ ☆ ☆ ☆

Mission: SPACE

FLIGHT SIMULATOR EST. 2003

Color in the missions you completed: GREEN ORANGE

Have you got the *right stuff* to be an astronaut? You'll cross Planetary Plaza to enter the International Space Training Center (ISTC). There are two experiences here you can choose from—the less intense *Green Mission* which orbits around the Earth and the more extreme *Orange Mission* which travels to Mars. You'll be assigned a job: *Commander, Engineer, Navigator* or *Pilot*. After a brief on-screen briefing, you and your team will load into a capsule with viewports that look out onto *stellar* scenery. Good luck and godspeed!

 **HOT TIP** — The **Green Mission** (for riders 40"+) **doesn't** spin but the **Orange Mission** (for riders 44"+) spins at speeds of **up to 35 miles per hour!** For **both** versions you sit in a row in a dark, enclosed flight simulator.

 FUN FACT — After your flight, you'll pass through the **Advanced Training Lab** with a **play area**, space-themed **games** and **video postcards**. Even if you don't go on a ride you can **still** visit areas like this by going in **through their exits**.

TIME MACHINE

1983 — A ride called Horizons, that shows how a family might live in the 21st century, debuts & closes in 1999.

2003 — Sean O'Keefe from NASA attends the ceremony when Mission: SPACE debuts where Horizons once was.

2006 — After having only one ride experience, the Green Mission is added to give riders a mellower option.

2017 — Mission: SPACE gets a new mural with Brava Centauri, the space station from Horizons. Far out!

🍴 Space 220 Table Service • Indoor Seating

For a meal with great atmosphere, take a "stellarvator" to dine aboard the Centauri Space Station, 220 miles above Earth. The windows at this restaurant and lounge look out on amazing day and evening views of Planet Earth and spaceships. The menus here feature "lift-off" appetizers like starry calamari and "star course" entrées like galactic miso salmon and space pad thai.

PLUS: **Refreshment Station** stand with frozen cola drinks
The Odyssey eatery (open seasonally) with an everchanging menu

☆☆☆☆☆

INDOOR CAR RIDE EST. 1999

MAY BE SCARY ⚠️

HEIGHT: 40"+

Test Track

The fun begins with cool exhibits in the queue about *vehicles* and the people who design them. Next, you'll get in the front or back row of a ride car to *cruise* through indoor scenes that show how the *world of motion* connects us as we find exciting new ways to get from point *A* to point *B*. Exiting the building, your car will hit an outdoor *track* where its *speed* capabilities will be put to the *test!*

 **HOT TIP** Across from Test Track is an outdoor **family play zone** and a **splash pad** where kids can cool off on hot days!

Create your dream car! Draw over the grey shape or design one in the blank area. ↓

Imagineers at Play   *Plans may change!*

Test Track debuted in **1999** and was first updated in **2012**. In **2024** Test Track **closed** to be **reimagined** with a new theme *(see above)* inspired by **World of Motion**. That Opening Day ride about the **history of transportation** was where Test Track is now until **1996**. The ride is due to reopen in **2025**.

What's **your take** on the upcoming changes to **Test Track**?
☐ I can't wait!   ☐ Sounds cool but I can wait...   ☐ Upcoming? It's open!

World Showcase

"Some go this way. Some go that way."
—CHESHIRE CAT

This showcase features the architecture, culture and history of countries around the globe. Here you'll find a path leading to World's Fair-style pavilions with replicas of iconic landmarks, and candy, food, drinks and snacks from—or inspired by—each nation!

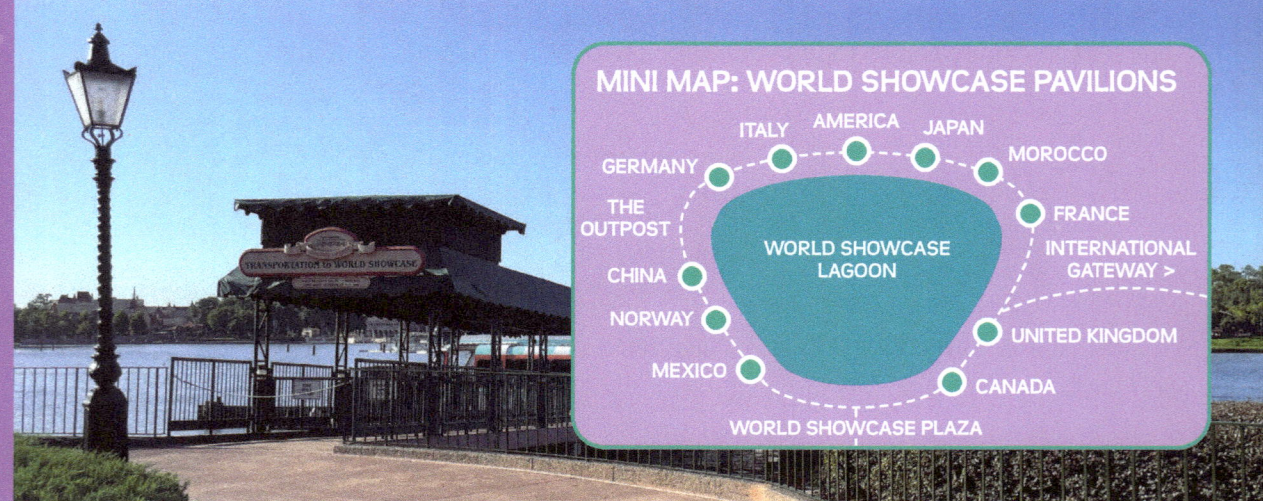

MINI MAP: WORLD SHOWCASE PAVILIONS

- GERMANY
- ITALY
- AMERICA
- JAPAN
- MOROCCO
- THE OUTPOST
- CHINA
- WORLD SHOWCASE LAGOON
- FRANCE
- INTERNATIONAL GATEWAY >
- NORWAY
- UNITED KINGDOM
- MEXICO
- CANADA
- WORLD SHOWCASE PLAZA

World Showcase Plaza

At the start of this part of the park you'll find World Showcase Plaza with a gazebo, a couple of shops, some quick-service food and drink stands and a waterfront promenade path. Now it's decision time! Do you go left or right? If you go left you'll soon end up in the Mexico Pavilion. Choose the right path and you'll head for the Canada Pavilion.

 HOT TIP There are **FriendShip Boats** you can catch here to ride across World Showcase Lagoon—but don't take one right away if this is your **first visit.** It's better to explore **each** pavilion and not **skip** past any!

 FUN FACT Many **World Showcase Cast Members** wear the **traditional clothing** of the country whose pavilion you are in—and they're actually **from** those countries! **Most** Cast Member name tags list where their **hometown** is.

The Fun Doesn't Stop

Kidcot is a free activity created for kids. You can begin at any of the **Kidcot Fun Stops**—which are in each World Showcase pavilion. These stops may be outside **or** inside at attraction exits, galleries or shops. At each station a **Cast Member** representing that country will chat with you about their homeland and give you **stickers** and **trivia cards.** When you've visited **ALL** the locations, let a Cast Member know and you'll get a **special card!**

📷 Meet n' Greets

You can meet Asha, the teen from *Wish*, at the World Showcase Friendship Ambassador Gazebo in World Showcase Plaza.

Sage Advice

During your **World tour**, take a sec to see what's **growing!** In the **Canada Pavilion**, you'll find **Victoria Gardens** with a lush lawn and flowerbeds around a lake. In the **United Kingdom Pavilion**, the garden beds have **herbs**, **flowers** that attract **butterflies**, and **plants** that are used to make **tea**. In the **Japan Pavilion**, a tucked-away garden has **koi fish ponds** and charming **footbridges**.

🎵 Entertainment

Luminous: The Symphony of Us closes out your day at EPCOT. This nighttime spectacular is set to music with fireworks, fountains and lights that can be viewed from all around World Showcase Lagoon.

If you want to see some of the REAL places that inspired World Showcase's pavilions, here's your Bucket List!

CANADA:
- ☐ Butchart Gardens
- ☐ Château Laurier Hotel

UNITED KINGDOM:
- ☐ Hampton Court Palace

FRANCE:
- ☐ Eiffel Tower

MOROCCO:
- ☐ The Blue Gate
- ☐ Koutoubia Minaret

JAPAN:
- ☐ Goju-no-to Pagoda
- ☐ Himeji Castle
- ☐ Itsukushima Torii Gate

ITALY:
- ☐ Doge's Palace
- ☐ St. Mark's Bell Tower

GERMANY:
- ☐ Statue of St. George

CHINA:
- ☐ Temple of Heaven

NORWAY:
- ☐ Detli House
- ☐ Gol Stave Church

MEXICO:
- ☐ El Castillo Pyramid

Might Solve a Mystery

Scrooge!

Launching in the **1980s**, the animated *DuckTales* TV series starred Donald's uncle **Scrooge McDuck** and playful nephews **Huey, Dewey** and **Louie** and their pal **Webby**. Now you can join the Duckburg crew on **DuckTales World Showcase Adventure,** a free, interactive game on the **Play Disney Parks** app. Taking place across **seven** pavilions, you'll defeat villains and solve clues to find the **Seven Plunders of the World.** As you play, your actions will trigger **special effects!**

🇨🇦 Canada Pavilion

The country of Canada is in North America. This pavilion has an elegant château, rugged mountains, rustic buildings and totem poles. Canada has two official languages: English and French, and Canadians sometimes say "eh" as in "Let's get some maple popcorn, eh?"

🎵 Entertainment
The outdoor Canada Mill Stage hosts Canadian bands and other acts!

🍴 Le Cellier Steakhouse Table Service • Indoor Seating

Hotel du Canada has a cellier—or cellar—where you'll find this handsome restaurant with stone arches and the warm glow of candlelight. The menu changes with the seasons but they're known for their cheddar cheese soup, pretzel bread sticks and, of course, steak!

PLUS: **Refreshment Port** stand with poutine (fries with gravy & cheese curds)

☆☆☆☆☆ Canada Far and Wide

INDOOR FILM — EST. 2020

Wind past a Rocky Mountain waterfall and enter the Maple Leaf Mine to see this live-action Circle-Vision 360 film. The visuals move across screens that encircle you 360 degrees as you stand along railings in the center of the theater. Canadian actors Eugene Levy and Catherine O'Hara will describe the sights as you travel far and wide all over Canada to see its amazing cities, coastlines, countryside, forests, mountains, snowscapes—and people!

SPY: While in this pavilion be sure to read the **signs** by the totem poles. The **Tsimshian** artist who crafted them carved one **in EPCOT** as Guests watched!

SO YOU KNOW... **Tsimshian** = Indigenous people of the Pacific Northwest

🇬🇧 United Kingdom Pavilion

The UK is in Europe and is made up of Great Britain (England, Wales and Scotland) and Northern Ireland. This pavilion has classic red phone booths, half-timbered buildings, a thatched cottage and a stone "palace" with roof crenellations that go up and down like square teeth. To say thanks like an Englishperson say "Cheers, mate!"

🍴 Rose & Crown Dining Room

Table Service • Indoor & Outdoor Seating

This cozy spot's dark wood paneling and leaded glass will make you feel like you're "across the pond." Tuck into hearty fare like bangers and mash, shepherd's pie and sticky toffee pudding. The front section has the Rose & Crown Pub with grown-up drinks.

🍴 Yorkshire County Fish Shop **Quick Service • Outdoor Seating**

Named for a county in northern England, this stand's specialty is their deep-fried fish n' chips (as in french fries) which you can take to a waterfront seating area off to the side.

🎵 Entertainment

Inside Rose & Crown Pub you'll find a lively Pub Musician on the piano. The UK Gazebo outdoor stage has bands like Command Performance who play British pop and rock.

SHOP SPOTLIGHT

The Crown & Crest has regal displays of armor, crests, flags, shields and swords.

Mini Quiz!

Can you guess which character was in the original book about Alice's adventures but not in Disney's 1951 animated movie? *Answer on page 203.*

☐ Bill the Lizard
☐ Mock Turtle
☐ The Dodo

📷 Meet n' Greets

No need to wonder where Alice is—find her in the UK Gardens. Follow the path past the gazebo to visit Winnie the Pooh inside Christopher Robin's Room.

🇫🇷 France Pavilion

The country of France is the largest in western Europe. This pavilion has chic boutiques and buildings with sloped mansard roofs and tall skinny windows, elegant fountains, artists' easels and vintage-style kiosks. To tell someone you hope they enjoy their meal say "Bon appétit!" (pronounced *bone ah-puh-teet*)

REMY | EMILE | LINGUINI | SKINNER | TATOU

☆☆☆☆☆

Remy's Ratatouille Adventure

See the world from Remy's point of view! You'll put on 3D glasses and climb into a *rat-shaped* ride car to scamper over the rooftops of Paris. As your *adventure* begins, Remy is chatting with his vision of Chef Auguste Gusteau about what to cook for a party. Suddenly Remy—and you—will *tumble* into the kitchen of Gusteau's restaurant where vermin like you are definitely not welcome. Remy scurries to avoid the feet of *Alfredo Linguini, Chef Skinner, Colette Tatou* and the rest of the kitchen staff. Next you'll follow the harried rat as he runs into his brother *Emile* in a cold pantry, then dashes under a hot oven, across a chaotic dining room and into the dark walls. Though Skinner tries to *trap* you, you'll make a clean getaway and join Remy and his fellow rats at a festive *Soirée!*

INDOOR DARK RIDE ★ EST. 2021 ★

SPY — When in **Place de Remy Courtyard** look for Remy on the **sewer covers** and **fountain.** Also, see if you can tell what food critic **Anton Ego** has been up to lately.

TIME MACHINE

1982
Place de Remy Courtyard doesn't exist when EPCOT opens. It's added to the France Pavilion in 2021.

2007
The animated "Ratatouille" movie hits theaters & Remy dreams of being like his idol Chef Gusteau.

2014
Ratatouille: L'Aventure Totalement Toquée de Rémy debuts in Disneyland Paris Resort.

2021
Remy's Ratatouille Adventure opens on the 50th Anniversary of Walt Disney World. Oui, oui!

🍴 La Crêperie de Paris

Table Service • Indoor Seating

The specialty here is a kind of thin French pancake called a crêpe. Choose the sweet dessert type or the ones made with buckwheat flour called galettes with savory fillings like cheese and meat. The restaurant's decor of rough stone walls and wood beams is inspired by France's Brittany region—which is where galettes traditionally come from!

PLUS: Crêpes À Emporter walk-up windows at La Crêperie de Paris with crêpes to go

FRENCH MINI DICTIONARY
Boulangerie = Bakery
Crêperie = Place where crêpes are made
L'Artisan des Glaces = The ice cream maker
Patisserie = Pastry shop
Ratatouille = Vegetable stew

📷 Meet n' Greets

Say "Bonjour!" to Princess Aurora from *Sleeping Beauty* at France Fragrance Gardens Gazebo or Belle from *Beauty and the Beast* on the France Promenade.

SHOP SPOTLIGHT

Swirling Art Nouveau shelves and a stained glass ceiling decorate **Plume et Palette.**

🍴 Chefs de France

Table Service • Indoor Seating

This Parisian-style café has globe lights, patterned tile floors and wood bistro tables. The chefs here prepare traditional French foods like escargot (snails!), onion soup and rotisserie roasted chicken. On the second floor the Monsieur Paul restaurant is for Guests ages 10 and up.

🍴 Les Halles Boulangerie & Patisserie

Quick Service • Indoor Seating

This hall, named for the famous Parisian food market, has metal arches like a 1900s-era train station and painted wall panels covered with signage like a classic French shop. Le menu includes baguettes, croissants, quiches and sandwiches.

PLUS: L'Artisan des Glaces parlor with ice cream and sorbet cones and sundaes
Les Vins de Chefs de France stand with grown-up drinks

Mini Museums

Seven pavilions have **small galleries** (where you can learn more about each country) including:

France's Palais du Cinema lobby—Cinema and stage costumes and props

Morocco's Gallery of Arts and History—Life and races in the Sahara Desert

Japan's Bijutsu-kan Gallery—Kawaii culture

America's American Heritage Gallery—Native American Indian art

China's House of the Whispering Willows Gallery—Shanghai Disneyland art

Norway's Stave Church Gallery—Viking myths and legends

Mexico's Mexican Folk Art Gallery—Day of the Dead art and displays

☆☆☆☆☆ Palais du Cinema

This luxurious movie palace features the animated *Beauty and the Beast Sing-Along*. This new twist on Belle's "tale as old as time" is narrated by **Mrs. Potts** who tells the story from LeFou's point of view. At select times of day you can catch *Impressions de France* here instead. Shown on a 200-degree-wide screen, this live-action film takes you on a **visual tour** of France's incredible cities, coastlines, vineyards and more, set to **music** by French composers.

INDOOR FILM EST. 1982

 "Impressions de France" is an Opening Day attraction and Belle's film joined the lineup in **2020**.

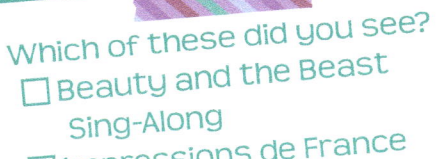
Which of these did you see?
☐ Beauty and the Beast Sing-Along
☐ Impressions de France

Legend Close-Up: Angela Lansbury

Angela Lansbury was born in 1925 in **London, England.** She loved to go to the movies, dance, play the piano, sing, and act in **school plays.** Angela moved to **America** and pursued her **acting dreams,** performing in movies, plays, radio programs and television shows over her long career. She starred in the 1971 Disney movie *Bedknobs and Broomsticks* which combined **animation** with **live-action.** From 1984 to 1996 Angela played amateur detective **Jessica Fletcher** in the TV show *Murder, She Wrote*. During that same time, she did the **voice acting** for the beloved **Mrs. Potts** in the 1991 animated movie *Beauty and the Beast.* More recently, she was the **Balloon Lady** in the 2018 live-action movie *Mary Poppins Returns*. Angela was named a Disney Legend in **1995.**

🇲🇦 Morocco Pavilion

The country of Morocco is in Northern Africa and borders the Mediterranean Sea. This pavilion, which opened in 1984, has carved plaster, mosaic tiles, keyhole arches and minaret towers. Many languages are spoken in Morocco but to say hi in Moroccan Arabic say "Ahlan!" (pronounced *ah-lin*)

🍴 Spice Road Table
Table Service • Indoor & Outdoor Seating

This exotic waterfront café has a Moroccan hot tea service and small plates of Mediterranean food like dolmas, hummus and spicy shrimp. In the entry area, you can see jars of colorful spices like the ones that were traded centuries ago along the Spice Route. The connected quick-service **Spice Road Table Bar** has small plates and specialty drinks.

🍴 Tangierine Café   Quick Service • Indoor & Outdoor Seating

Tangiers is a port city in Morocco and is where the tangerine fruit gets its name. This inviting café beneath an ancient-looking minaret has swags of fabric and colored glass lanterns. "Flavors of the Medina" are served here, like couscous, kebabs and pitas.

PLUS: **Oasis Sweets & Sips** stand with Baklava pastries & frozen mint tea

🎵 Entertainment

An outdoor stage near Spice Road Table hosts Moroccan bands like Atlas Fusion.

📷 Meet n' Greets

Jasmine awaits your visit inside the sumptuous Lamps of Wonder.

Marvelous Medina

The **King of Morocco** sent his own artisans over to EPCOT to help create the Morocco Pavilion. In the back area you'll find the **Marketplace in the Medina**, a walled "city center" with **wares** on display and shaded **seating areas**. Don't miss the **Fez House**—a beautiful tiled courtyard!

🇯🇵 Japan Pavilion

The country of Japan is an island nation off the coast of the Asian mainland. This pavilion has a red torii gate beside the World Showcase Lagoon, natural wood buildings with gracefully curved tile rooftops and a Japanese castle. To say excuse me in Japanese say "Sumimasen." (pronounced *soo-mee-mah-sen*)

SHOP SPOTLIGHT

Mitsukoshi Dept. Store has pop culture and traditional-style Japanese items.

🍴 Mitsukoshi Restaurants — Table Service • Indoor Seating

There are three eateries with Japanese cuisine in the Mitsukoshi building. On the first floor you can indulge in an upscale experience at **Takumi-Tei** which means "house of the artisan." The stylish dining rooms are themed to earth, stone, washi paper, water and wood. Upstairs you'll find **Shiki-Sai: Sushi Izakaya,** a sushi bar and grill with sharable plates like skewers, tempura and sushi rolls—many with a seasonal flair. Also upstairs is the lively **Teppan Edo** restaurant where each table has an attached grill on which a chef chops and stir-fries meats n' veggies—and entertains the Guests while they're at it!

🍴 Katsura Grill

Quick Service • Indoor & Outdoor Seating

Stop in to this thatch-roofed eatery for Japanese dishes like sushi, udon noodles or teriyaki chicken. The indoor seating area is nice but the outdoor tables are even nicer because they are by the pavilion's peaceful garden. Look for clever gizmos called shishi-odoshi. These bamboo tubes fill with water, tip over and make a clacking sound to scare away deer—who are known for nibbling on gardener's flowers and plants.

PLUS: **Kabuki Café** stand with edamame, sushi & Japanese shave ice

🎵 Entertainment

Catch a thundering performance from Taiko drummers Matsuriza near the pagoda tower.

Sam the Eagle illustration by Mariana Koontz • www.landandworld.com

🇺🇸 The American Adventure

The USA's early days are the inspiration at this midpoint of the World Showcase loop. This pavilion has a sailing ship docked along the shore, and a traditional Colonial brick building with columns, a clocktower and an inner rotunda with changing exhibits. To say you're hungry like someone from 1700s America say "I'm gut-foundered!"

★ ☆ ☆ ☆ ☆

The American Adventure

INDOOR SHOW — EST. 1982

Take a trip through the adventurous history of America! This Opening Day show has a mix of Audio-Animatronic figures and on-screen visuals that illustrate the days of the Pilgrims in the 1600s up to modern times. It all begins with the show's narrators, Founding Father Ben Franklin and author Mark Twain, having a fireside chat. Notable figures from the past like President Jefferson, Native American Indian Chief Joseph, activist Susan B. Anthony and many more also make appearances in this historical highlight reel!

SPY: Alcoves in the theater hold the 12 Spirits of America statues sculpted by Disney Legend Blaine Gibson. Each of them represents an ideal that Americans hold dear like Compassion, Freedom and Knowledge.

🎵 Entertainment

The Voices of Liberty group sing "a cappella" (without music) inside the rotunda. Outside near the lagoon, live acts perform at the American Gardens Theatre.

🍴 Regal Eagle Smokehouse — Quick Service • Indoor & Outdoor Seating

Regal Sam the Eagle the Muppet is hosting a BBQ cook-off! The smoker outside barbecues meats in a variety of styles from across the nation, and sides like beans, pickles and mac n' cheese complete the meal. The brick walls inside the eatery have signs featuring Sam—and other Muppets.

PLUS: **Funnel Cake** stand with deep-fried funnel cake desserts
Block & Hans stand with Mickey pretzels & grown-up drinks
Fife & Drum Tavern stand with popcorn & turkey legs

🇮🇹 Italy Pavilion

The country of Italy is one of the southernmost parts of mainland Europe. This pavilion has gondola boats floating in the lagoon, arched arcade walkways, an 83-foot bell tower, a pair of statue-topped pillars, a handcrafted donkey cart and warm-toned stucco walls lining its piazza. To say let's eat in Italian say "Mangiamo!" (pronounced *mon-gee-yam-oh*)

SHOP SPOTLIGHT

Masks are displayed (and for sale) inside gorgeous **La Gemma Elegante.**

ITALIAN MINI DICTIONARY
- **Al Taglio** = By the slice
- **Gelateria** = Gelato shop
- **La Bottega Italiana** = The Italian shop
- **La Gemma Elegante** = The elegant gem
- **Napoli** = Italian city of Naples
- **Toscana** = Italy's Tuscany region
- **Tutto Gusto** = All the flavors

Do you collect or study coins?
☐ Yes, I do!
☐ Nah, not me.

Calling All Numismatists

If you collect or study coins, then YOU are a **"NOO-MIZ-MUH-TIST!"** Pressed coins celebrating **Italian explorer** Christopher Columbus became a popular souvenir in America in 1893 during the **Chicago World's Fair.** Today in Walt Disney World, **Coin Press** machines offer **many** everchanging and unique designs to choose from with themes like attractions, characters, lands and more. After you pay the fee, the machine imprints a coin with the artwork of your choice, turning it into a more **oval** shape. The Walt Disney World **app** and **website** list where the Coin Press machines can be found all over the resort. The one in the **Italy Pavilion** is at **La Bottega Italiana.** An even **fancier** type of keepsake is available from **Collectible Medallion** machines. These **round** coins come in gold or silver and already have designs on them. Like the Coin Press machines, they are **usually** found in or near shops.

🎵 Entertainment

Performing here and there in the piazza is Sergio the cheery master juggler and mime!

Place Settings!

Write the name of the **country** where each movie below is **set**. One has been done for you. *Answers on page 203.*

(1) Turning Red
_____
(2) The Aristocats
_____
(3) Lady and the Tramp
_____
(4) Luca
_____Italy_____
(5) Coco
_____

🍴 Via Napoli Table Service • Indoor Seating

This Ristorante e Pizzeria has wood-fired ovens made to look like the gods of the Italian volcanoes Stromboli, Vesuvius and Etna. And into their gaping mouths go the pizzas to be cooked! The specialty at this bustling eatery is thin-crust pizza but there are a few other options like salad or pasta.

🍴 Tutto Italia Table Service • Indoor & Outdoor Seating

This handsome Ristorante has comfy booths, crystal chandeliers and murals showing scenes from ancient Rome inside as well as an outdoor covered patio. Choose Italian standards like lasagna or spaghetti, or try roasted fish or grilled steak.

PLUS: **Gelateria Toscana** stand with creamy gelato & icy sorbetti
Tutto Gusto wine cellar with snacks, desserts & grown-up drinks
Pizza al Taglio walk-up window with thick-crust pizza by the slice

Germany Pavilion

The country of Germany is in central Europe and shares borders with nine other countries. This pavilion has a miniature village with tiny trains, and Bavarian buildings that are straight out of a fairytale with balconies, leaded-glass windows, flower boxes and turrets. To say please in German say "Bitte." (pronounced *bit-tuh*)

GERMAN MINI DICTIONARY
Biergarten = Beer garden
Glaskunst = Glass art
Karamell Küche = Caramel kitchen
Sommerfest = Summer party

📷 Meet n' Greets
Meet Snow White outside by the scenic Wishing Well.

🍴 Sommerfest Quick Service • Indoor & Outdoor Seating

A clock tower building with painted shields and vines has two archways, each leading to one of the pavilion's restaurants. The right one leads to this casual spot for bratwurst sausages and huge hot pretzels and the left to Biergarten. The clock is a glockenspiel with two tots inside who come out of the doors on the balcony to ring the bell on the hour!

🍴 Biergarten Buffet • Indoor Seating

Oktoberfest is an annual fall festival that began in Munich, Germany but it takes place daily at Biergarten! This indoor restaurant looks like a traditional village square with a night sky, streetlights, trees and a watermill. It's the perfect setting to enjoy German cuisine like sauerkraut, sausages, schnitzel and spätzle.

PLUS: **Karamell-Küche** cottage has all things caramel-covered like apples & popcorn

🎵 Entertainment

Inside Biergarten, performers dance, yodel and play oompah music while you dine. Other German-style folk & pop bands play outside at the Germany Gazebo.

🇨🇳 China Pavilion

The country of China is in eastern Asia. This pavilion has bamboo plants, footbridges over a serene pond, a tiered temple, a triple-arched gate, tubular roof tiles and intricate patterns covering most surfaces. Many language dialects are used in China but to say hello in Mandarin say "Ni hao!" (pronounced *knee how*)

☆ ☆ ☆ ☆ ☆

Reflections of China

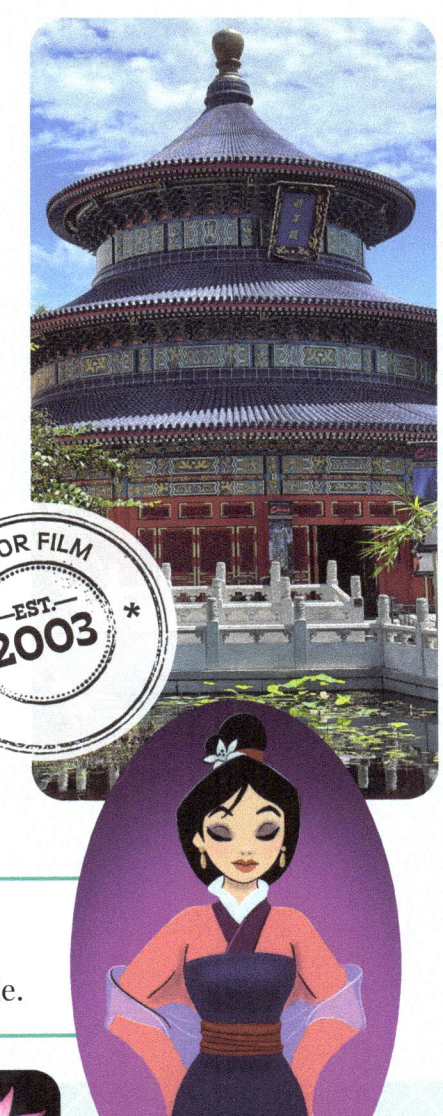

Discover the ageless *beauty* of China! The theater inside the Temple of Heaven debuted on Opening Day with *"Wonders of China"* and now features this film. Your guide through this lovely visual tour is the 8th-century Chinese poet *Li Bai*. He will describe the sights as you travel through China's ravishing cities, countryside, desert, mountains and rivers. This live-action *Circle-Vision 360* film has wraparound screens and there are railings for you to lean against in the center of the theater.

INDOOR FILM EST. 2003

 The **Temple of Heaven** has a **dazzling** domed ceiling with a dragon and phoenix on a central golden **medallion.**

 ## Meet n' Greets
Meet Mulan inside the Great Hall or strolling outside.

 ## Lotus Blossom Café

Quick Service • Indoor & Outdoor Seating
A swooping tile roof tops this café where you'll find Chinese cuisine like egg rolls, fried rice, noodles, pot stickers and lychee ice cream. The lotus is a symbol of purity in Chinese culture and you may see some blooming in the pavilion's pond.

🍴 Nine Dragons **Table Service • Indoor Seating**

Chinese legends tell of the nine sons of the Dragon King, a water deity. This stylish restaurant has silk lanterns and carved wooden screens—many featuring dragons. Dishes like spring rolls, dumplings and stir fry are served here with a modern flair.

Illustration by Melissa Chan Stone • www.amuseboosh.com

🇳🇴 Norway Pavilion

The country of Norway is in a northern part of Europe called Scandinavia. This pavilion opened in 1988 and has a cluster of brightly painted buildings, a medieval church, castle turrets and walls, and a log house with a living grass roof. To say thank you in Norwegian (the country's most widely spoken language) say "Tusen takk!" (pronounced *too-sen tok*)

🍴 Akershus Royal Banquet Hall

Family Style • Indoor Seating

Named for a region of Norway, this grand castle hall has soaring beamed ceilings hung with royal flags. Princesses like Belle and Snow White host this Character Meal where you can enjoy American and Norwegian foods like pastries, waffles, kjøttkaker (meatballs) and kylling og melboller (chicken and dumplings).

☆☆☆☆☆ Frozen Ever After

INDOOR BOAT RIDE • EST. 2016

Visit *Arendelle* during a summer snow day! Lanterns light the way to your awaiting *Nordic* vessel. Once aboard, you and your group will float under twinkling branches and stars past Sven and singing Olaf. Next you'll *cruise* by Grand Pabbie telling the younger trolls stories about the royal sisters. As you approach the *Ice Palace,* you'll see Olaf, Sven, Anna and Kristoff have gathered there. The gates open up to reveal Elsa belting out "Let It Go" and making her snowy *magic.* Before you head back to go ashore, you'll see *Marshmallow* and the *Snowgies* watching the Kingdom's skies aglow with icy fireworks!

 FUN FACT: In the 2015 animated short *Frozen Fever,* Elsa throws a surprise birthday party for Anna with **sunflowers** and **cake.** Because she has a cold, Elsa keeps sneezing—which creates the **snow babies** called **Snowgies.**

TIME MACHINE

1844 — Scandinavian author Hans Christian Andersen's "Snedronningen" (or "The Snow Queen") is published.

2013 — The animated movie "Frozen" hits theaters & is loosely based on "The Snow Queen."

2014 — Frozen fractals all around! A live Frozen sing-along show opens in Disney's Hollywood Studios.

2016 — Frozen Ever After debuts where a ride called Maelstrom was from 1988 until 2014.

Kringla Bakeri Og Kafe
Quick Service • Outdoor Seating

"Go ahead. I won't judge."
—ANNA

This charming wooden bakery and café has cupboards, plates and trim painted with the pretty swirls and whirls of rosemaling, a folk art that originated in Norway. Sandwiches and salads are served here but the line out the door is for popular treats like pretzel-shaped kringla (ring) cookies and skolebrød (school bread) buns made with custard and coconut!

Replica of King Sverre's ancient castle ruins in Norway!

Have you ever built a snowman?
☐ Yes! ☐ Not yet...

Meet n' Greets
Meet Anna and Elsa inside Royal Sommerhus, a cozy summer cabin with handpainted flowers and a lovely mountain view.

SHOP SPOTLIGHT
Don't forget to say hei to the huge wooden troll sitting inside **The Fjording**.

The Story of...Frozen
Young Princess Elsa of Arendelle and her little sister Anna love playing together and having fun with Elsa's magical ability to make snow and ice. When Anna gets hurt, their parents get Grand Pabbie (the Troll King) to help her and then they close the castle to hide Elsa's secret from the world. Years later on Elsa's Coronation Day, Anna meets Prince Hans and agrees to marry him—even though they just met. Queen Elsa gets angry at her sister's hasty actions and loses control of her powers. She runs into the mountains and builds an ice palace hideaway. Anna sets off in search of Elsa and meets an ice salesman named Kristoff and his reindeer Sven at Wandering Oaken's Trading Post who agree to help her with her search. Along the way, they meet a funny snowman called Olaf who shows them where Elsa's hideaway is. To chase everyone away Elsa creates Marshmallow, a huge snow monster. When Anna gets injured again, kind Kristoff takes her to see the trolls who tell them that her heart is freezing and she needs to be saved by an act of true love. While selflessly saving her sister from danger, Anna is accidentally turned to ice and in fact it's the true love between her and Elsa that ends up saving her.

🇲🇽 Mexico Pavilion

The country of Mexico is America's neighbor to the south. This pavilion has a stucco building and a grass-roofed hut along the promenade, and a massive Aztec pyramid with a charming Mexican village and market plaza inside it. To say goodbye in Spanish (the language most people in Mexico speak) say "Adios!" (pronounced *ah dee-yoh-sss*)

☆☆☆☆☆

Gran Fiesta Tour

It's time for a *big party* with The Three Caballeros—Donald Duck, José Carioca (a Brazilian parrot) and Panchito Pistoles (a Mexican rooster). Inside the pavilion's *pyramid*, you'll board a boat to join other riders on a tour of Mexico's Rio Grande. José and Panchito begin to perform—but soon realize Donald is missing! As the *sightseeing* duck races through *madcap* adventures, his bandmates pursue him on a flying *serape* shawl. You'll float through a village where dancing dolls and a band of skeletons are having a fun *fiesta* and then it won't be long until the *bird buddies* are reunited at last!

INDOOR BOAT RIDE • EST. 2007

HOT TIP: More of the **action** can be seen on the **left** side of the boat—including **screens** that show animated and live-action scenes set in **Mexico!**

TIME MACHINE

1941 — Walt & some Disney artists visit Latin America & later create the 1943 "Saludos Amigos" movie with José.

1945 — Panchito debuts in "The Three Caballeros," a second Latin-themed movie with animation & live-action.

1982 — The Mexico Pavilion debuts with an Opening Day boat ride called El Rio del Tiempo.

2007 — ¡Que lindo! Gran Fiesta Tour Starring The Three Caballeros replaces El Rio del Tiempo.

Illustration by Mariana Koontz • www.landandworld.com

🍴 San Angel Inn Table Service • Indoor Seating

Named after a Mexico City neighborhood, this 17th-century-style Restaurante has views of the Gran Fiesta Tour boats floating by with ancient Mayan ruins and a smoking volcano in the distance. Candles on the tables light up the always-nighttime setting as you enjoy Mexican foods like chips and guacamole, tortilla soup, enchiladas, tacos, and desserts like sweet corn ice cream sprinkled with chile powder.

PLUS: **La Cava del Tequila** table-service or to-go lounge with snacks & grown-up drinks

📷 Meet n' Greets

¿Dónde estás Donald Duck? You may find him outside on the Mexico Promenade.

SPANISH MINI DICTIONARY
Caballeros = Gentlemen
Cantina = Saloon
Cava = Cellar for drinks
Choza = Hut
Gran Fiesta = Big party
Hacienda = House on an estate
Saludos Amigos = Greetings friends

🍴 La Hacienda de San Angel

Table Service • Indoor Seating
Inside this waterfront restaurant you'll find a tall, peaked ceiling with dark wooden beams hung with star lanterns, and tables and booths with great views of World Showcase Lagoon. You'll find Mexican dishes like queso fundido, carne asada, enchiladas, and nieve for dessert (a type of sorbet).

PLUS: **La Cantina de San Angel** eatery with nachos, rice bowls & tacos
Choza de Margarita stand with snacks & grown-up drinks

🎵 Entertainment

The music of Mexico is played outside near La Hacienda de San Angel by bands like the traditional folk musicians Mariachi Cobre, and Marimba de las Américas whose instruments include a marimba which is sort of like a large xylophone.

📖 Sample Souvenirs

"I decide what everyone deserves."
—KING MAGNIFICO

Time Talisman
Marvel movie fans know that each Infinity Stone is linked to a Relic. World Discovery's Treasures of Xandar has quite the collection including the Eye of Agamotto which holds the Time Stone.

Passport to Adventure
As you travel the globe in World Showcase you can track your progress—and create a special keepsake—with a passport booklet. These are sold at most of the land's shops. As you visit each country, you can add stickers of characters, flags and landmarks onto the pages and add notes about your adventures. Cast Members at each Kidcot location *(see page 112)* will validate your passport.

Global Goodies
Shops in World Showcase's pavilions sell all sorts of wares that the countries are known for like French berets, Moroccan lanterns, German cuckoo clocks and Norwegian trolls. The Japan Pavilion even has a fun pick-a-pearl activity where you choose a live oyster and watch as it's opened to reveal your pearl! In the Mexico Pavilion some of the handicrafts sold there are made by artisans on-site including custom-engraved glass at La Princesa de Cristal, handpainted Alejibre sculptures in Plaza de los Amigos and engraved rings at a small outdoor stand called Ring Carvers.

Your Own Handiwork
There are some chances for you to get crafty in World Showcase including mask painting inside the Italy Pavilion's La Gemma Elegante shop or glass art making at the Germany Pavilion's Glaskunst.

The Outpost
This area between the Germany and China pavilions is inspired by **Equatorial Africa**. There's a **Refreshment Outpost** snack stand and a rural shop called **Village Traders** with African handicrafts—many made onsite. **Bongo drums** and **umbrella tables** are set up here for all to use and enjoy. Peek over the wall to see some colorful **canoes** docked on the sandy beach.

This Land is That Land!

Draw a line connecting the number of the photo on the **left** to the letter of the photo on the **right** that was taken in the **same land** in EPCOT. *Answers on page 203.*

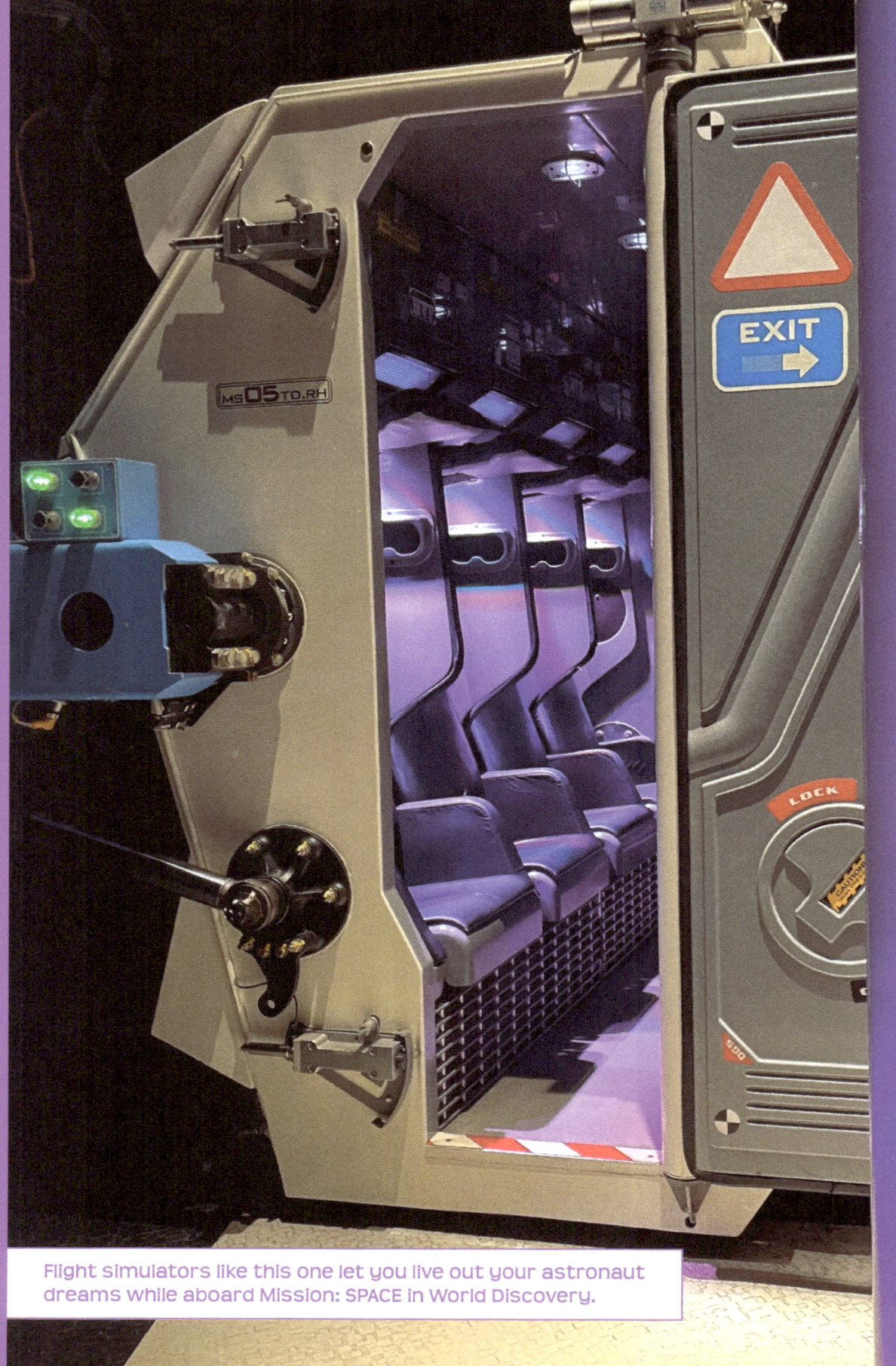

Flight simulators like this one let you live out your astronaut dreams while aboard Mission: SPACE in World Discovery.

Disney's Hollywood Studios

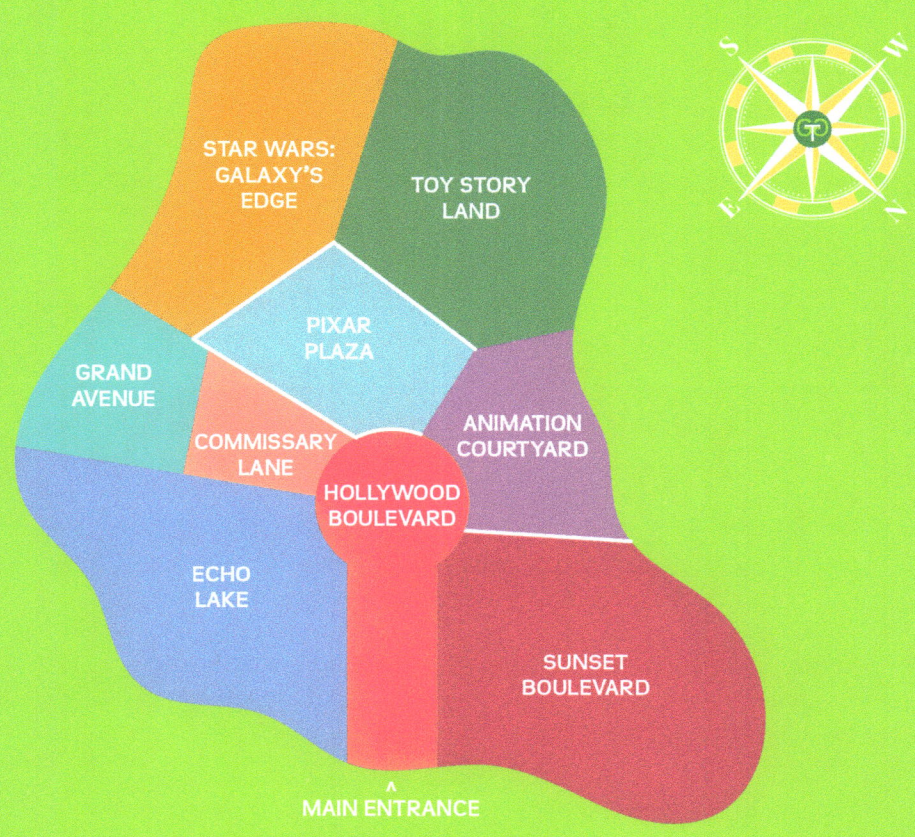

Lands in Brief!

Put a **dot** in the circle next to the **land** that you **think** you'll like best. Once you've visited them all, **color in** the circle by your **favorite**.

- ○ **Animation Courtyard:** educational, entertaining
- ○ **Commissary Lane:** polished, retro
- ○ **Echo Lake:** dramatic, whimsical
- ○ **Grand Avenue:** charming, quirky
- ○ **Hollywood Boulevard:** glitzy, vintage
- ○ **Pixar Plaza:** colorful, fashionable
- ○ **Star Wars: Galaxy's Edge:** distant, rugged
- ○ **Sunset Boulevard:** glamorous, mysterious
- ○ **Toy Story Land:** oversized, playful

DISNEY'S HOLLYWOOD STUDIOS AT A GLANCE

HOLLYWOOD BLVD. ATTRACTIONS	MEET N' GREETS	ENTERTAINMENT
• Mickey & Minnie's Runaway Railway		• Disney Movie Magic • Wonderful World of Animation

ECHO LAKE ATTRACTIONS	MEET N' GREETS	ENTERTAINMENT
• A Frozen Sing-Along Celebration (For the First Time in Forever) • Indiana Jones Epic Stunt Spectacular • Star Tours • Vacation Fun	• Olaf	

COMMISSARY LN. ATTRACTIONS	MEET N' GREETS	ENTERTAINMENT
	• Mickey • Minnie	

GRAND AVENUE ATTRACTIONS	MEET N' GREETS	ENTERTAINMENT
• Muppet Vision 3D		

GALAXY'S EDGE ATTRACTIONS	MEET N' GREETS	ENTERTAINMENT
• Millennium Falcon: Smugglers Run • Star Wars: Rise of the Resistance	• Star Wars Characters	• First Order Searches for the Resistance

TOY STORY LAND ATTRACTIONS	MEET N' GREETS	ENTERTAINMENT
• Alien Swirling Saucers • Slinky Dog Dash • Toy Story Mania!	• Buzz Lightyear • Jessie • Woody	• Green Army Drum Corps

PIXAR PLAZA ATTRACTIONS	MEET N' GREETS	ENTERTAINMENT
	• Edna Mode & Pixar Pals	

ANIMATION CTYRD. ATTRACTIONS	MEET N' GREETS	ENTERTAINMENT
• Disney Junior Play and Dance! • Star Wars Launch Bay • The Little Mermaid (stage show) • Walt Disney Presents	• Ariel • Disney Junior Pals • Pluto • Star Wars Characters	

SUNSET BLVD. ATTRACTIONS	MEET N' GREETS	ENTERTAINMENT
• Beauty and the Beast—Live on Stage • Fantasmic! • Rock 'n' Roller Coaster • The Twilight Zone Tower of Terror		

Picture if you will...

❖ **QUICK-SERVICE EATERY**

FOOD & DRINKS
- The Hollywood Brown Derby
- The Trolley Car Café ❖

FOOD & DRINKS
- 50's Prime Time Café
- Backlot Express ❖
- Dinosaur Gertie's ❖
- Dockside Diner ❖
- Epic Eats ❖
- Hollywood & Vine
- Tune-In Lounge

SHOPS
- Celebrity 5 & 10
- Oscar's Super Service
- Keystone Clothiers
- Mickey's of Hollywood
- Sid Cahuenga's

SHOPS
- Frozen Fractal Gifts
- Hollywood & Vine
- Indiana Jones Adventure Outpost
- Tatooine Traders

FOOD & DRINKS
- ABC Commissary ❖
- Sci-Fi Dine-In Theater

FOOD & DRINKS
- BaseLine Tap House ❖
- Ice Cold Hydraulics ❖
- Mama Melrose's
- PizzeRizzo ❖

SHOPS

SHOPS
- Stage 1 Company Store

FOOD & DRINKS
- Docking Bay 7 Food and Cargo ❖
- Kat Saka's Kettle ❖
- Milk Stand ❖
- Oga's Cantina
- Ronto Roasters ❖

SHOPS
- Dok-Ondar's Den of Antiquities
- Droid Depot
- First Order Cargo
- Savi's Workshop
- The Market Merchants

FOOD & DRINKS
- Roundup Rodeo BBQ
- Woody's Lunch Box ❖

FOOD & DRINKS
- Neighborhood Bakery ❖

SHOPS
- Jessie's Trading Post

SHOPS

FOOD & DRINKS

SHOPS

FOOD & DRINKS
- KRNR The Rock Station ❖
- Sunset Ranch Market ❖
  5 eateries: Anaheim Produce, Catalina Eddie's, Fairfax Faire, Hollywood Scoops and Rosie's All-American Café

SHOPS
- Beverly Sunset Boutique
- Legends of Hollywood
- Once Upon a Time
- Rock Around the Shop
- Sunset Club Couture
- Tower Hotel Gifts

135

Hollywood Boulevard

"What does this lever do?"
—GOOFY

This first land past the Main Entrance is similar to Magic Kingdom's Main Street USA—but with a vintage Tinseltown flair. Here you'll find glitzy neon, glamourous Art Deco decor and retro traffic lights that ding when they switch between stop and go!

Inspired by Hollywood

One of the most famous streets in Los Angeles, CA is Hollywood Boulevard. To recreate a version of that glamorous town, Imagineers took inspiration from real landmark buildings all around L.A. like a bank, camera shop, drugstore, gas station, makeup studio and pet hospital. From the Crossroads of the World souvenir stand just inside the Main Entrance to the Chinese Theatre at the end of the lane, you'll see replicas here of some of the most famed California architecture from the 1920s through 1940s.

FUN FACT When creating Disneyland, Walt would call tall, eye-catching things off in the distance **"wienies."** Just as he'd tempt his pet dogs with wiener hot dogs, these structures draw you closer to them for a **treat.** Wienies in this park include the **Chinese Theatre** and the **Tower of Terror.**

The Hollywood Brown Derby

Table Service • Indoor Seating

Starting in the 1920s, celebrities flocked to dine at Hollywood's Brown Derby restaurant on Vine Street. Today the tradition of fashionable dining continues at this elegant indoor restaurant and outdoor lounge made to look like the popular hotspot. Like its namesake, there are derby hat-shaped lamps and framed caricature drawings of stars, along with a book in a display case with celebrity autographs. Specialties here include char-grilled beef, their famous Cobb salad, Faroe Island salmon and grapefruit cake.

PLUS: **The Trolley Car Café** with pastries, sandwiches, specialty coffees & teas

☆ ☆ ☆ ☆ ☆
Mickey & Minnie's Runaway Railway

Now showing at the Chinese Theatre: *Perfect Picnic.* In this **short cartoon** Mickey, Minnie and Pluto are heading for a picnic in a red roadster as Engineer Goofy toots alongside aboard the **Runnamuck Railroad.** After things go amuck on screen, Goofy will invite you and the other moviegoers to actually enter his **cartoon world** and ride on his train! Once you get settled onboard, Mickey and Minnie will drive up and say **hiya** but when the track switch gets accidentally bumped, your train becomes a **runaway!** You'll **twist and turn** through risky adventures in a desert canyon, an amusement park, a tropical paradise and a bustling city as brave Mickey and Minnie try to get you **back on track!**

♫ Entertainment

The nighttime shows Disney Movie Magic and Wonderful World of Animation feature clips projected on the front of the Chinese Theatre!

 You'll see **old pals** like Daisy, Donald and Pete the cat and **new** faces, like **Chuuby** *(Choo-bee),* a golden **bird** who made his debut on this ride!

 Sometimes cartoon characters have **"pie eyes"** where the **circle** or **oval** of each eye is shaped like a pie with a **slice missing** to look like a **reflection** of light.

TIME MACHINE

1927 — Grauman's Chinese Theatre in L.A. opens & stars press their hands & feet in cement out front.

1989 — Opening Day attraction The Great Movie Ride debuts in the replica of the Chinese Theatre.

2017 — Roll credits! The Great Movie Ride closes—the park's last remaining Opening Day attraction.

2020 — Mickey & Minnie's Runaway Railway opens where The Great Movie Ride used to be.

Echo Lake

"Ice is my life!"
—KRISTOFF

The bustling Echo Park neighborhood in L.A. is centered around Echo Park Lake. Here you'll find a central lake too along with theaters, a forest village and "California Crazy" buildings—a term for structures built in whimsical shapes to attract people passing by!

☆ ☆ ★ ☆ ☆

A Frozen Sing-Along Celebration

With its glass block walls and shining silver trim, the pale icy blue Hyperion Theater is the perfect site for *the First Time in Forever: A Frozen Sing-Along Celebration*. The comical Royal Historians of Arendelle will tell the tale of the kingdom's regal sisters and share clips of musical numbers from the 2013 animated movie *Frozen* on a screen behind them. It's easy to sing along because the song lyrics are shown over the scenes—though you may already know them by heart? The historians are joined on stage by Anna, Kristoff and Elsa too. For a big finish, you'll "Let It Go" with the whole crew as swirling snow falls from above!

INDOOR LIVE SHOW · EST. 2014

FUN FACT: Walt and Roy Disney started their business on Kingswell Avenue in L.A. in 1923. Their second location on Hyperion Avenue from 1926 to 1940 is where this theater gets its name! After the success of the Snow White movie, the studio moved across town to its current location in Burbank.

TIME MACHINE

1989 — Opening Day attraction SuperStar Television debuts in what is now the Hyperion Theater.

2014 — For the First Time in Forever: A Frozen Sing-Along Celebration debuts in the now-gone Premiere Theater.

2015 — The Frozen sing-along moves to the Hyperion Theater & gets a holiday version starting in 2017.

2016 — Test the limits! The Frozen Ever After ride debuts in EPCOT's Norway Pavilion.

Dockside Diner Quick Service • Outdoor Seating

The S.S. Down the Hatch is based on a 1930 live-action MGM movie called *Min and Bill*. This boat is actually a stand that serves up plain or loaded hot dogs, milkshakes and more. Buoy, oh buoy!

Hollywood & Vine Buffet • Indoor Seating

Join Disney Junior stars here for a Character Meal breakfast with French toast, omelets, waffles and more. Sometimes Minnie Mouse hosts lunch and dinner parties here with food, drinks and decor that changes with the seasons. This casual spot, named after the corner of Hollywood Boulevard and Vine Street in L.A., has the chrome, curves and neon of a 1930s Art Deco-style cafeteria.

50's Prime Time Café Table Service • Indoor Seating

You better keep your elbows off the table! The sassy waiters here entertain—and treat you like family—as they serve up comfort foods like fried chicken, meatloaf and pot roast. This nifty fities style diner looks like a mid-century mom's kitchen with boomerang wallpaper and kitschy knickknacks. Many tables have their own vintage TV set playing clips from popular old shows that aired during "prime time"—the evening hours when most people watch TV. Finish your meal and you'll be in the Clean Plate Club! Also in the café is Tune-In Lounge which serves grown-up drinks and looks like a retro den.

What would you name a pet dino?
_____

Dinosaur Gertie's Ice Cream of Extinction

Quick Service • No Seating

Though this eatery with ice cream and snacks is not always open, you can't miss it towering over Echo Lake! This big, green stand is a tribute to Gertie the Dinosaur, an animated character created by Winsor McCay in 1914. Look for an info sign nearby to learn more about this dino—and see if you can spot her footprints.

⭐⭐⭐⭐⭐

Indiana Jones Epic Stunt Spectacular

Movie magic comes alive here at the Indiana Jones Ampitheater! The show begins with a performance of the *thrilling* scene from *Raiders of the Lost Ark* where Indiana Jones is chased through a temple by a giant boulder! Once that's a wrap, the assistant director hits the stage and explains how *stunt work* works as the crew transform the *massive* set into a marketplace. The stunt doubles for the main characters—*Indiana* and *Marion*—are introduced, along with the Epic Stunt Team. These skilled pros train for years to be able to perform the amazing acrobatics, fake fights and falls from buildings you'll witness before the show comes to a *fiery* ending. And…cut!

 Outside of this attraction, there's a sign on a well that says **"Do Not Pull Rope!"** (But you should totally pull it.)

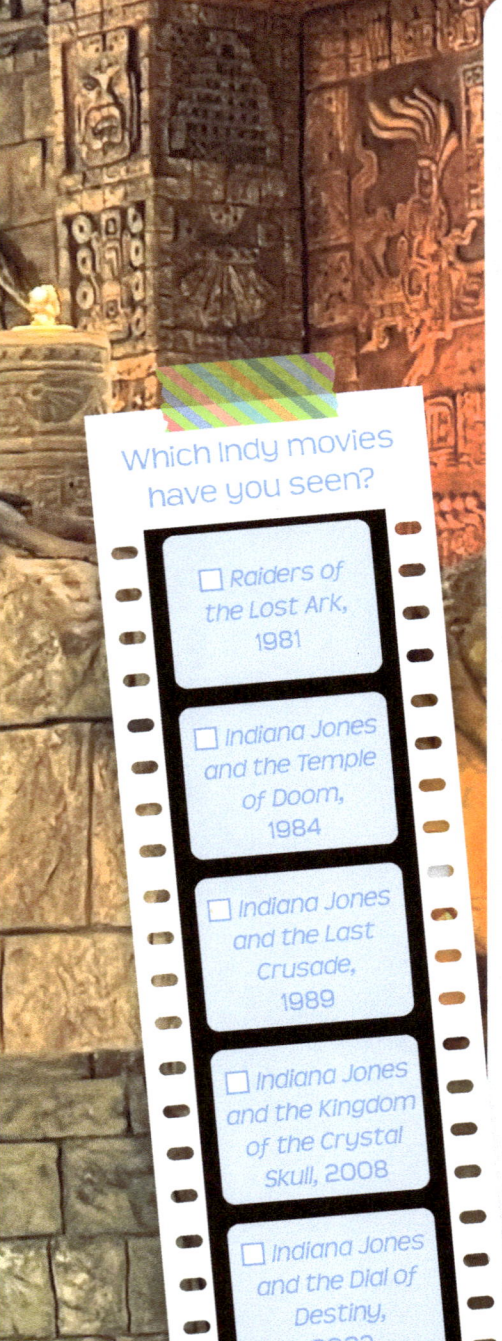

Which Indy movies have you seen?
- ☐ Raiders of the Lost Ark, 1981
- ☐ Indiana Jones and the Temple of Doom, 1984
- ☐ Indiana Jones and the Last Crusade, 1989
- ☐ Indiana Jones and the Kingdom of the Crystal Skull, 2008
- ☐ Indiana Jones and the Dial of Destiny, 2023

TIME MACHINE

1981 — The live-action "Raiders of the Lost Ark" movie hits theaters with Dr. Indiana Jones & his ex Marion.

1989 — Based on "Raiders of the Lost Ark," the stunt show debuts a few months after the park opens.

1993 — An Indy roller coaster debuts in Disneyland Paris & it's the first Disney ride ever to go upside down.

1995 — Earthly riches! Indiana Jones Adventure: Temple of the Forbidden Eye debuts in California's Disneyland.

Showbiz Terms

You may hear these **moviemaking words** and **phrases** during the **Indiana Jones stunt show**:

- **Action** = Start performing
- **Assistant Director** = Person who runs the set during production
- **Cut** = Stop filming
- **Director** = Person in charge of the project's creative vision
- **Mark** = The location where an actor begin a scene
- **Pick-up shot** = Short reshot scene
- **Places please** = Actors need to hit their marks
- **Roll cameras** = Start recording
- **Stunt Coordinator** = Person who plans out the action scene stunts
- **Stunt Double** = Person who does dangerous action scenes in place of an actor
- **Take one** = The first time a scene is shot

Vacation Fun

Toodle on in to the Mickey Shorts Theater to catch an *Original Animated Short with Mickey & Minnie!* This collection of clips are memories Mickey's having as he packs his bags for a trip with Minnie. He's had oodles of action-packed *travels* all around the world in places like China's *Beijing Zoo,* a castle in *France* and fabulous *Potatoland.* You'll see friends like Daisy, Donald and Goofy, and faithful Pluto joining in on the *vacation fun* too!

 In the **photo spot** area at the theater's exit, look for **details** from the cartoons you just saw like the camera-shy **panda** and...a **potato**!

 ## Meet n' Greets

Do you wanna meet a snowman? Huggable Olaf from *Frozen* chills out at a sunshiny summer setting inside Celebrity Spotlight.

SO YOU KNOW... **backlot** = area with sets used for filming outdoor scenes

Backlot Express Quick Service • Outdoor Seating

This industrial metal prop warehouse building houses a restaurant with burgers and fries, chicken strips, salads and more.

PLUS: *Epic Eats* stand with funnel cake & ice cream floats

FLIGHT SIMULATOR EST. 1989

MAY BE SCARY
HEIGHT: 40"+

Which characters have appeared in transmissions during your tours?
_____
_____

⭐⭐⭐⭐⭐

Star Tours

Located within an Ewok village on the forest moon of Endor, you'll find a *spaceport terminal* where you can go inside to catch convenient daily departures to places seen in the Star Wars movies! Droids C-3PO and R2-D2 ready your *Starspeeder 1000* for the captain as you and your *tour group* board and don 3D flight glasses. When menacing military troops approach to search among the passengers for a *rebel spy*, it's time for a getaway! Launching into space, the Starspeeder will *careen* through a hair-raising flight. There's no telling *who* you'll run into...Chewbacca in the woodlands of Kashyyyk, Sebulba at a Tatooine pod race, Poe Dameron near the red crystal mines of Crait? Wherever you end up, may the *Force* be with you!

 Look for the **footprint** left by the All Terrain Armored Transport (AT-AT). You can also see Andy's **25-foot-long sneaker tread** in Toy Story Land, and celebrity handprints and footprints outside Hollywood Boulevard's **Chinese Theatre** and Sunset Boulevard's **Theater of the Stars.**

 This ride was renamed **Star Tours—The Adventures Continue** in **2011** when new characters, destinations and effects were added. Over time, more **variations** have come along—like **Ahsoka Tano, Cassian Andor** and the **Mandalorian** joining the ranks in **2024.**

Commissary Lane

"Life is a dance so let's twirl and whirl!"
—MINNIE MOUSE

Believe it or not, this path is officially a land! Here you'll find palm trees and large soundstage buildings along both sides of the lane along with banners and billboards about various entertainment projects in production.

🍴 Sci-Fi Dine-In Theater

Table Service • Indoor Seating

Enjoy a drive-in movie theater experience inside this unique restaurant. Most seating is in "automo-booths"—1950s-style convertibles with built-in tables! The cars face a large movie screen where old commercials and clips of science-fiction movies play. Lighting up the darkness is a starry night sky and the glow of car taillights. The menu features classic American cuisine like burgers, fries and milkshakes.

🍴 ABC Commissary Quick Service • Indoor & Outdoor Seating

This Art Deco **commissary** serves up meals like salads, sandwiches and tacos to keep your crew fueled up and ready for action. Around the restaurant, posters and props from Disney-owned shows are on display.

> SO YOU KNOW…
> **commissary** = studio cafeteria

📷 Meet n' Greets

You'll find Mickey Mouse in the sorcerer's castle from *Fantasia* and Minnie Mouse on a ritzy garnet and gold movie set inside Red Carpet Dreams!

The Wonderful World of Disney

Since it began in **1923**, The Walt Disney Company has grown into one of the **biggest entertainment companies** in the world! They now own a book publishing company, a cruise line, radio stations, television channels and theme parks—and these businesses all use the **Disney name** in some form. But they also own many **media companies** that **don't** have Disney in their names including ABC, ESPN, Hulu, Lucasfilm, Marvel, National Geographic, Pixar **and** 20th Century Studios!

Grand Avenue

"What foolishness would you like to see?"
—THE GREAT GONZO

Muppet fans will have a grand time on this avenue. Here you'll find brick city buildings with fire escapes, lamp lights, park benches and a fountain in the center of the courtyard with a statue of Miss Piggy herself dressed as Lady Liberty!

🍴 BaseLine Tap House

Quick Service • Indoor & Outdoor Seating

The story goes that this building was once a California print shop. Mostly grown-up drinks are on tap here but they also serve lemonade, charcuterie plates and giant pretzels.

PLUS: **Ice Cold Hydraulics** stand with mini churros, popcorn & slushies

☆☆☆☆☆ Muppet Vision 3D

The best Muppet is: _____

INDOOR 3D FILM • EST. 1991

It's time to *get things started* inside the Grand Arts Theatre! You'll put on a pair of 3D safety goggles to see Kermit the Frog share the Muppets' *really* top secret research. Grouchy Statler and Waldorf *heckle* the show from their balcony seats as the klutzy Swedish Chef works the film projector in back. As Miss Piggy the diva and patriotic Sam the Eagle prepare their *acts,* Kermit runs into corny Fozzie Bear and then introduces you to the bumbling Dr. Honeydew and his assistant Beaker. That's when a *wacky* flying character called *Waldo C. Graphic* gets loose! After Piggy scolds cute Bean Bunny for ruining her musical number, he runs away and the Muppets need your help to find him. But with Waldo around, *nothing* goes as planned!

 FUN FACT: **Before** the main show, you can see stage manager **Scooter** on screens inside the **theater's prop warehouse** as he tries to keep the **show's prep** on track. At times, promos for **new Muppet movies** are shown here instead.

Marvelous Muppets!

The Muppets were created by Disney Legend Jim Henson in **1955** and their first TV show aired on ABC in **1977.** Many more Muppet shows and movies have followed! Can you name **ALL** of these **characters?** *Answers on page 203.*

ROW 1

ROW 2

ROW 3

ROW 4

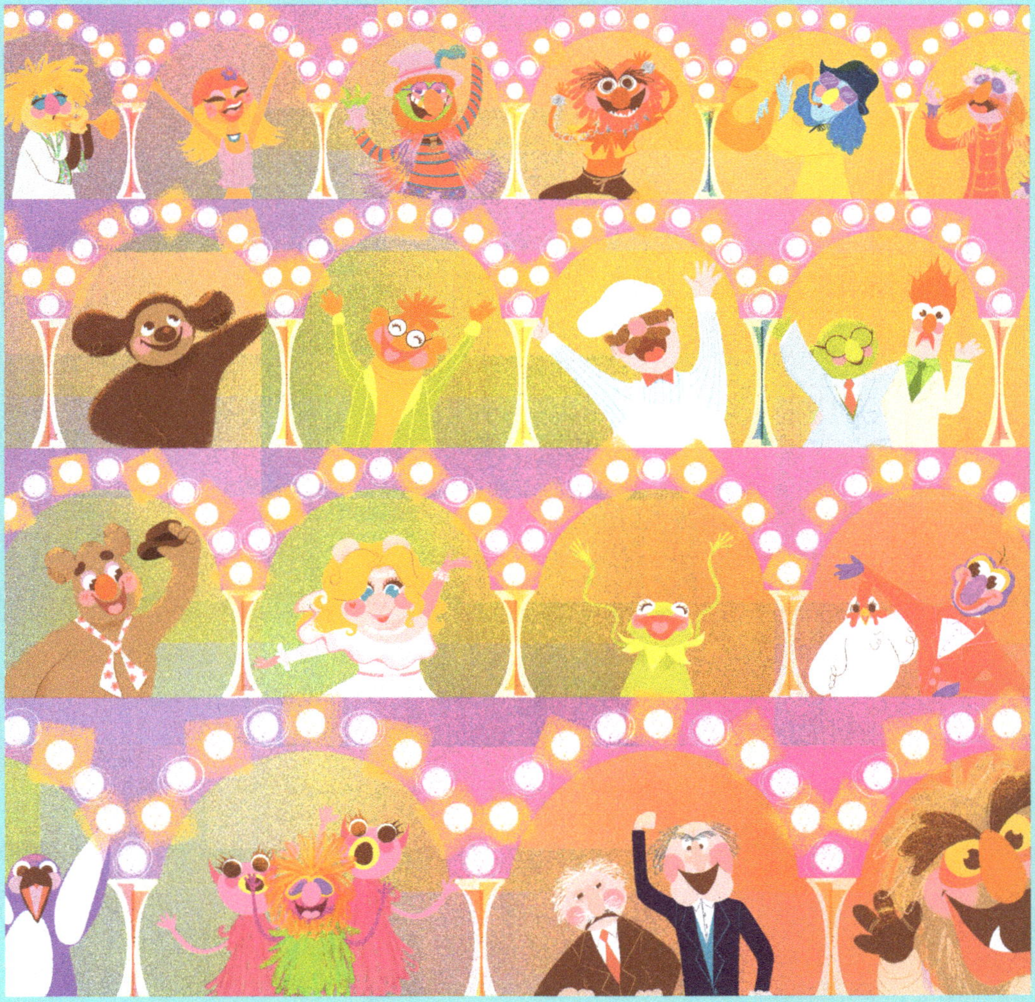

Illustration by Mary Pavlou • www.etsy.com/shop/MareBearPress

PizzeRizzo Quick Service • Indoor & Outdoor Seating

Decorated in the green, white and red of the Italian flag, this pizza joint is run by the scrappy Muppet, Rizzo the Rat. Salads, submarine sandwiches and "100% Authentic New Yorkish Pizza" are served here. Notice what the neon sign on the roof does at night!

Mama Melrose's Table Service • Indoor Seating

Once a backlot warehouse, this is now a cozy Ristorante Italiano with checked curtains, twinkle lights and hanging grapes. Mama recreates her papa's recipes like minestrone soup, pasta, pizza and cannoli.

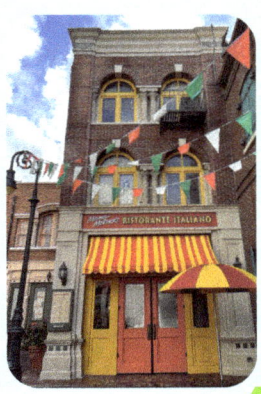

Star Wars: Galaxy's Edge

> "I know all about waiting."
> —REY

Travel to the edge of the galaxy to land in Black Spire Outpost on the planet Batuu. Here you'll find weathered buildings and ruins, unique vegetation, towering petrified spires and a bustling marketplace where a strange creature lives in a water tank!

☆☆☆☆☆

Star Wars: Rise of the Resistance

MAY BE SCARY

HEIGHT: 40"+

Welcome to the cause! Deep inside a Resistance camp, droid BB-8 has a vital message from Rey. Appearing as a **hologram,** she urges you to keep the rebel base's location a secret from the evil First Order. Next, you and the other Resistance recruits will board a transport to fly to the planet Pacara —but the bad guys have other plans. Though Lieutenant Bek, Nien Nunb and Poe Dameron fight to keep your transport from being captured, you'll be taken prisoner aboard a Star Destroyer. After entering the spaceship's hangar bay, you'll pass legions of imposing Stormtroopers and be taken to see First Order leaders Armitage Hux and Kylo Ren. With help from Finn and other Resistance rebels, you'll have a shot at reaching an escape pod. An R5 droid will give you a lift in a hijacked vehicle but you'll have to get past a probe droid, enormous AT-ATs and more before you can make it back to Batuu!

HOT TIP: Listen for **"I have a bad feeling about this."** A form of this phrase is said in **every** Star Wars movie.

SO YOU KNOW... hologram = projected 3D image

INDOOR DARK RIDE ★ EST. 2019 ★

TIME MACHINE

1989 — Star Tours opens a few months after the park does & is its first Star Wars-themed attraction.

2007 — The interactive show Jedi Training Academy opens outside Star Tours & closes in 2020.

2015 — The park gets more Star Wars fun when Launch Bay opens in Animation Courtyard.

2019 — Bright suns! Galaxy's Edge opens with Smuggler's Run, & Rise of the Resistance opens soon after.

MINI MAP: GALAXY'S EDGE

- MILLENNIUM FALCON: SMUGGLERS RUN
- DOCKING BAY 7 FOOD AND CARGO
- OGA'S CANTINA
- DOK-ONDAR'S DEN OF ANTIQUITIES
- FIRST ORDER CARGO
- RONTO ROASTERS
- KAT SAKA'S KETTLE
- DROID DEPOT
- MILK STAND
- THE MARKET MERCHANTS
- SAVI'S WORKSHOP
- GRAND AVENUE ∨
- RESISTANCE SUPPLY
- RISE OF THE RESISTANCE
- TOY STORY LAND ∨

SHOP SPOTLIGHT

See the elusive alien's curious collections at **Dok-Ondar's Den of Antiquities.**

♫ Entertainment

Report to First Order Cargo Bay to see Kylo Ren in action as the First Order Searches for the Resistance.

Ronto Roasters Quick Service • Outdoor Seating

A dreary smelter robot mutters to himself as he endlessly roasts ronto beasts from the planet Tatooine under a podracer engine here. Ronto morning wraps with eggs, ronto wraps with sausage and specialty drinks are served at this rugged counter. At an outdoor garage nearby, you'll find the starting point for the Play Disney Parks app's Star Wars: Batuu Bounty Hunters game *(requires a MagicBand+)*.

Docking Bay 7 Food and Cargo

Quick Service • Indoor & Outdoor Seating

Artiodac alien chef Strono "Cookie" Tuggs has gathered ingredients from all over the universe to create meals like Endorian fried chicken tip-yip, Peka tuna poke and a plant-based garden spread. This industrial hangar bay has a cement floor, cables snaking across the walls, and cargo pods with rugged tables and metal drums for seats. The numbers 77, 80 and 83 on the cargo loads inside and out on the roof represent the years that the movies in the original Star Wars trilogy were released: 1977, 1980 and 1983.

PLUS: **Kat Saka's Kettle** stand with sweet & spicy popcorn & drinks

SCORECARD

DATE: YOUR SCORE: YOUR ROLE:

☆ ☆ ☆ ☆ ☆

Millennium Falcon: Smugglers Run

MAY BE SCARY

HEIGHT: 38"+

Climb into the cockpit of the fastest *hunk o' junk* in the galaxy to take off on a smuggling run for space pirate Hondo Ohnaka. After he briefs you on the mission, you'll board the Millennium Falcon to take on one of three roles during your flight: Engineer, Gunner or Pilot. *Engineers* have wall panels that make sounds and light up to show which buttons need to be pushed to repair the ship. The controls next to the *Gunners* signal when it's time to shoot down any TIE Fighters who may be getting in the way. Sitting up front, the two *Pilots* work together to fly the ship with levers—the one sitting on the *left* steers side to side while the one sitting on the *right* steers up and down and makes the jump to *hyperspace*. At the end of your run, you can check out your *score* and hear what Hondo thinks of your crew's performance on the job!

 **HOT TIP** If it lights up, then **PUSH IT** or **PULL IT!** Plus, listen for **Hondo** giving you advice. As you exit, there may be **exposed wires** and **sparks** if your ship was "damaged" in flight.

 FUN FACT In **2024** Disney announced that, when the **Mandalorian movie** is released in **2026**, they'll add new missions with that masked bounty hunter and his apprentice **Grogu**.

🍴 Oga's Cantina — Table Service • Indoor Seating

Oga Garra, originally from Blutopia, runs Batuu's black market and this popular watering hole that's mostly standing room only. The curved bar in the center of the space wraps around a mass of tubes and wires, and tanks of bubbling liquids. Nosh on easy-to-share nibbles like Batuu bits and the Happabore sampler, and try exotic drink concoctions like blurrgfire or Jabba juice. DJ Rex—who started his career as a Star Tours pilot—works at this hotspot, cranking out tunes created just for Galaxy's Edge!

PLUS: **Milk Stand** with frozen fruity blue or green milk & snacks

📷 Meet n' Greets

Keep a look out for sightings of bad guys like First Order Stormtroopers or Kylo Ren and heroes like Chewbacca, Rey, the Mandalorian with Grogu, or Vi Moradi roaming around Batuu!

Aurebesh Decoder!

Use this chart to read and write **Aurebesh,** one of the languages you'll see written throughout Galaxy's Edge. To practice, decode the name of the **Star Wars character** written in **green** in the box below. *Answer on page 203.*

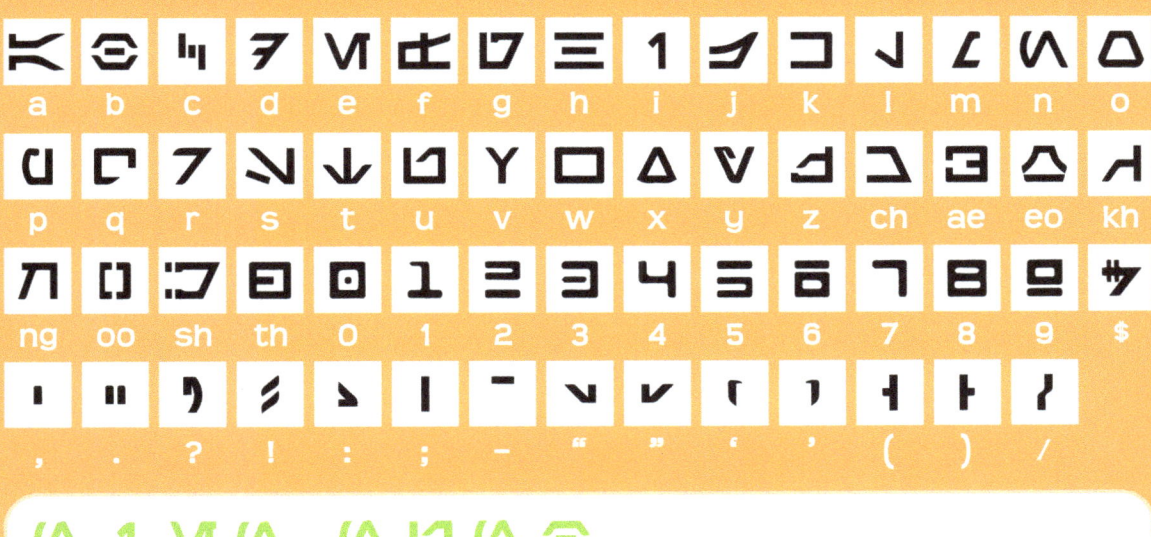

Toy Story Land

"You. Are. A. Toy!"
—WOODY

To make you feel like you're the size of a toy, everything is supersized in this land. Here you'll find Andy's backyard where the creative kid has built everything you see with art supplies, board games, building toys and playthings!

★★★★★

Alien Swirling Saucers

 COVERED SPINNER ★ EST. 2018 ★ — HEIGHT: 32"+

The *Little Green Men* have left Pizza Planet behind and now these three-eyed goofy aliens are ready to take you for a *spin* behind one of their flying saucers! As *peppy* futuristic music plays, your spaceship will whip from side to side as it whirls around under *planets* covered in pizza toppings, a colorful starry ceiling and an alien being chosen by... *The Claw!*

🎵 Entertainment

Atten-hut! Green Army Drum Corps toy soldiers drum up lots of fun near Alien Swirling Saucers.

 SPY — Starting with the Pizza Planet **robot guards** at its entrance, see how many **pizza shapes** you can find at this attraction.

TIME MACHINE

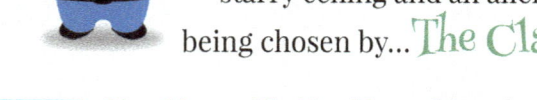

1995 — The animated "Toy Story" movie hits theaters with number 2 in 1999, 3 in 2010, 4 in 2019 & 5 due in 2026.

1998 — Buzz Lightyear's Space Ranger Spin debuts in Magic Kingdom—the resort's first Toy Story ride.

2008 — Toy Story Mania! opens in what is now Pixar Plaza & its entrance moves when Toy Story Land opens.

2018 — Golly bob howdy! Toy Story Land opens with Alien Swirling Saucers & Slinky Dog Dash.

🍴 Woody's Lunch Box

Quick Service • Outdoor Seating

Andy's "Woody's Roundup" lunchbox has been turned on its side with the lid propped open with a drink thermos and a Tinkertoy stick to create this stand! Grilled sandwiches, tater tot nachos and pastry tarts are served here.

☆☆☆☆☆ Slinky Dog Dash

HEIGHT: 38"+

Dash and dodge with *Slinky!* This darling outdoor roller coaster has ride cars that look like the *wiener dog* pull toy. You'll even sit *within* the Slinky spring that makes up his middle. The pace starts off smooth and mellow, and then launches through a row of rings to GO! GO! GO! GO! even faster. Just before you disem*bark,* a toy you may recognize will make a guest appearance.

 **SPY** The story goes that Andy built this ride with a **Mega Coaster Play Kit.** See if you can find the kit's **box** in the standby line.

Mini Quiz!
Can you guess the word some early ads used for the sound a Slinky toy makes?
Answer on page 203.
☐ Boing ☐ Slinkety ☐ Zing

📖 The Story of... Toy Story

In *Toy Story*, Sheriff Woody and his friends Bo Peep, Hamm the piggy bank, Mr. Potato Head, Rex the Tyrannosaurus Rex, Slinky Dog, the Green Army Men and other toys live in Andy's room and come to life when he and the other humans aren't around. Andy's toys welcome Buzz Lightyear, a Space Ranger action figure who doesn't know he's a toy. At the Pizza Planet restaurant Buzz meets the three-eyed Little Green Men toys when he ends up inside an arcade claw game. When Buzz realizes he really is a toy he becomes depressed but Woody convinces him that it's a great thing! In *Toy Story 2* Woody is stolen by a collector while he's trying to save a squeaker toy penguin named Wheezy. While he's being held captive Woody meets toys Jessie the cowgirl, Bullseye the horse and Stinky Pete the prospector and learns the four of them were in a "Woody's Roundup" TV show. During their adventures they run into an evil Emperor Zurg action figure—who tries to destroy Buzz. In *Toy Story 3,* Woody and some of his friends end up finding a new home with a girl named Bonnie and her toys like Buttercup the unicorn, Dolly, Mr. Pricklepants the hedgehog and Trixie the Triceratops.

☆☆☆☆☆
Toy Story Mania!

Grab some 3D glasses and pile in to a two-sided ride car to take a spin through Andy's **Midway Games Play Set**, a collection of carnival games. The Toy Story gang will show you just what to do, give you a chance to *practice*—and then cheer you on along the way. You'll **zip** past blocks, board games, crayons and more, as you take aim at targets and pull the string on your **Spring-Action Shooter**. The five fun games are hosted by Buttercup and Hamm, Rex and Trixie, the Green Army Men, Buzz and Woody. At the end you'll find out how many points you earned, who got the highest score in your tram and which **virtual critter** is your prize!

INDOOR DARK RIDE ★ EST. 2008 ★

HOT TIP: In the last game, fire at the **mine carts** as **fast** as possible to reveal some that are worth **more points**.

Write your top scores below!

📷 Meet n' Greets

Catch up with Buzz Lightyear near Roundup Rodeo BBQ and Woody or Jessie near Toy Story Mania!

🍴 Roundup Rodeo BBQ *Table Service • Indoor Seating*

Just past a huge statue of Woody you'll find this Western-style barbeque joint. More larger-than-life Toy Story toys are inside this eatery too like Bo Peep with her sheep (Billy, Goat and Gruff), Jessie and Trixie, along with frontier town and outer space playsets. The vittles at this family-style meal include biscuits, salad, sides like beans or coleslaw, a platter of house-smoked meats and a choice of desserts. Yee-haw!

Pixar Plaza

"Luck favors the prepared."
—EDNA MODE

This teensy-tiny land is dedicated to all things Pixar. Here you'll find columns topped with blue-and-yellow Pixar balls with red stars, industrial brick buildings, and panels and gates decorated with dynamic artwork inspired by the animation studio's movies!

🍴 Neighborhood Bakery Quick Service • No Seating

In *Incredibles 2*, the Parr family's baby loves to chomp on chocolate chip cookies. Now you can try his favorite treat—the great big Jack-Jack's Num Num Cookie. This stand has popcorn, pretzels and specialty drinks too.

📷 Meet n' Greets

Cool costume displays line the halls on your way to rub elbows with the famous fashion designer Edna Mode inside The Edna Mode Experience. Along the plaza you may see other characters from *The Incredibles* like Mr. or Mrs. Incredible or Frozone. Joy from *Inside Out* and Sulley from *Monsters, Inc.* often stop by the plaza too!

🔍 Legend Close-Up: Joe Ranft

Joe Ranft was born in 1960 in **California** and grew up enjoying drawing, being in school plays and doing magic tricks for his friends and family. After high school, he studied character animation at the **California Institute of the Arts**. In 1980, Joe got a job at **Disney** and worked as a **story artist** and **storywriter** on *Who Framed Roger Rabbit, Oliver & Company, Beauty and the Beast* and more. After moving on to **Pixar,** he was a major player in the creation of *Toy Story* (1 and 2), *A Bug's Life, Monsters, Inc., Finding Nemo* and *Cars*. He did **character voices** in those movies too--like **Heimlich** the caterpillar, a blue monster named Pete **"Claws"** Ward, **Jacques** the shrimp and **Red** the fire engine! One of his favorite sayings hung on his office door: **"The journey is the reward."** Joe was named a Disney Legend in **2006.**

Animation Courtyard

"Getting cold fins?"
—ARIEL

A hulking rectangular arch like you'd see at a studio entrance graces this courtyard. Here you'll find theaters lined with chrome and neon, an open plaza with rows of palm trees and space to explore another galaxy!

☆ ☆ ☆ ☆ ☆

Walt Disney Presents

INDOOR EXHIBITS • EST. 2001

Learn about Walt Disney's career highlights and legacy here! The first section you'll enter is a *gallery* with exhibits that start with his early *inspirations* and go forward through time to The Walt Disney Company's more modern-day projects. You can see awards, costumes, memorabilia, props and detailed *miniature models*—including some Walt built himself! Some of the displays are permanent and others change out from time to time. *The Walt Disney Theater* here features a live-action film narrated by actress Julie Andrews called *Walt Disney: One Man's Dream*.

HOT TIP: Sometimes the **featured film** is replaced for a short time by a sneak peek of a **new movie**.

Which did you go to?
☐ Gallery ☐ Meet n' Greet
☐ Movie theater

Meet n' Greets

Inside Walt Disney Presents, you can visit with characters like Ariel (from the 2023 live-action *The Little Mermaid* movie) on the seaside terrace of Prince Eric's castle.

The Studio System

From Disney's Hollywood Studios' Opening Day until the early **2000s**, there were real, working **studios** where **films** and **TV** shows were created. In the spot where **Star Wars Launch Bay** *(see opposite page)* is today, Guests could take the **Studio Backlot Tour** and later **The Magic of Disney Animation** tour. These unique experiences let Guests see backstage areas and peek in as artists worked at their **computers** and **drawing boards** on animated movies like *The Little Mermaid* (1989), *Lilo & Stitch* (2002) and *Brother Bear* (2003).

Fill in the year this new show opened on the dotted line. Not sure? Ask a Cast Member!

INDOOR LIVE SHOW EST. _____

Star Wars Launch Bay

This mecca for Star Wars fans opened in 2015. Today you can head inside to visit three separate Meet n' Greets and an exhibit area. The displays include character costumes, concept artwork, models of spaceships and starfighters, movie props, and replicas created just for this location.

 **SPY** Walled walkways outside of Launch Bay have framed **posters** from various **Star Wars** movies.

☆☆☆☆☆
The Little Mermaid

Have fun with Ariel at this toe-tapping **Musical Adventure!** The show uses a unique combo of on-screen animation, live performers and **delightful** puppets. You'll see the mermaid's pals Flounder and Sebastian, and family members like her sisters and proud papa King Triton—but villainous **Ursula** will be there too. **Eeks!**

📷 Meet n' Greets

You can meet BB-8 the adorable astromech droid, Chewbacca the wonderful Wookiee and diabolical Darth Vader in outer space environments inside Star Wars Launch Bay.

 FUN FACT This show uses **UV black lights** that make the **fluorescent colors glow.** If you're wearing **white clothing** here, it may **also** glow!

Imagineers at Play

Plans may change!

The **Voyage of the Little Mermaid** stage show ran from **1992** until **2020**. In **2023** Disney announced it would be replaced by a **reimagined** version called **The Little Mermaid—A Musical Adventure** (see above).

Do tell—was this **new show** open during your visit?
☐ No, not yet...   ☐ Yes, I went to it!   ☐ Yes, but I didn't go this time.

⭐⭐⭐⭐⭐
Disney Junior Play and Dance!

It's time to play and dance! Fans of the Disney Junior *television shows* Doc McStuffins, Mickey and the Roadster Racers, The Lion Guard and Vampirina won't want to miss this energetic, *interactive* show. A music-playing *DJ* on stage will get the party started and invite you to move and *groove* along with the tunes. *Disney Junior* characters will take turns hitting the stage to join you in dancing—including friendly Vampirina, imaginative Doc McStuffins and zany Timon. Last but not least, *Mickey Mouse* will burst onto the scene to show you his amazing moves. *Hot dog!*

INDOOR LIVE SHOW * EST. 2020 *

 FUN FACT: Mickey's red-and-yellow **racing suit** has **black-and-white checkered stripes** (like a car racing **finish line** flag) and the **number 28** as a nod to the year *Steamboat Willie* hit theaters!

📷 Meet n' Greets

Disney Junior TV show stars like to meet their fans outside of their theater. Look for Doc McStuffins in her backyard playhouse clinic, outgoing Fancy Nancy in her play palace and Vampirina at her Scare B&B. You may even spot Mickey's pal Pluto hanging around.

TIME MACHINE

1989
Nice ambience! Soundstage Restaurant debuts on Opening Day & changes to be a theater in 1999.

1999
The theater hosts shows for younger kids & the first "Disney Junior" version launches in 2011.

2012
Disney Junior launches Doc McStuffins's TV show, then Vampirina's in 2017 & Fancy Nancy's in 2018.

2015
Based on "The Lion King," "The Lion Guard" TV show begins on Disney Junior with Timon the meerkat.

Sunset Boulevard

> "Take it with you so you'll always have a way to look back and remember me."
> —THE BEAST

This land, which opened in 1994, is named for a famous street in L.A. Here you'll find vintage California vibes up and down the stylish boulevard with retro billboards and neon movie marquee signs atop 1920s through 1940s-era buildings!

⭐⭐⭐⭐⭐

Beauty and the Beast – Live on Stage

OUTDOOR LIVE SHOW • EST. 1991

This Broadway-style musical in the *Theater of the Stars* is a feast for your eyes and ears with beautiful sets, elaborate costumes and those *superb songs!* Main characters like the Beast, Belle, Gaston, Cogsworth, Lumiere, Mrs. Potts and Chip are joined by lively villagers and enchanted dancing dishware to take you back through highlights of the *beloved* story. This show actually debuted the same day the animated *Beauty and the Beast* movie was released in 1991!

 **HOT TIP** Many shows, including this one, have **signs** out front that list the **times** of its **performances** that day.

 FUN FACT In the **2017** live-action *Beauty and the Beast* movie, the floor of the ballroom features the swirly letters "W" and "D" as a tribute to **Walt Disney!**

SHOP SPOTLIGHT

Fairytales come true inside a classic Hollywood theater at **Once Upon a Time.**

🍴 Sunset Ranch Market — Quick Service • Outdoor Seating

Like L.A.'s historic Farmers Market, this open-air market has white buildings trimmed in green with red roofs and a clock tower. A shared seating area is near five eateries: **Anaheim Produce** with fresh fruit and Mickey pretzels; **Catalina Eddie's** with pizza and sandwiches; **Fairfax Faire** with Mickey-shaped waffle platters; **Hollywood Scoops** with ice cream treats; and **Rosie's All-American Café** with burgers, hot dogs and lemonade.

☆ ☆ ☆ ☆ ☆

Rock 'n' Roller Coaster

MAY BE SCARY

HEIGHT: 48"+

This indoor ride *Starring Aerosmith* is one of the resort's most thrilling! You'll go inside a studio at *G-Force Records* where the legendary rock band are recording their song "Walk This Way." When their limousine car pulls up, lead singer Steven Tyler invites you fans to come along to their *concert!* You'll board a *super-stretch limo* to careen into the darkness as Aerosmith music blasts from the onboard speakers. As you pass palm trees and street signs, the track will *twist* like a corkscrew and even loop upside down!

ROLLER COASTER EST. 1999

HOT TIP: Put your **head back** on the headrest—the launch is **FAST** and you'll feel the **G-force!**

SPY: The arch that leads to this area has an **upside-down limo** on it—but look closely at the track it's attached to. That track is actually the long, extended neck of a **giant red guitar** near the entrance to this ride!

SET LIST - Cross out the songs you've heard on this ride!
* Back in the Saddle * Love in a Roller Coaster * Nine Lives * Sweet Emotion
* Walk This Way * Others? _____

🍴 KRNR The Rock Station

Quick Service • Outdoor Seating

Before or after you rock out with Aerosmith, you can eat to the beat at this radio station's tricked-out trailer which has snicky snackies like corn dog nuggets, mini churros, root beer floats and ice cream.

Villain Vanity Plates!

Draw a line connecting the **car license plate** to the **cad** who it would belong to. One has been done for you. *Answers on page 203.*

License plates:
- FAIREST1
- NOBLL4U
- HEDZOFF
- H8-PAN
- FURFAN
- INOBEST
- SPINWME
- C-WITCH
- HOTHEAD
- EMPR-Z

Villains:
- Captain Hook
- Cruella de Vil
- Evil Queen
- Hades
- Lady Tremaine
- Maleficent → (SPINWME)
- Mother Gothel
- Queen of Hearts
- Ursula
- Zurg

Imagineers at Play

Plans may change!

Rock 'n' Roller Coaster's neighbor **Sunset Showcase** debuted in **2015** with a dance spot called **Club Disney**. From **2019** to **2024** this building was home to the **Lightning McQueen's Racing Academy** show. In **2024** Disney announced that the venue would get an all-new **villain-themed stage show** soon.

What was **brewing** at **Sunset Showcase** during your visit?
☐ It was closed! ☐ I'm not sure... ☐ The villain show was there!

☆☆☆☆☆

The Twilight Zone Tower of Terror

MAY BE SCARY

HEIGHT: 40"+

INDOOR DROP TOWER • EST. 1994 •

*C*ross over into…The Twilight Zone! You'll enter the lobby of the *deserted* 1930s-era Hollywood Tower Hotel where you'll be directed to a library. The room darkens and a TV flickers on to show Rod Serling, the host and narrator of *The Twilight Zone.* He'll explain what happened here in 1939 when lightning struck an *elevator* and the people inside disappeared! Next, it's on to the boiler room to ride in a service elevator—*if you dare.* After you strap yourself in to one of the rows of seats, the elevator rises and its doors open to reveal a long hallway and…*mysteries* of the Fifth Dimension. Hold on tight as the elevator *plummets* towards the ground floor and *rockets* towards the rooftop where the doors fly open to reveal a one-of-a-kind view of the park. Enjoy it while it lasts. You won't be there long before the next *drop!*

SPY

You may be able to spy **tributes** to episodes of *The Twilight Zone* TV series like the name **Cadwallader,** a small **spacesuit** and a ventriloquist **doll** wearing a tuxedo.

Do you like scary rides?
☐ Oh, yes!
☐ Not really…

TIME MACHINE

1959
"The Twilight Zone" live-action CBS TV show (in which very odd things happen) runs until 1964.

1983
The Warner Bros. live-action "Twilight Zone: The Movie" hits theaters & recreates parts of the TV series.

1994
YIKES! The Twilight Zone Tower of Terror debuts & is so tall it can be seen from EPCOT.

1997
The live-action "Tower of Terror" movie is released with some scenes filmed in Disney's Hollywood Studios.

⭐⭐⭐⭐⭐

Fantasmic!

OUTDOOR LIVE SHOW • EST. 1998

MAY BE SCARY ⚠

Join Mickey Mouse in a journey beyond your **wildest imagination** in the outdoor Hollywood Hills Ampitheater. Fountains dance in a ring of water around the stage as the **magical** mouse gets the show started. In Mickey's dream world, you'll hear **songs** and see **scenes** from Disney's treasured animated movies projected on screens made of **water mist.** A large cast of characters can be seen in the clips, on stage, and atop barges that cruise by on the water. As the princes and princesses waltz, it's all so lovely —but suddenly the **Evil Queen** appears and casts a spell for Mickey's dream to turn into a **nightmare!** Other villains join her but they're no match for our **brave** hero. With a wave of Tinker Bell's wand, a large paddleboat rounds the bend driven by Mickey and filled with dancing characters!

SHOP SPOTLIGHT

Near the hotel's exit you'll find the luxe, lower-level gift shop, **Tower Hotel Gifts.**

HOT TIP — Fantasmic only happens **after dark** and may not take place every night. As with any live show, **check the schedule!**

Illustration by Mary Pavlou • www.etsy.com/shop/MareBearPress

🎁 Sample Souvenirs

"I see you have constructed a new lightsaber."
—DARTH VADER

Games with a Twist
If you love Disney and games then you'll really love the Disney Parks theme park editions of games like Battleship, Candy Land, Clue, The Game of Life and Yahtzee! Look for them in Hollywood Boulevard's Mickey's of Hollywood—one of this park's largest shops. They can be found in other stores around the resort too.

Sabers and Droids
Star Wars: Galaxy's Edge has two high-end souvenirs that you create yourself. At Savi's Workshop, you can create your ultimate lightsaber. The guides here, known as Gatherers, pass down legends about the Jedi while builders choose a sword theme and bring it to life with a kyber crystal. At Droid Depot, an astromech droid unit can be customized at a Build Station. After deciding which type of robot to make, you'll fill a basket with parts and follow plans to create and activate your new remote-controlled buddy!
NOTE: Reservations are recommended for both experiences.

Light-up Pooch
At what's got to be the cutest stand in the whole park, you can find fun toys like a light-up Slinky Dog. Push a button and his spring lights up and blinks in colorful patterns. This Play Family Camper stand is parked in Toy Story Land.

Rhythm Sticks
Riders who are exiting Rock 'n' Roller Coaster in Sunset Boulevard pass through Rock Around the Shop but you can also reach it by going up the exit path to the left of the ride. Inside you'll find drums filled with wooden drumsticks. Pick up a pair, pay for 'em, practice hard and maybe you'll become the next big rock star!

Imagineers at Play

Plans may change!

In **2024** Disney announced that a new land with a **Monstropolis** theme was coming to Disney's Hollywood Studios! They didn't say **where** this would be built, but they shared that Guests will be able to ride through the **door vault** at the **Monsters, Inc.** factory in ride cars that hang from an **overhead** track. This will be the first **suspended** roller coaster **ever** in a Disney park.

So how does all this news **grab** ya?
☐ Yesss, I love *Monsters, Inc.!* ☐ Dunno... ☐ Sounds like a lot of paperwork

This Land is That Land!

Draw a line connecting the number of the photo on the **left** to the letter of the photo on the **right** that was taken in the **same land** in Disney's Hollywood Studios. *Answers on page 203.*

Modeled after the 1931 Oakland Floral Depot in California, this shop in Sunset Boulevard has the rich colors and bold geometric shapes that the Art Deco style is known for.

Disney's Animal Kingdom

AFRICA

ASIA

DISCOVERY ISLAND

DINOLAND USA

PANDORA—THE WORLD OF AVATAR

OASIS

^ MAIN ENTRANCE

Lands in Brief!

Put a **dot** in the circle next to the **land** that you **think** you'll like best. Once you've visited them all, **color in** the circle by your **favorite**.

- ○ **Africa:** lively, rustic
- ○ **Asia:** exotic, vibrant
- ○ **DinoLand USA:** amusing, prehistoric
- ○ **Discovery Island:** leafy, scenic
- ○ **Oasis:** lush, tropical
- ○ **Pandora:** dramatic, otherworldly

DISNEY'S ANIMAL KINGDOM AT A GLANCE

OASIS ATTRACTIONS	MEET N' GREETS	ENTERTAINMENT
• The Oasis Exhibits	• DiVine	

DISCOVERY ISLAND ATTRACTIONS	MEET N' GREETS	ENTERTAINMENT
• Discovery Island Trails • It's Tough to Be a Bug!	• Dug • Kevin • Mickey • Minnie • Moana • Russell	• Discovery Island Drummers Flotilla • Viva Gaia Street Band • Winged Encounters—The Kingdom Takes Flight

PANDORA ATTRACTIONS	MEET N' GREETS	ENTERTAINMENT
• Avatar Flight of Passage • Na'vi River Journey		

AFRICA ATTRACTIONS	MEET N' GREETS	ENTERTAINMENT
• Festival of the Lion King • Gorilla Falls Exploration Trail • Kilimanjaro Safaris • Rafiki's Planet Watch —Affection Section —Conservation Station —The Animation Experience		• Harambe Village Acrobats • Harambe Village Street Band—Burudika • Kora Tinga Tinga • Tam Tam Drummers of Harambe

ASIA ATTRACTIONS	MEET N' GREETS	ENTERTAINMENT
• Expedition Everest—Legend of the Forbidden Mountain • Feathered Friends in Flight! • Kali River Rapids • Maharajah Jungle Trek		• Beats and Strings

DINOLAND USA ATTRACTIONS	MEET N' GREETS	ENTERTAINMENT
• DINOSAUR • Finding Nemo: The Big Blue... and Beyond • The Boneyard • TriceraTop Spin	• Chip • Daisy Duck • Dale • Donald Duck • Goofy	

❖ QUICK-SERVICE EATERY

FOOD & DRINKS	SHOPS
• Rainforest Café	• Garden Gate Gifts

FOOD & DRINKS	SHOPS
• Creature Comforts ❖ • Eight Spoon Café ❖ • Flame Tree Barbecue ❖ • Isle of Java ❖ • Nomad Lounge • Pizzafari ❖ • Terra Treats ❖ • The Smiling Crocodile ❖ • Tiffins	• Discovery Trading Company • Island Mercantile

FOOD & DRINKS	SHOPS
• Pongu Pongu ❖ • Satu'li Canteen ❖	• Color of Mo'ara • Windtraders

FOOD & DRINKS	SHOPS
• Dawa Bar ❖ • Harambe Fruit Market ❖ • Harambe Market ❖ • Kusafiri Coffee Shop & Bakery ❖ • Mahindi ❖ • Tamu Tamu Refreshments ❖ • Tusker House	• Africa Hub Cart • Mariya's Souvenirs • Mombasa Marketplace • Ziwani Traders • Zuri's Sweet Shop

FOOD & DRINKS	SHOPS
• Anandapur Ice Cream Truck ❖ • Caravan Road ❖ • Drinkwallah ❖ • Mr. Kamal's ❖ • Royal Anandapur Tea Co. ❖ • Thirsty River Bar & Trek Snacks ❖ • Warung Outpost ❖ • Yak & Yeti Local Food Cafés • Yak & Yeti Quality Beverages ❖ • Yak & Yeti Restaurant	• Mandala Gifts • Serka Zong Bazaar • Yak & Yeti Bhaktapur Market

FOOD & DRINKS	SHOPS
• Dino-Bite Snacks ❖ • Restaurantosaurus ❖ • Trilo-Bites ❖	• Chester & Hester's Dinosaur Treasures • The Dino Institute Shop

Oasis

"Let's not be too hasty."
—ALADDIN

Unlike Walt Disney World's other theme parks, this first land beyond the Main Entrance has few structures and no main walkway. Here you'll find winding paths where you can wander through a tropical garden oasis with rocks, streams, tunnels and waterfalls.

The Oasis Exhibits

Tucked among the lush landscape of the Oasis are the habitats of many animals including birds and fish. Pause along the paths to read the info signs and watch the antics of exotic species like adorable Asian barking deer, Australian wallabies (which look like small kangaroos), African Mozambique tilapia fish, and Coscoroba swans and giant anteaters from South America— who eat up to 30,000 insects a day!

 Disney's Animal Kingdom is a **zoological** theme park. To keep the **residents** safe, balloons, fireworks and plastic straws are **not** allowed. Eateries do have **paper** straws though.

 Meet n' Greets

Blink and you might miss tall, leafy DiVine who blends in with her surroundings perfectly!

Rainforest Café Table Service • Indoor Seating

Just outside the Main Entrance is this restaurant with fish tanks and robotic animals— and an alternate entrance into the park. Options include pasta, seafood, soup and more.

Join the Wilderness Explorers

You can **explore the wilderness** just like **Russell** from the 2009 animated movie **Up**. To take part in this free activity, report to **headquarters** (near the bridge from Oasis to Discovery Island) or any of the park's many **Troop Leader locations** to pick up a **Wilderness Explorer handbook**. The uniformed Troop Leaders will give you a **merit badge** sticker each time you complete one of the **25+ nature-themed challenges!**

Discovery Island

"Sometimes the right path is not the easiest one."
—GRANDMOTHER WILLOW

This land is the hub of the park with its leafy landmark, the Tree of Life, at its center. Here you'll find clusters of metal-roofed buildings decorated with colorful folk art, animal dwellings, and bridges that take you across Discovery River to other lands!

SHOP SPOTLIGHT

There's a bounty of carved beasts, bees, birds and butterflies in **Island Mercantile**.

♫ Entertainment

Marvel at a flock of South American macaws at the Winged Encounters—The Kingdom Takes Flight outdoor bird show. Animal experts will share how smart these colorful parrots are and answer your questions.

Which type of bird is your fave?
_____

☆ ☆ ☆ ☆ ☆

Discovery Island Trails

SO YOU KNOW...
lappet = loose, wrinkly skin hanging down from the chin or neck

The best way to *discover* the wildlife on this *island* is to wander along its many *trails*. The landscape here is filled with exotic plants and flowers, rushing waterfalls and peaceful ponds. Footbridges, cave-like tunnels and snaking pathways lead to observation stations where you can observe critters like frolicking small-clawed *otters*, freewheeling cotton-top tamarin *monkeys* and large **lappet**-faced *vultures* who have a wingspan up to 9 feet wide!

 **SPY** You can get **up-close views** of the incredible **Tree of Life** *(see next page)* from these trails.

OUTDOOR TRAILS — EST. 1998

Tree of Life

From afar this looks like a real **baobab** tree but it was actually made by Imagineers. Standing **14 stories tall,** the branches, roots and trunk are carved with **over 300** members of the animal kingdom. When night falls, colorful lights and projections play across the great tree during **Tree of Life Awakenings.**

HEY KIDS COLOR ME IN!

Flik

MAY BE SCARY

☆ ☆ ☆ ☆ ☆

It's Tough to Be a Bug!

Scuttle *bee-neath* the Tree of Life to enjoy this *3D film* hosted by Flik the ant from the 1998 animated movie *A Bug's Life.* You'll put on a pair of *bug eye* glasses to become an honorary insect and see what their life is like. The show is filled with *surprises* that you'll see—*and feel.* Things get a little hairy when *ornery* Hopper the grasshopper bursts into the theater and tries to *exterminate* the audience but the show ends on an upbeat note with a cheery song about how much *creepy-crawlies* help our planet!

★ INDOOR 3D CARTOON ★ EST. 1998

 FUN FACT — Animal expert **Dr. Jane Goodall** gave advice about this park so a likeness of **David Greybeard**—a **chimp** she studied and befriended—was included on the Tree of Life.

Imagineers at Play

Plans may change!

In **2024** Disney announced that the Opening Day attraction **It's Tough to Be a Bug!** *(see above)* is being replaced by a **new** 3D show inspired by the 2016 animated movie *Zootopia* to be called **Zootopia: Better Zoogether!**

What was at the **Tree of Life Theater** during your visit? _____

🍴 Flame Tree Barbecue
Quick Service • Outdoor Seating

This haven for meat eaters serves barbecued chicken and pork with sides like baked beans, coleslaw and cornbread. The covered dining pavilions have views of Discovery River and decorations that reflect the circle of life. Flame trees have red flowers that make them look like they're on fire when seen from a distance!

PLUS: **Isle of Java** stand with breakfast sandwiches, specialty coffees & sweet treats
The Smiling Crocodile stand with nachos & street tacos
Eight Spoon Café stand with churros, mac n' cheese & pulled pork

🎵 Entertainment

Celebrate the good life with the Viva Gaia Street Band as they dance and play Caribbean music on the outdoor Discovery Island Stage. The Discovery Island Drummers Flotilla musicians can be seen from various lands as they zip across Discovery River on a barge.

📷 Meet n' Greets

Dug the dog and Russell hang out at the rustic Wilderness Explorers Clubhouse and their bird pal Kevin roams the island too. Moana may be outside near a woven reed panel at Character Landing. Inside Adventurers Outpost, Mickey and Minnie take a break from their travels to visit with you!

🍴 Pizzafari Quick Service • Indoor Seating

This color-drenched pizza place has a zoo's worth of animal in the murals and figures on the ceiling beams, chairs and walls. Find a seat in one of the dining rooms to enjoy foods like garlic knot bread rolls, lasagna, meatballs or pizza.

SO YOU KNOW... nomad = wanderer

🍴 Tiffins Table Service • Indoor & Outdoor Seating

When Imagineers were creating Disney's Animal Kingdom they explored the globe snapping pix, taking notes and drawing quick sketches. This research inspired the art and decor of this restaurant and **Nomad Lounge** next door. Both spots have a bread service (a stand with breads and dipping sauces) and small plates. Tiffins also has internationally-inspired main dishes like Szechuan noodles, South African shrimp, and Oaxacan pork. You can see the metal meal tins called tiffins on top of the sign out front.

PLUS: **Creature Comforts** café with pastries, sandwiches, specialty coffee & tea
Terra Treats stand with cookies, pizza slices & specialty drinks

Fabric illustration by www.iStock.com/serazetdinov

Pandora—The World of Avatar

Be transported to the moon that the Na'vi call home in this land of Pandora. Here you'll find the Valley of Mo'ara's floating mountains, dramatic waterfalls, unusual plants that glow in the dark, ex-military structures and native-crafted environments!

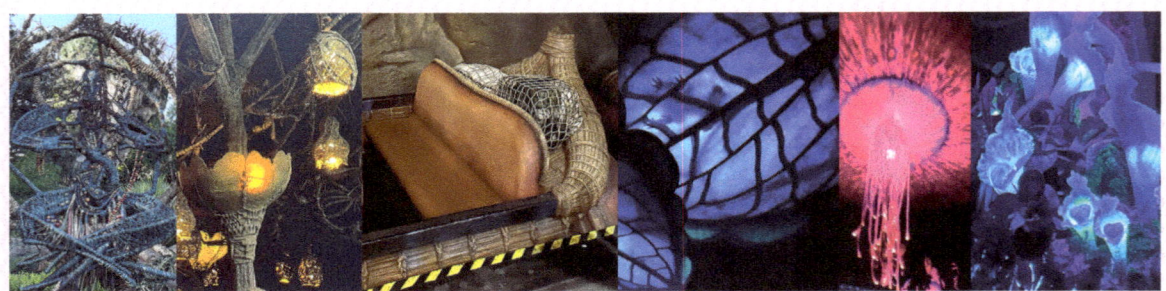

☆ ☆ ☆ ☆ ☆

Na'vi River Journey

INDOOR BOAT RIDE — EST. 2017

The troubles between human miners and the blue-skinned Na'vi are in the past and now eco-tourists like you are **welcome** to visit and enjoy the **beauty** and **culture** of this magnificent moon. The good people at ACE run this expedition where you can take a peaceful cruise on the **Kasvapan River** into a rainforest like no other! You'll board a woven reed boat with the other journeyers and float into darkness past **bioluminescent flora** and unusual **fauna** like direhorses, fan lizards and viperwolves. You'll see the Na'vi moving through the forest to visit their **Shaman of Songs.** This gentle giant sits on the shoreline, singing about her connection to nature and the goddess **Eywa**, and gracefully waving her long arms.

 **HOT TIP**: Explore this land and see if you can discover any interesting **effects**—like what happens when you touch the huge, pod-shaped **Flaska Reclinata** plant along the path from **Africa** to **Pandora.**

SO YOU KNOW… flora = plant life fauna = animal life

TIME MACHINE

1998 — Camp Minnie-Mickey is an Opening Day land where Pandora is now. It closes in 2014.

2009 — "Avatar" hits theaters with sequels "The Way of Water" in 2022 & "Fire & Ash" scheduled for 2025.

2017 — Pandora—The World of Avatar opens with Na'vi River Journey & Avatar Flight of Passage. Sivako!

2024 — Disney announces that an Avatar land will be coming to Disney California Adventure in Anaheim.

Which outer space movie series do you like best?
- ☐ Avatar
- ☐ Guardians of the Galaxy
- ☐ Star Wars

HEY KIDS COLOR ME IN!

Species Traits!

Fill in the **missing words** (blue, four, nose, tail, ten or toes) to describe how the **Na'vi** differ from **humans**. One has been done for you.
Answers on page 203.

Na'vi are about _____ feet tall with ___blue___ skin & a flat, cat-like _____. They have _____ digits per hand, opposable _____ & a _____ with a tuft at the end!

Pandora Basics

Not from around here? **No worries!** Here's what you need to know to feel right at home!

HUMAN WORDS & PHRASES:
ACE = Alpha Centauri Expeditions
AMP = Amplified Mobility Platform, an exoskeleton combat suit for soldiers

Avatar = A body that looks similar to a Na'vi but is controlled by a human mind
PCI = Pandora Conservation Initiative, a program that restores and protects nature on Pandora
RDA = Resources Development Administration, a group that ran mining on Pandora

NA'VI WORDS & PHRASES:
Ikran = What the Na'vi call the mountain banshee creature they ride to hunt or travel
Iknimaya = The rite of passage when young Na'vi first bond with their ikran
Omatikaya = The clan of Na'vi who were first to settle in the Valley of Mo'ara
Pongu = Party
Satu'li = Heritage
Sivako = Rise to the challenge

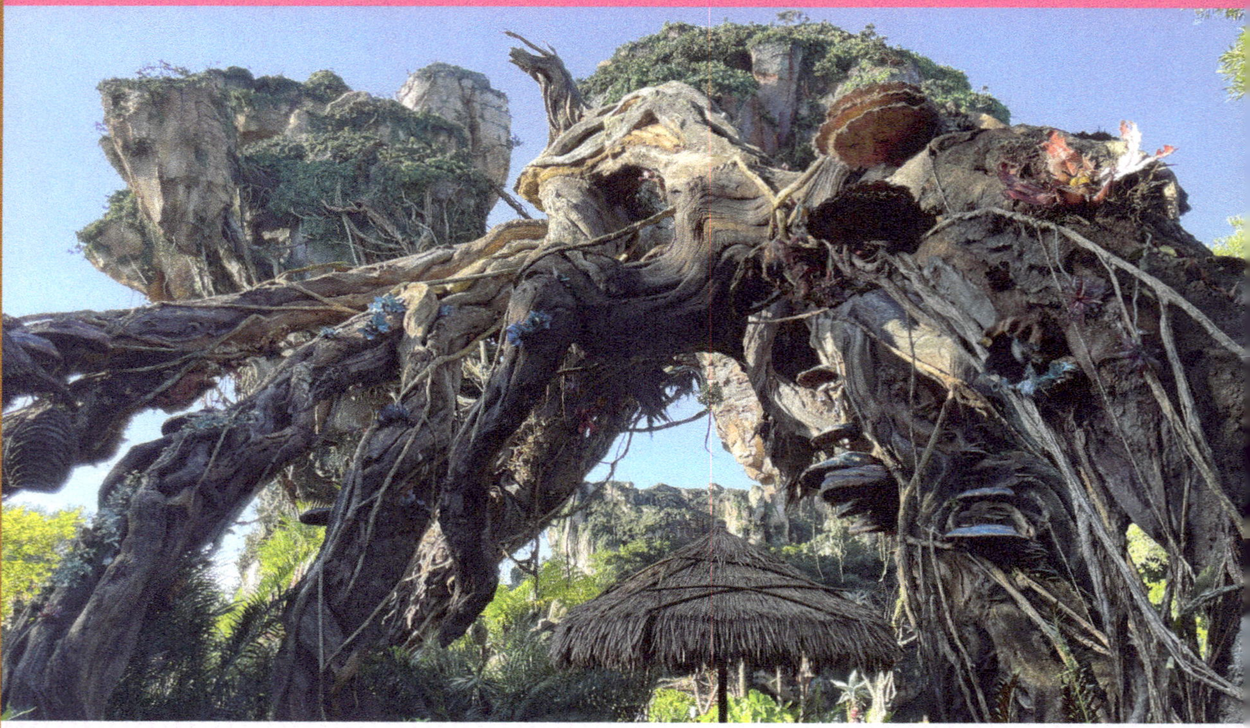

☆ ☆ ☆ ☆ ☆

Avatar Flight of Passage

Within Pandora's breathtaking mountains are the remains of the RDA's **mining operations.** Now doctors and scientists from ACE have turned the facility into a lab where they work with the Na'vi to **conserve** and **restore** the banshee population. Inside their lab, Doctor Stevens and later Doctor Ogden will appear on screens to explain how you'll be **linked** with an avatar to experience a simulated flight on the back of your own personal banshee! Once you're in the **Link Chamber,** you'll climb onto one of the motorbike-style seats and put on 3D goggles. You can see what your creature looks like on a small monitor in front of you and then your eye-popping flight begins via a screen that covers an **entire** wall. During this **rite of passage,** you'll dive and swoop through forest, mountain and ocean environments as gentle **winds** and light **mists** make you feel as if you're really there!

Your exit path **may** take you past a wall with the **handprints** of **James Cameron** (the director of *Avatar*), **Jon Landau** (the producer of *Avatar*) and Disney Legend **Joe Rohde** *(see opposite page)*.

This ride **simulates** the movements of a mountain banshee and it will **rock, sway** and **tilt** during the flight. When your animal takes a rest, you'll even feel it **breathe** beneath you!

🍴 Satu'li Canteen Quick Service • Indoor & Outdoor Seating

You'll find native crafts decorating this metal military Quonset hut, along with displays of Omatikaya heritage items. This former RDA mess hall serves Bao buns, bowls with noodles or slaw topped with chicken, shrimp or tofu, and a fruity drink called Pandoran sunrise.

PLUS: **Pongu Pongu** hut with a few snack options & specialty drinks

Shop Spotlight

Twisting carvings, painted patterns and crafty weavings fill **Windtraders**.

🎀 Mini Quiz!

Can you guess where mountain banshees live? *Answer on page 203.*
☐ Burrow ☐ Drey ☐ Hive ☐ Rookery

Legend Close-Up: Joe Rohde

Joe Rohde was born in Sacramento in **1955** and was mostly raised in Hawaii. Back in California, he graduated from high school and then earned an **art degree** from Occidental College. While teaching **theater** at his former high school, Joe was **recruited** by a Disney executive who saw the stage sets he'd designed. In **1980** Joe started in the Imagineering Department as a **model designer** and then **scenic painter** for EPCOT's **Mexico Pavilion** and later led the research team for the **Norway Pavilion**. Though he's done work for the Disney resorts in **California, Tokyo** and **Paris**, and Disney's **Aulani** hotel in **Hawaii,** his biggest project was **Disney's Animal Kingdom** where he was the **lead designer.** An avid world traveler, Joe led his team in explorations around the globe for inspiration—collecting **earrings** to hang from one ear during his journeys! He also oversaw the additions of **Expedition Everest** and **Pandora.** In 2020 a limited-edition **mouse ear hat** was created in Joe's honor that had the **opening dates** of Disney's Animal Kingdom (Earth Day in 1998) and Expedition Everest (April 7, 2006) printed on each ear. Joe was named a Disney Legend in **2024.**

Africa

"Remember who you are."
—MUFASA

The rustic East African portside village of Harambe is the setting of this land. Here you'll find massive carved wooden gates, rough stucco walls, woven grass roofs, a water tower and handpainted patterns, murals and signs in the African language of Swahili!

⭐⭐⭐⭐⭐

Festival of the Lion King

INDOOR LIVE SHOW · EST. 1998

This joyous *celebration* of the 1994 animated movie *The Lion King* is an Opening Day attraction that now takes place in a *theater in the round* called the Harambe Theatre. Singers dressed in African attire will start the show which features *splendidly* costumed acrobats, dancers, stiltwalkers and even a fire juggler. Also joining in the party are Puumba, Timon and King Simba on parade-style floats. This *musical revue* includes unique versions of beloved songs like "Circle of Life" and "Hakuna Matata"—what a *wonderful* phrase!

HOT TIP: A **face painting** stand by **Mombasa Marketplace** specializes in **animal** designs. These stands are all over WDW and the **cost** depends on the **style** you choose.

 The Story of... The Lion King

The Pride Lands of Africa are ruled over by the good King Mufasa the lion, whose advisor is a mandrill monkey named Rafiki. The king and queen have a son named Simba who loves to explore with a lioness called Nala—while a hornbill bird called Zazu tries to keep tabs on them. Mufasa's younger brother Scar is jealous and plots to overthrow the king with the help of some rowdy hyenas. When Mufasa is trampled in a stampede of wildebeests, Scar tricks Simba into thinking it was his fault and tells him to run away from home. In the desert Simba makes friends with meerkat Timon and warthog Pumbaa who teach him to embrace their "no worries" lifestyle. Nala finds Simba and convinces him to return home—which is in shambles under Scar's reign. After courageous Simba overthrows his uncle, he and Nala become king and queen, and have a cub of their own!

🍴 Tusker House Buffet • Indoor Seating

Donald is your host at this Character Meal. You'll find the dashing duck and pals like Daisy, Goofy and Mickey dressed in adventurous outfits here. The bountiful buffet has eggs, pastries and waffles for breakfast, and foods like Tandoori chicken with cauliflower curry for lunch and dinner. The buffet area here looks like an outdoor open-air market!

🍴 Tamu Tamu Refreshments

Quick Service • Outdoor Seating

This weathered, half-built corner building has sweet treats like croissants, muffins or the Simba sunset—a mix of pineapple, watermelon and strawberry soft-serve with coconut syrup.

PLUS: **Dawa Bar** patio with grown-up drinks
Mahindi stand with cinnamon-glazed nuts & popcorn
Kusafiri Coffee Shop & Bakery with breakfast items, coffee & hot cocoa
Harambe Fruit Market stalls with fresh fruit, spicy corn on the cob & pretzels

Illustration by Lindsay Gibson • www.emandsprout.com

SWAHILI MINI DICTIONARY
Dawa = Medicine
Fichwa = Hidden
Jambo = Hello
Kilimanjaro = Mountain of greatness
Kusafiri = To journey
Mahindi = Corn
Tamu = Delicious

Have you ever been to the continent of Africa?
☐ Yes! ☐ Not yet...

🎵 Entertainment

Africa has three dynamic acts: Harambe Village Acrobats who form human pyramids and tumbling towers; Harambe Village Street Band—Burudika who play lively Afro-pop; and Tam Tam Drummers of Harambe who dance and play conga drums, shekeres and other African instruments. You can also find the strolling musician Kora Tinga Tinga who strums peaceful melodies on a kora harp.

⭐⭐⭐⭐⭐

Kilimanjaro Safaris

SO YOU KNOW... **safaris** = journeys to view animals in the wild

You'll board a rough n' ready truck with your fellow explorers to travel through the **Harambe Wildlife Reserve** which over 30 species native to Africa call home. The driver of your vehicle is an **expert guide** who will slow down or stop as needed to give the animals the right of way. Along the way, your guide will point out **what** and **who** you're seeing and **why** they act the way they do. The landscapes here recreate the grassy savannas, muddy pools, rocky wetlands and shady forests that each creature prefers. During your jaunt over bumpy roads and bridges, you may see a **cackle** of hyenas, a **dazzle** of zebras, a **herd** of elephants or a **pride** of lions—among others. These are real, live animals and you never know what they may do, so no two safaris are **ever** the same!

FIELD NOTES
Sketch or write here about what you observed in the Reserve:

HOT TIP: A stand near the entrance to the safari has info on **behind-the-scenes tours** *(cost extra)* that offer a closer look at the animals in this park **or at** the nearby **Animal Kingdom Lodge** hotel. You can ask about **same-day** tours but it's best to reserve a spot in **advance**.

FUN FACT: All of **Magic Kingdom** could fit inside the land used for **Kilimanjaro Safaris** and, in fact, Disney's Animal Kingdom is the **world's largest** theme park!

TIME MACHINE

1954 — Walt wants to use live animals on the original Jungle Cruise but it's not practical at the time. Drat!

1973 — Tanzania's Kilimanjaro National Park is created to protect Africa's highest peak & its forests.

1998 — Kilimanjaro Safaris is an Opening Day attraction & is one of the longest ride experiences in WDW.

2020 — A warden's home is added to the scenery & Nigerian dwarf goats can be seen by it today.

☆ ☆ ☆ ☆ ☆

Gorilla Falls Exploration Trail

This walking trail through *Pangani Forest* leads to observation stations dotted here and there along a meandering pathway. You'll see striped *okapis*, curious *meerkats* and burrowing *naked mole-rats*, to name just a few. The enclosures recreate each animal's natural habitat and have displays and signs with *trivia* and *info* about some of the challenges they face in the wild. Inside the *Bird Forest* area, you can borrow a printed *guide* to identify which types you see. This Opening Day attraction gets its name from a troop of western lowland *gorillas* who live on a hillside near the trail's waterfall.

HOT TIP: Some animals can be hard to spot when they're **sleeping**. Many have more **pep** in their **step** in the **morning**—so that's a good time to visit!

🍴 Harambe Market   Quick Service • Outdoor Seating

This open-air watering hole has taken over an old train depot to serve hot foods and cool drinks. You'll find Chef Mwanga's rice bowls, pita sandwiches, salads and specialty drinks. If you choose a table near the water tower in the back part of the market, you may catch sight of the Wildlife Express Train *(see page 180)* clattering past.

An Easy Way To Help Animals

You may notice **signs** for the **Disney Conservation Fund**. Part of the price of some food, drinks and souvenirs goes to this cause. The money from these **special purchases** is matched **100%** by Disney and given to **non-profit organizations** who are working to protect and save **endangered species** and their **environments** around the globe. If you'd rather, you can also make a **donation** without buying anything at some eateries and shops in the park.

⭐⭐⭐⭐⭐
Rafiki's Planet Watch

WALK-THROUGH EST. 1998

Open your eyes to the world around you! Since Opening Day, Guests have reached this area by taking the *Wildlife Express Train* from Harambe Railway Station. During the 1.2-mile journey, you'll get a glimpse at the *housing* where the elephants and rhinos *snooze* at night. Once you arrive, you'll take a *nature trail* past Habitat Habit exhibits to reach Affection Section and Conservation Station.

Affection Section

In this outdoor petting zoo you can visit with cute critters like cows, donkeys, goats, pigs and sheep. If you have questions about any of your new four-legged friends, you can ask any of the animal experts standing by. They sometimes take the animals to a small stage nearby to share their Care Story.

HOT TIP: To keep the **wild birds** and other animals all over the resort **healthy**, you must **never** share your human food with them!

If you took a drawing class, who did you draw?
_____

Conservation Station

This building has giant animal murals inside and out. Within its walls you may see nutritionists making meals in the Nutrition Center or scientists experimenting in the Science Center. You might even catch veterinary doctors treating one of their feathered, fluffy, furry, horned, scaly, sharp-clawed, slimy, spiky, spotty or stripy patients in the Veterinary Treatment Room. There's also a drawing class called The Animation Experience where a talented artist will lead you through easy, step-by-step instructions to teach you how to draw a Disney animal character using a pencil, paper and drawing board. Which character you learn to draw changes for each session—and you get to keep your masterpiece!

FUN FACT: Many creatures **just visit** Conservation Station for healthcare but others (like **millipedes, scorpions, snakes** and **tarantulas**) live there full time.

Asia

"I am here with the bird and I will bring it back and then you will like me."
—DUG

The Asian-style Kingdom of Anandapur and the Serka Zong village are in this land. Here you'll find plantlife creeping over aging stone structures, intricately carved wood, pointed arches, skinny boats along the water's edge and signs in the Sanskrit language!

☆☆☆☆☆
Feathered Friends in Flight!

OUTDOOR LIVE SHOW • EST. 2022

In this bird show at the Anandapur Theater, a Cast Member duo demonstrate what makes our *feathered friends* so special. The *lineup* may change but you might see an Amazon parrot, a bald eagle, a crowned crane, a great horned owl, a long-beaked toucan or a marabou stork strutting their stuff. These free-flying stars will even *swoosh* right over the heads of the audience! You'll discover *amazing facts* about the fascinating—and sometimes funny—birds and learn how people like you can help to make a difference in their lives. Be ready to *volunteer* if you want to try and lend a hand with the show.

 **SPY** See if you can find **stone statues** of **Russell** and **Dug** near the Anandapur Theater. Since Opening Day in **1998** there has been a **bird show** here and one of them was *Up* themed.

♫ **Entertainment**
Beats and Strings beat tabla drums and pluck a long-necked sitar to play Hindustani raga music on the outdoor stage near the Anandapur Theater.

Mandala illustration from www.all-free-download.com

～ Birds of a Feather!

Number each **bird character** 1 through 6 based on the **year** they made their **first** appearance, starting with **1** for the **oldest** movie and ending with **6** for the **newest**. **One** has been done for you. *Answers on page 203.*

- ③ Flit in *Pocahontas*
- ○ Iago in *Aladdin*
- ○ Pico in *Encanto*
- ○ Heihei in *Moana*
- ○ Kevin in *Up*
- ○ Zazu in *The Lion King*

🍴 Yak & Yeti Table Service • Indoor Seating

Beautiful artifacts, beaded crystal chandeliers and golden statues fill this lavish restaurant. This luxurious pitstop for travelers visiting the nearby mountains serves pot stickers, lettuce cups, soups and salads, noodle bowls, grilled meats and more. There are also two quick-service spots next door with outdoor seating called **Yak & Yeti Local Food Cafés** with breakfast bowls and English muffins and **Yak & Yeti Quality Beverages** with egg rolls, fried rice, desserts like mango pie, and specialty drinks.

PLUS: **Caravan Road** stand with shaved ice & grown-up drinks
Mr. Kamal's stand with seasoned french fries
Warung Outpost shack with a few snacks & specialty drinks
Drinkwallah roadside stand with ice cream, nuts & specialty drinks
Royal Anandapur Tea Company hut with iced & hot tea & coffee

SO YOU KNOW... yak = longhaired Himalayan cattle

☆☆☆☆☆ Maharajah Jungle Trek

OUTDOOR TRAIL — EST. 1999

Within this walking trail, animals native to **Asia** live among the romantic **ruins** of crumbling palaces and temples, overgrown with plants creeping in from the surrounding **Anandapur Royal Forest**. During your **trek** you'll see animals like prowling Bengal tigers, lounging Komodo dragon lizards and grazing water buffalo. There's an **aviary** with printed guides you can borrow and signs that tell you the **breeds** of the birds flying all around you. When you enter the Malayan flying fox building, you can go left to see those **fruit bats** or keep going straight to bypass them!

FUN FACT The story goes that Indian **Maharajahs** once hunted game here but after one of these princes died, they decided to live in **harmony** with the animals.

> The rafts have fun names like Java Jumper. Did you notice the name on the side of the first raft you rode on? If so, what was it?
>
> _____

☆ ☆ ☆ ☆ ☆

Kali River Rapids

OUTDOOR BOAT RIDE — EST. 1999

MAY BE SCARY

HEIGHT: 38"+

Kali Rapids Expeditions welcomes tourists like you to enjoy a *white water adventure!* The standby line goes through open-air rooms like an ancient temple filled with exotic *bric-a-brac* and the rafting company's offices. An ornate *pagoda* graces the center of the loading platform where you'll strap into a 12-passenger round raft. After you travel uphill on a moving conveyer belt, it's all *downhill* from there! As your raft *bobs* and *bounces* along, spinning freely with the water currents through a forest, you'll pass geysers, a waterfall, rocky caves and damage caused by loggers. During your jaunt, the mellow waves turn into fast-moving *rapids* and you'll either get lightly *spritzed* or totally *soaked* by the drips, sprays and splashes!

HOT TIP — Worried about your stuff getting **wet?** Many of the park's shops sell **plastic ponchos** and this ride has **lockers** nearby that are **free** for up to two hours. There are water play **fountains** near the lockers!

SPY — Between **Kali River Rapids** and **Maharajah Jungle Trek,** you'll see an island where two types of **gibbon** apes live. They are fun to watch—and **listen** to— because they really know how to **whoop** it up!

Raft illustration by Chris Buchholz • www.etsy.com/shop/buchworks

🍴 Thirsty River Bar & Trek Snacks
Quick Service • Outdoor Seating

This roughly textured tan building has metal awnings over the ordering counters of these two grab n' go spots. Thirsty trekkers will find a specialty drink called the pink lotus, and snacks like frozen lemonade, ice cream, popcorn and pretzels.

PLUS: **Anandapur Ice Cream Truck** food truck with frozen treats

☆☆☆☆☆

Expedition Everest

ROLLER COASTER ★ EST. 2006 ★

MAY BE SCARY ⚠

HEIGHT: 44"+

The *Legend of the Forbidden Mountain* is that a huge, hairy *Yeti* is living there—and he doesn't like company! The Royal Anandapur Tea Company used to ship their wares from *Serka Zong* through the mountain pass by railroad but the Yeti put a stop to that. If you dare to risk coming face-to-face with this abominable snowman, you'll board an *Anandapur Rail Services* train car. First you'll coast through the trees at the base of the mountain range and then begin the *ascent* towards its *icy, snow-covered* peaks. After you go through a short tunnel strung with tattered prayer flags, something seems amiss—and is that *growling* you hear? Hold on tight because what comes next is a high-speed journey in and out of dark **chasms** with *you-know-who* hot on your heels!

FUN FACT: When your train car first sets off on its *expedition*, listen for the cry of a *peacock*. These *birds* are often found in *Nepal* and *Tibet* where the real Mount Everest is—in the *Himalayan mountains*. That peak is considered the highest point on *Earth!*

SO YOU KNOW... **chasms** = narrow openings in rock

Illustration by Eva Sowinski • www.critterosityshop.com

TIME MACHINE

1953 — Nepalese-Indian sherpa Tenzing Norgay & New Zealand explorer Edmund Hillary summit Everest first.

1998 — When the park opens, the bird show where Feathered Friends is now is Asia's only attraction.

1999 — Maharajah Jungle Trek debuts, followed soon after by Kali River Rapids. A roaring good time!

2006 — WDW gets its highest point (199.5 feet) when Expedition Everest—Legend of the Forbidden Mountain debuts.

SANSKRIT MINI DICTIONARY
Anandapur = City of happiness
Himalayas = Abode of snow
Kali = The Goddess of time
Maharajah = Indian prince
Serka Zong = Fortress of the chasm
Wallah = A worker or someone in charge
Warung = A small shop or café

Have you ever been to the continent of Asia?
☐ Yes!
☐ Not yet...

Shop Spotlight

Asian artifacts and tributes to the Yeti abound inside **Serka Zong Bazaar**.

Not the same Yeti that's in Expedition Everest!

Mythical Quest!

Draw a line connecting the type of **being** to the **movie** they were in. *Answers on page 203.*

Alebrije   *Aladdin*
Dragon   *Coco*
Fairy   *Hercules*
Genie   *Monsters, Inc.*
Satyr   *Mulan*
Yeti   *Peter Pan*

DinoLand USA

> "Today's the day!"
> —PEACH

This land is a must for dinosaur fans. Here you'll find a large building with statues out front called The Dino Institute and a kitschy amusement park area dubbed Chester & Hester's Dino-Rama that's full of carnival-style fun!

☆☆☆☆☆ Finding Nemo: The Big Blue...and Beyond

INDOOR LIVE SHOW — EST. 2022

When Nemo was caught by the dentist in *Finding Nemo* he ended up in an *aquarium* in a dental office with the *Tank Gang*. This colorful crew—including Bloat the blowfish, Deb the blue damselfish, Gill the moorish idol fish and Peach the starfish—are now living at the *Marine Life Institute*. Inside the *Theater in the Wild* (which has offered live entertainment since Opening Day), you'll see the Tank Gang tell the tale of their little lost clownfish buddy with the help of Bruce, Crush, Dory and Marlin. This *live stage show* has beautiful bubbly sets, dancers, puppets and singers. One of the songs you'll hear called "In the Big Blue World" was written for an earlier version of this show—and that *catchy tune* also plays over in EPCOT's Nemo ride!

HOT TIP: Between **Asia** and **DinoLand USA** is the outdoor waterfront **Discovery River Theater** which has hosted shows like **KiteTails, Rivers of Light** and **The Jungle Book: Alive with Magic.** It's a great spot to **take a break** and enjoy the view!

Bloat • Deb • Gill • Peach

☆ ☆ ☆ ☆ ☆

TriceraTop Spin

*OUTDOOR SPINNER * EST 2001 *

Bright colors and rows of lights decorate this attraction which looks like a giant spinning *top* toy. To take a *spin*, you'll sit in one of two rows on a **Triceratops**, each with different controls. If you're up front, you can move a *joystick* to tilt forward or backward. If you're in back, you can move a *lever* to go up and down. *Bop* along to *pop music* as you ride!

FUN FACT The story goes that locals **Chester** and **Hester** created an **amusement park** with this ride and the **Fossil Fun Games** pay-to-play area after **T-Rex bones** were discovered nearby.

SO YOU KNOW... **Triceratops** = dinosaur with 3 horns & neck frill

 ## Meet n' Greets

You might catch Donald or Goofy hanging around outside the Welcome Center, Daisy hatching ideas at her outdoor Design Studio or Chip 'n Dale chilling by the plants and trees of the Cretaceous Trail.

SHOP SPOTLIGHT

A small train runs around the celing of **Chester & Hester's Dinosaur Treasures.**

Imagineers at Play. *Plans may change!*

In **2022** Disney shared that they were thinking about replacing **DinoLand USA.** Then in **2024** they revealed plans to turn it into a new land with a **Tropical Americas** theme and attractions related to *Encanto* and *Indiana Jones,* as well as a carousel with Disney animals. Different sections of the land are closing in **phases** and the **new version** is due to open in the next few years.

What are **your thoughts** on DinoLand's **extinction?**
☐ Literally can't wait!   ☐ Sounds cool but I can wait...   ☐ I'll miss DinoLand!

Cretaceous Trail

A curving pathway goes between the World's Largest Pin Truck exhibit outside of Chester & Hester's Dinosaur Treasures and the gateway to The Dino Institute. This trail has one of the largest collections of plants that have been on Earth ever since the final days of the dinosaur.

DINOSAUR

★ ★ ★ ★ ★

MAY BE SCARY

HEIGHT: 40"+

We may never know why dinosaurs went *extinct*, but one theory is that they died when the Earth was struck by a *meteor*. Inside The Dino Institute research facility, director Dr. Helen Marsh appears on screen to welcome you to a peaceful sightseeing trip back to the *Cretaceous* time period. But a self-serving doctor named Grant Seeker plots to sends you to a more recent *time coordinate* so you can bring him back an *Iguanadon* dinosaur! You and the other daring souls will board a *Time Rover* vehicle to set off on your thrilling adventure through a dark, *primeval* forest. The bad news is, you'll arrive just as the meteor is about to hit! As you bump and bounce over the *choppy* terrain, the onboard computer identifies each ferocious beast you cross paths with. Will you make it back to the present day *unscathed?* Only time will tell!

INDOOR DARK RIDE ★ EST. 1998 ★

 **SPY** — A replica called **Dino-Sue** near The Dino Institute was based on an actual **Tyrannosaurus skeleton** found by fossil collector **Sue Hendrickson**.

Illustration by Chris Buchholz • www.etsy.com/shop/buchworks

TIME MACHINE

1998
Countdown to Extinction & The Boneyard attractions debut on Opening Day.

2000
The movie "Dinosaur" hits theaters & Countdown to Extinction is rethemed & renamed DINOSAUR.

2001
TriceraTop Spin debuts as part of Chester & Hester's Dino-Rama. Whee-eee!

2024
Disney announces that DINOSAUR will be replaced by an Indiana Jones-themed ride.

Archival Quality

What happens to all the **STUFF** when a whole land changes themes? Some items are **reused** in other parts of the resort. Others are stored at the **Walt Disney Archives** in Burbank where artifacts from **film, theme parks** and other projects are preserved. Though the warehouses aren't usually open to the general public, select pieces are showcased in **traveling exhibitions!**

Restaurantosaurus
DAK-2024

Restaurantosaurus Quick Service • Indoor & Outdoor Seating

Rooms used by the paleontology students who study dinosaurs and fossils at The Dino Institute can be found at this large, lively restaurant. The former dorm, camping hut, greasy garage and 1950s-style rec room are now dining rooms where you can dig in to your feast. There's also an outdoor **Pterodactyl** Pterrace with umbrella tables. Stop that growling in your tummy with classics like burgers (meat or plant-based), fried chicken sandwiches, hot dogs and milkshakes.

PLUS: **Dino-Bite Snacks** stand with ice cream, cookies & pretzels
Trilo-Bites shack with chips, churros & soft-serve ice cream

> SO YOU KNOW...
> **Pterodactyl** = flying prehistoric reptile with a beak and teeth

☆☆☆☆☆

The Boneyard

OUTDOOR PLAY AREA • EST. 1998

This open-air fossil-filled play area is designed for kids ages 10 and under. There are mysterious caves to explore, twisty slides to zip down and bridges to hightail it across—including one that goes through the legs of a dinosaur skeleton! Junior paleontologists will have a blast discovering and uncovering T-Rex and Triceratops bones in the sand.

 **HOT TIP:** The Boneyard has a **shaded seating area** with fans where people who aren't playing can hang out.

Sample Souvenirs

"You must choose your own ikran and he must choose you."
—NEYTIRI

Your Own Banshee

Pandora's Windtraders shop has lots of unique souvenirs—like Na'vi ear headbands and tails, real venus flytrap plants, wings that glow in the dark, and even a custom Avatar—but, for those dreaming of adopting a banshee, there are two options. The larger style is a shoulder puppet with a controller that you use to move it and make sounds. The smaller one (which comes in an egg) is made to strap onto your wrist. It will move and make noises if it senses other banshees nearby or when you pet it or give it a treat. You may find banshees for sale in other stores like Island Mercantile in Discovery Island.

Hand-beaded Adornments

A stand outside of Africa's Mombasa Marketplace has handcrafted bracelets, earrings and necklaces. Each piece takes hours to make and you can often see an artisan here crafting these one-of-a-kind treasures.

Cool Carvings

Next to Africa's bead stand is a woodcarving stand with figurines, masks, statues and walking sticks. You can watch as the carvers create some of these souvenirs. The Outpost in EPCOT has a spot like this too.

Personalized Chopsticks

Wooden chopsticks with names already carved on them are sold at Bhaktapur Market in Asia. If you don't find any with your name, look through the other styles that say things like "best friend" or "princess" and you might see a set you like. You'll also find chopsticks in EPCOT's Japan Pavilion (at Mitsukoshi Department Store) and the China Pavilion (at House of Good Fortune).

Animal Roll Call!

Using a **light color** like yellow, highlight the **types** of **animal** you spotted in Disney's Animal Kingdom! Write in any **others** you saw in the box below.

ANTEATER • BAT • CHEETAH • ELEPHANT • GIRAFFE
GORILLA • HIPPO • LEMUR • LION • MEERKAT • OTTER
PORCUPINE • RHINO • TIGER • WILDEBEEST • ZEBRA

This Land is That Land!

Draw a line connecting the number of the photo on the **left** to the letter of the photo on the **right** that was taken in the **same land** in Disney's Animal Kingdom. *Answers on page 203.*

 1

 A

 2

 B

 3

 C

 4

 D

This wall near Africa's Harambe Market has a unique "hidden" Mickey photo spot.

MY TRIP JOURNAL—ABOUT MY VISIT

What was your **favorite** part of your visit? ....

....

....

Was it **crowded** overall? ☐ Yes ☐ Kinda ☐ No

Rank the theme parks from 1 to 4 in the **order** you like them:

◯ Magic Kingdom
◯ EPCOT
◯ Disney's Hollywood Studios
◯ Disney's Animal Kingdom

Why did you pick the park you did as your number one favorite?

....

....

....

Which of these other **places** in Walt Disney World did you visit?

☐ Blizzard Beach water park
☐ Typhoon Lagoon water park
☐ ESPN Wide World of Sports Complex
☐ Golf courses
☐ Disney Springs
☐ Disney's BoardWalk

Did you visit any **hotels?** If so, which ones?

....

....

MY TRIP JOURNAL–ABOUT MY VISIT

What were the **best** rides of all? ....
....
....

Did you see any **characters?** If so, which ones?
....
....

Did you see any **entertainment?** If so, what did you see?
....
....

What were the most **delicious** things you ate or drank?
....
....

Did you get any **souvenirs?** If so, what?
....
....

Was there **anything** you wanted to do but couldn't? Why?
....
....

Are you hoping to go **back** to Walt Disney World soon? ☐ Yes ☐ Maybe ☐ Nah

MY TRIP JOURNAL—MEMORIES

It's **time** to write down **stories** from your trip. What awesome, exciting, interesting, funny or **special things** happened during your visit? Did anything **not-so-great** happen? Reflect on your **memories** below!

....
....
....
....
....
....
....
....
....
....

MY TRIP JOURNAL—MEMORIES

....
....
....
....
....
....
....
....
....
....
....
....

Draw a **picture** of one of your **memories** from Walt Disney World:

MY TRIP JOURNAL—SCRAPBOOK

Fill these pages with **souvenirs** from your visit to Walt Disney World like a coaster, receipt, sticker or the **autograph** of someone special you meet!

MY TRIP JOURNAL–SCRAPBOOK

Pop Quiz!

Now that you've read this guide, you can put your knowledge to the test! Put a ✓ in the bubble next to the correct answers below. If you're **not sure** of an answer, you can **look back** through the book. **Still** stumped? *Answers on page 203.*

1. Something in WDW that dates back to 1971 is:
- ○ Blizzard Beach
- ○ The Electrical Water Pageant

2. Getting to a theme park before it opens is called:
- ○ Gate Crashing
- ○ Rope Drop

3. Magic Kingdom's singing barbershop quartet is called:
- ○ The Dapper Dans
- ○ Harmony

4. The Country Bear who performs on a swing is named:
- ○ Big Al
- ○ Teddi Barra

5. The statue of Walt Disney in EPCOT is called:
- ○ Walt the Dreamer
- ○ Partners

6. The bamboo tubes in the Japan Pavilion garden are called:
- ○ Shiki-Sai
- ○ Shishi-odoshi

7. A bird's name in Mickey & Minnie's Runaway Railway is:
- ○ Chuuby
- ○ Orange Bird

8. The robot at Ronto Roasters in Disney's Hollywood Studios is named:
- ○ 8D-J8
- ○ DJ Rex

9. The Disney Legend who mostly grew up in Hawaii was:
- ○ Joe Ranft
- ○ Joe Rohde

10. The theater in Disney's Animal Kingdom with a bird show is called:
- ○ Anandapur
- ○ Serka Zong

Game Answers

PAGE 19—Mini Quiz "When You Wish Upon a Star"

PAGE 21—A Home Away from Home
Top row: 18 = Riviera; 14 = Polynesian Village; 20 = Wilderness Lodge
Bottom row: 7 = BoardWalk Inn; 12 = Grand Floridian; 16 = Port Orleans—French Quarter

PAGE 23—Guess the Goner Mr. Toad's Wild Ride

PAGE 29—Park Bag Match-Up
(1) Moana from *Moana* (2) Russell from *Up*
(3) Flynn Rider from *Tangled* (4) Belle from *Beauty and the Beast*

PAGE 31—Say What: Attraction Edition
Festival of the Lion King = "Something tells me this ain't the floor show."; Gran Fiesta Tour = "Excuse me, we are looking for a duck."; Mission: SPACE = "I know you're probably feeling a little nervous right now."; Pirates of the Caribbean = "Don't tell him, Carlos! Don't be chicken!"; Spaceship Earth = "Here, in this hostile world, is where our story begins."; The Twilight Zone Tower of Terror = "That door's opening once again and, this time, it's opening for you."; Toy Story Mania! = "Ready, aim, break those plates!"

PAGE 42—Name That Locomotive LILLY BELLE; ROGER E. BROGGIE; ROY O. DISNEY; WALTER E. DISNEY

PAGE 45—Mini Quiz Fantasy in the Sky

PAGE 49—Who Plays What (1) Drum (2) Guitar (3) Steel drums (4) Flute Extra credit: Trumpet

PAGE 63—Titles of Nobility
(1) Evil Queen (2) Prince Naveen (3) King Triton (4) Princess Aurora (5) King Louie (6) Prince Charming (7) Princess Rapunzel (8) Prince John (9) Queen Atta (10) Queen Elinor

PAGE 67—Talk Like an Astronaut Gravity Bar; Oxygen Dome; Rocket Ready

PAGE 70—Antiquated Lingo
(1) Cans or jars (2) Water (3) Clumsy (4) Dance (5) Lower back (6) Recreation (7) 3D

PAGE 72—Mini Quiz Cyclops

PAGE 73—Say What: Laughs Edition
Buzz Lightyear = "My eyeballs could have been sucked from their sockets!"; Cruella de Vil = "I worship furs!"; Gramma Tala = "Whatever just happened…blame it on the pig."; Hades = "Wow, is my hair out?"; Kronk = "The poison. The poison for Kuzco. The poison chosen especially to kill Kuzco. Kuzco's poison. That poison?"; Lilo = "I'm sorry I bit you. And pulled your hair. And punched you in the face."; Olaf = "I don't have a skull. Or bones."; Sulley = "I don't believe I ordered a wake-up call, Mikey."; Timon = "Not in front of the kids!"

PAGE 81—Mini Quiz Iago and Zazu

PAGE 86—Melody Time
(1) TRUE (2) TRUE (3) FALSE—Casey played baseball (4) TRUE (5) FALSE—Pecos Bill's favorite gal was named Slue-Foot Sue and his horse was called Widowmaker
(6) FALSE—It was about Ichabod Crane, not Obadiah

PAGE 91—Coin a Phrase
BONANZA; FORTY NINER; GOLD FEVER; GOLD NUGGET; HIT PAY DIRT; MOTHER LODE; PANNED OUT; PETERED OUT; PROSPECTOR; SHENANIGANS; UNION SUIT

PAGE 93—This Land is That Land
Pix 1 and B were taken in Frontierland; Pix 2 and D were taken in Fantasyland;
Pix 3 and A were taken in Adventureland; Pix 4 and C were taken in Tomorrowland

I shall elucidate.

PAGE 101—Color Connections (1) Red (2) Pink (3) Green (4) Yellow (5) Blue (6) Orange
PAGE 103—Mini Quiz French bread
PAGE 115—Mini Quiz Mock Turtle
PAGE 123—Place Settings (1) Canada (2) France (3) America (4) Italy (5) Mexico
PAGE 131—This Land is That Land
Pix 1 and A were taken in World Discovery; Pix 2 and C were taken in World Nature; Pix 3 and D were taken in World Celebration; Pix 4 and B were taken in World Showcase

PAGE 145—Marvelous Muppets
Row 1: Lips, Janice, Dr. Teeth, Animal, Zoot, Floyd Pepper
Row 2: Rowlf the Dog, Scooter, Swedish Chef, Dr. Bunsen Honeydew and Beaker
Row 3: Fozzie Bear, Miss Piggy, Kermit the Frog, Camilla the Chicken and Gonzo
Row 4: Nicky Napoleon, Mahna Mahna and the Snowths, Waldorf and Statler, Sweetums
PAGE 149—Aurebesh Decoder Nien Nunb
PAGE 151—Mini Quiz Slinkety
PAGE 159—Villain Vanity Plates
Captain Hook = H8-PAN (Hate Pan); Cruella de Vil = FURFAN (Fur fan); Evil Queen = FAIREST1 (Fairest one); Hades = HOTHEAD (Hothead); Lady Tremaine = NOBLL4U (No ball for you); Maleficent = SPINWME (Spin with me); Mother Gothel = INOBEST (I know best); Queen of Hearts = HEDZOFF (Heads off); Ursula = C-WITCH (Sea witch); Zurg = EMPR-Z (Emperor Z)
PAGE 163—This Land is That Land
Pix 1 and C were taken in Star Wars: Galaxy's Edge; Pix 2 and A were taken in Hollywood Boulevard; Pix 3 and D were taken in Grand Avenue; Pix 4 and B were taken in Echo Lake

PAGE 173—Species Traits
Na'vi are about <u>ten</u> feet tall with <u>blue</u> skin & a flat, cat-like <u>nose</u>. They have <u>four</u> digits per hand, opposable <u>toes</u> & a <u>tail</u> with a tuft at the end!
PAGE 175—Mini Quiz Rookery
PAGE 181—Birds of a Feather
(1) *Aladdin,* 1992 (2) *The Lion King,* 1994 (3) *Pocahontas,* 1995
(4) *Up,* 2009 (5) *Moana,* 2016 (6) *Encanto,* 2021
PAGE 185—Mythical Quest
Alebrije = *Coco;* Dragon = *Mulan;* Fairy = *Peter Pan;* Genie = *Aladdin;* Satyr = *Hercules;* Yeti = *Monsters, Inc.*
PAGE 191—This Land is That Land
Pix 1 and C were taken in Pandora; Pix 2 and D were taken in Asia; Pix 3 and A were taken in Discovery Island; Pix 4 and B were taken in Africa

PAGE 201—Pop Quiz
(1) The Electrical Water Pageant (2) Rope Drop (3) The Dapper Dans (4) Teddi Barra (5) Walt the Dreamer (6) Shishi-odoshi (7) Chuuby (8) 8D-J8 (9) Joe Rohde (10) Anandapur

More Fun from GOING TO GUIDES

It all started with the guidebooks and now the wonderful world of GTG has expanded to include a website with a Blog and a Fan Club page with freebies like "This Just In" printable bookmarks. PLUS, there's an Etsy shop filled with goodies like bandanas, buttons, digital downloads, patches, postcards, stickers & even a card game!

- www.GoingToGuides.com
- www.GoingToGuides.Etsy.com

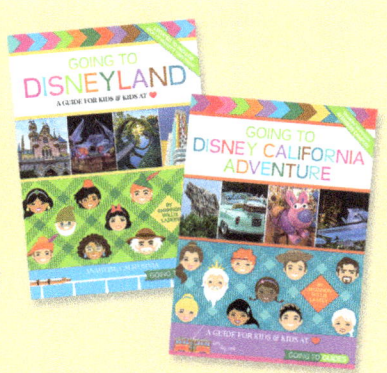

Don't miss these guides for California's Disneyland Resort!

Index

● = Walt Disney's World ● = EPCOT
● = Planning to Have Fun ● = Disney's Hollywood Studios
● = Magic Kingdom ● = Disney's Animal Kingdom

■ **ATTRACTIONS & DESTINATIONS**

- A Frozen Sing-Along Celebration (For the First Time in Forever), pg. 138
- A Pirate's Adventure—Treasures of the Seven Seas, pg. 83
- Advance Training Lab, pg. 110
- Affection Section, pg. 180
- Alien Swirling Saucers, pg. 150
- Astro Orbiter, pg. 69
- Avatar Flight of Passage, pg. 174
- Awesome Planet, pg. 102
- Beauty and the Beast—Live on Stage, pg. 157
- Beauty and the Beast Sing-Along, pg. 118
- Bibbidi Bobbidi Boutique, pg. 47
- Big Thunder Mountain Railroad, pg. 90
- Buzz Lightyear's Space Ranger Spin, pg. 71
- Canada Far and Wide, pg. 114
- Casey Jr. Splash 'n' Soak Station, pg. 59
- Cinderella Castle, pg. 46
- Conservation Station, pg. 180
- Country Bear Musical Jamboree, pg. 85
- DINOSAUR, pg. 188
- Discovery Island Trails, pg. 169
- Disney & Pixar Short Film Festival, pg. 101
- Disney Junior Play and Dance, pg. 156
- Dumbo the Flying Elephant, pg. 58
- Enchanted Tales with Belle, pg. 54
- Expedition Everest, pg. 184
- Fantasmic, pg. 161
- Feathered Friends in Flight, pg. 181
- Festival of the Lion King, pg. 176
- Finding Nemo: The Big Blue...and Beyond, pg. 186
- Fire Station, pg. 40
- Gorilla Falls Exploration Trail, pg. 179
- Gran Fiesta Tour, pg. 128
- Guardians of the Galaxy: Cosmic Rewind, pg. 108
- Harmony Barber Shop, pg. 41
- Haunted Mansion, pg. 76
- ImageWorks—The "What If" Labs, pg. 100
- Impressions de France, pg. 118
- Indiana Jones Epic Stunt Spectacular, pg. 140
- It's a Small World, pg. 52
- It's Tough to Be a Bug, pg. 170
- Journey Into Imagination With Figment, pg. 100
- Journey of Water, pg. 105
- Jungle Cruise, pg. 80
- Kali River Rapids, pg. 183
- Kidcot Fun Stops, pg. 112
- Kilimanjaro Safaris, pg. 178
- Liberty Square Riverboat, pg. 75
- Mad Tea Party, pg. 60
- Maharajah Jungle Trek, pg. 182
- Main Street Vehicles, pg. 43
- Mickey's PhilharMagic, pg. 49
- Mickey & Minnie's Runaway Railway, pg. 137
- Millennium Falcon: Smugglers Run, pg. 148
- Mission: SPACE, pg. 110
- Monsters, Inc. Laugh Floor, pg. 72
- Morocco Pavilion Medina, pg. 119
- Muppet Vision 3D, pg. 144
- Palais du Cinema, pg. 118
- Peter Pan's Flight, pg. 50
- Prince Charming Regal Carrousel, pg. 48
- Project Tomorrow, pg. 98
- Na'vi River Journey, pg. 172
- PeopleMover (Tomorrowland Transit Authority), pg. 68
- Pirates of the Caribbean, pg. 82
- Rafiki's Planet Watch, pg. 180
- Reflections of China, pg. 125
- Remy's Ratatouille Adventure, pg. 116
- Rock 'n' Roller Coaster, pg. 158
- SeaBase, pg. 106
- Seven Dwarfs Mine Train, pg. 62
- Slinky Dog Dash, pg. 151
- Soarin' Around the World, pg. 103
- Space Mountain, pg. 66
- Spaceship Earth, pg. 98
- Star Tours, pg. 142
- Star Wars Launch Bay, pg. 155
- Star Wars: Rise of the Resistance, pg. 146
- Swiss Family Treehouse, pg. 78
- Tangled Rest Area, pg. 53
- Tiana's Bayou Adventure, pg. 88
- Test Track, pg. 111
- The American Adventure, pg. 121
- The Animation Experience, pg. 180
- The Barnstormer, pg. 59
- The Boneyard, pg. 189
- The Hall of Presidents, pg. 74
- The Little Mermaid (stage show), pg. 155
- The Magic Carpets of Aladdin, pg. 79
- The Many Adventures of Winnie the Pooh, pg. 61
- The Oasis Exhibits, pg. 168
- The Outpost, pg. 130
- The Seas with Nemo & Friends, pg. 106
- The Twilight Zone Tower of Terror, pg. 160
- Tom Sawyer Island, pg. 87
- Tomorrowland Speedway, pg. 64
- Toy Story Mania, pg. 152
- Tree of Life, pg. 170
- TriceraTop Spin, pg. 187
- TRON Lightcycle Run, pg. 65
- Turtle Talk with Crush, pg. 107
- Under the Sea—Journey of The Little Mermaid, pg. 56
- Vacation Fun, pg. 141
- Walt Disney Presents, pg. 154
- Walt Disney's Carousel of Progress, pg. 70
- Walt Disney's Enchanted Tiki Room, pg. 81
- Walt Disney World Railroad, pg. 42
- Wilderness Explorers, pg. 168
- World Showcase Galleries, pg. 118
- World Showcase Gardens, pg. 113

■ FOOD & DRINKS

- 50's Prime Time Café, pg. 139
- ABC Commissary, pg. 143
- Aloha Isle, pg. 81
- Anaheim Produce, pg. 157
- Anandapur Ice Cream Truck, pg. 184
- Auntie Gravity's Galactic Goodies, pg. 67
- Backlot Express, pg. 141
- Baseline Tap House, pg. 144
- Be Our Guest, pg. 55
- Biergarten, pg. 124
- Block & Hans, pg. 121
- Caravan Road, pg. 182
- Casey's Corner, pg. 44
- Catalina Eddie's, pg. 157
- Chefs de France, pg. 117
- Cheshire Café, pg. 60
- Choza de Margarita, pg. 129
- Cinderella's Royal Table, pg. 47
- Columbia Harbour House, pg. 77
- Connections Café, pg. 99
- Connections Eatery, pg. 99
- Coral Reef, pg. 106
- Cosmic Ray's Starlight Café, pg. 64
- Creature Comforts, pg. 171
- Crêpes À Emporter, pg. 117
- Dawa Bar, pg. 177
- Dino-Bite Snacks, pg. 189
- Dinosaur Gertie's Ice Cream of Extinction, pg. 139
- Docking Bay 7 Food & Cargo, pg. 147
- Dockside Diner, pg. 139
- Drinkwallah, pg. 182
- Eight Spoon Café, pg. 171
- Epic Eats, pg. 141
- Energy Bytes, pg. 64
- Fairfax Faire, pg. 157
- Fife & Drum Tavern, pg. 121
- Flame Tree Barbecue, pg. 171
- Funnel Cake, pg. 121
- Garden Grill, pg. 103
- Gaston's Tavern, pg. 55
- Gelateria Toscana, pg. 123
- Golden Oak Outpost, pg. 86
- Harambe Fruit Market, pg. 177
- Harambe Market, pg. 179
- Hollywood & Vine, pg. 139
- Hollywood Scoops, pg. 157
- Ice Cold Hydraulics, pg. 144
- Isle of Java, pg. 171
- Kabuki Café, pg. 120
- Karamell-Küche, pg. 124
- Kat Saka's Kettle, pg. 147
- Katsura Grill, pg. 120
- KRNR The Rock Station, pg. 159
- Kusafiri Coffee Shop, pg. 177
- La Cantina de San Angel, pg. 129
- La Cava del Tequila, pg. 129
- La Crêperie de Paris, pg. 117
- La Hacienda de San Angel, pg. 129
- L'Artisan des Glaces, pg. 117
- Le Cellier Steakhouse, pg. 114
- Les Halles Boulangerie & Patisserie, pg. 117
- Les Vins de Chefs de France, pg. 117
- Liberty Square Market, pg. 75
- Liberty Tree Tavern, pg. 75
- Lotus Blossom, pg. 125
- Mahindi, pg. 177
- Main Street Bakery, pg. 44
- Mama Melrose's, pg. 145
- Milk Stand, pg. 149
- Monsieur Paul, pg. 117
- Mr. Kamal's, pg. 182
- Neighborhood Bakery, pg. 153
- Nine Dragons, pg. 125
- Nomad Lounge, pg. 171
- Oasis Sweets & Sips, pg. 119
- Oga's Cantina, pg. 149
- Pecos Bill Tall Tale Inn and Café, pg. 86
- Pinocchio Village Haus, pg. 53
- Pizza al Taglio, pg. 123
- Pizzafari, pg. 171
- PizzeRizzo, pg. 145
- Plaza Ice Cream Parlor, pg. 44
- Pongu Pongu, pg. 175
- Prince Eric Village Market, pg. 57
- Rainforest Café, pg. 168
- Refreshment Outpost, pg. 130
- Refreshment Station, pg. 111
- Regal Eagle Smokehouse, pg. 121
- Restaurantosaurus, pg. 189
- Ronto Roasters, pg. 147
- Rose & Crown Dining Room, pg. 115
- Rose & Crown Pub, pg. 115
- Rosie's All-American Café, pg. 157
- Roundup Rodeo BBQ, pg. 152
- Royal Anandapur Tea Co., pg 182
- San Angel Inn, pg. 129
- Satu'li Canteen, pg. 175
- Sci-Fi Dine-In Theater, pg. 143
- Shiki-Sai: Sushi Izakaya, pg. 120
- Skipper Canteen (Jungle Navigation Co. LTD), pg. 78
- Sleepy Hollow, pg. 74
- Sommerfest, pg. 124
- Space 220, pg. 111
- Spice Road Table, pg. 119
- Spice Road Table Bar, pg. 119
- Storybook Treats, pg. 63
- Sunset Ranch Market, pg. 157
- Sunshine Seasons, pg. 104
- Sunshine Tree Terrace, pg. 78
- Takumi-Tei, pg. 120
- Tamu Tamu Refreshments, pg. 177
- Tangierine Café, pg. 119
- Teppan Edo, pg. 120
- Terra Treats, pg. 171
- The Crystal Palace, pg. 45
- The Diamond Horseshoe, pg. 75
- The Friar's Nook, pg. 63
- The Hollywood Brown Derby, pg. 136
- The Lunching Pad, pg. 68
- The Odyssey, pg. 111
- The Plaza, pg. 45
- The Smiling Crocodile, pg. 171

CONTINUES ON THE NEXT PAGE...

...CONTINUED FROM THE PREVIOUS PAGE

- The Trolley Car Café, pg. 136
- Thirsty River Bar & Trek Snacks, pg. 184
- Tiffins, pg. 171
- Tomorrowland Terrace, pg. 73
- Tony's Town Square Restaurant, pg. 41
- Tortuga Tavern, pg. 82
- Trilo-Bites, pg. 189
- Tune-In Lounge, pg. 139
- Tusker House, pg. 177
- Tutto Gusto, pg. 123
- Tutto Italia, pg. 123
- Via Napoli, pg. 123
- Warung Outpost, pg. 182
- Westward Ho, pg. 86
- Woody's Lunch Box, pg. 151
- Yak & Yeti Local Food Cafés, pg. 182
- Yak & Yeti Quality Beverages, pg. 182
- Yak & Yeti Restaurant, pg. 182
- Yorkshire County Fish Shop, pg. 115

■ GAMES & ACTIVITIES
- A Home Away from Home, pg. 21
- Animal Roll Call, pg. 190
- Antiquated Lingo, pg. 70
- Birds of a Feather, pg. 181
- Color Connections, pg. 101
- Coin a Phrase, pg. 91
- Decoders, pg. 76, 149
- Guess the Goner, pg. 23
- Happiness Worldwide, pg. 19
- In Walt's Footsteps, pg. 15
- Lands in Brief, pg. 37, 95, 133, 165
- Marine Life Roll Call, pg. 107
- Marvelous Muppets, pg. 145
- Melody Time, pg. 86
- Mini Quiz, pg. 19, 35, 45, 72, 81, 103, 115, 151, 175
- Mythical Quest, pg. 185
- Name That Locomotive, pg. 42
- Park Bag Match-Up, pg. 29
- Place Settings, pg. 123
- Rank Your Options, pg. 25
- Rock On, pg. 105
- Say What, pg. 31, 73
- Species Traits, pg. 173
- Talk Like an Astronaut, pg. 67
- This Land is That Land, pg. 93, 131, 163, 191
- Titles of Nobility, pg. 63
- Vehicle Challenge, pg. 43
- Villain Vanity Plates, pg. 159
- Waiting Games, pg. 208
- Who Plays What, pg. 49

■ MAPS AND CHARTS AT A GLANCE
- Disney's Animal Kingdom, pg. 165, 166-167
- Disney's Hollywood Studios, pg. 133, 134-135
- EPCOT, pg. 95, 96-97
- Magic Kingdom, pg. 37, 38-39
- Walt Disney World Resort, pg. 25
- Walt Disney's World, pg. 15

■ MEET N' GREETS
- Disney's Animal Kingdom, pg. 168, 171, 187
- Disney's Hollywood Studios, pg. 141, 143, 149, 152, 153, 154, 155, 156
- EPCOT, pg. 99, 101, 105, 113, 115, 117, 119, 124, 125, 127, 129
- Magic Kingdom, pg. 41, 50, 57, 59, 60, 61, 63, 71, 79, 83, 85

■ PARK ENTERTAINMENT
- Disney's Animal Kingdom, pg. 169, 171, 177, 181
- Disney's Hollywood Studios, pg. 137, 147, 150
- EPCOT, pg. 99, 113, 114, 115, 119, 120, 121, 123, 124, 129
- Magic Kingdom, pg. 41, 43, 44, 45, 84, 89

■ TIDBITS & INFO
- Accessibility, pg. 29
- Activities Beyond the Theme Parks, pg. 22, 69
- Attractions—General Info, pg. 30
- Character Meet n' Greets—General Info, pg. 32
- Collectible Coins and Medallions, pg. 122
- Disney and Walt Disney World History, pg. 16-19, 154
- Disney Companies and Projects, pg. 102, 143, 179
- Disney Legend Close-Ups, pg. 53, 118, 153, 175
- DuckTales World Showcase Adventure, pg. 113
- Entertainment—General Info, pg. 33
- EPCOT Festivals, pg. 109
- Extinct Attractions, pg. 23
- Food and Drinks—General Info, pg. 34
- Helpful Spots, pg. 35
- Hotel Info, pg. 21, 22, 27
- Imagineers at Play, pg. 83, 87, 91, 111, 155, 159, 162, 170, 187
- Key to the World, pg. 26
- Lightning Lanes, pg. 31
- MagicBand+, pg. 26
- MagicMobile, pg. 26
- Main Street Window Honors, pg. 44
- Mouse Ear Hats, pg. 92
- Pandora Basics, pg. 173
- PhotoPass, pg. 32
- Rider Switch, pg. 30
- Rope Drop, pg. 30
- Shopping—General Info, pg. 35
- Show Biz Terms, pg. 141
- Single Rider, pg. 30
- Ticket Sources and Types, pg. 27
- Transportation, pg. 28
- Seasonal Events, pg. 33
- Security Tips, pg. 29
- Tours, pg. 33
- Virtual Queue, pg. 30
- Walt Disney Archives, pg. 189
- Walt Disney World Resort App and Website, pg. 26

Contributor Credits

Throughout this book, art and photos without a credit are by author Shannon W. Laskey. Illustrations and photographs with a credit are courtesy of Going To Guides Contributing Artists. Many of these images are available for purchase as art prints or on other products. Support your favorite artists and check out more of their amazing art on their websites! *NOTE: All images are the property of their respective owners.*

Aaron Albarran
See page 126
www.manandthemouse.com

Morgane Barret
See pages 138 and 155
www.morganebrretshop.com

Chris Buchholz
See pages 20, 28, 31, 35, 43, 44, 46, 64, 65, 66, 69, 77, 103, 106, 179, 183 and 188
www.etsy.com/shop/buchworks

Sam Carter
See page 23
www.samcarterart.com

Dave DeCaro
See pages 17, 47, 75 and 80
www.davelandweb.com

Fiona Joy Dulieu
See pages 7, 61, 72 and 73
www.fionadulieu.com

J. Shari Ewing
See page 91
www.linktr.ee/jshariewing

Lindsay Gibson
See pages 33, 62, 81, 95, 111, 133, 142, 150, 177 and 199
www.emandsprout.com

Danamarie Hosler
See pages 2 and 79
www.danamariehosler.com

Mariana Koontz
See pages 15, 16, 27, 85, 115, 121, 128 and 146
www.landandworld.com

Lauren Kurtz
See page 86
www.coppertopink.com

Rosa C. Lopez
See pages 153 and 186
www.rosaclopez.wordpress.com/hello

Christopher Michon
See pages 63 and 170
https://failedimagineer.com

Sara Newman
See page 27
www.instagram.com/artofsaranewman

Kristen O'Dell
See page 71

Mary Pavlou
See pages 54, 56, 57, 64, 89, 100, 145 and 161
www.etsy.com/shop/marebearpress

Lisa Penney
See pages 6 and 81
www.lisapenney.com

Eva Sowinski
See pages 165 and 184
www.critterosityshop.com

Melissa Chan Stone
See pages 60, 92, 99, 113, 119, 125 and 157
www.amuseboosh.com

Kirsten Ulve
See pages 5, 30 and 155
www.kirstenulve.com

Heather Dixon Wallwork
See page 77
www.instagram.com/story_monster

Megan Woods
See pages 74 and 178
www.etsy.com/shop/popcutouts

My first visit to Walt Disney World!

💗 Heartfelt Thanks 💗

Creating this book was a major undertaking and I have many people to recognize! First I'd like to thank the artists above for allowing their wonderful creations to be included in these pages. I love the mix of art styles inside Going To Guides books and that's all due to them! Thank you to *The Twilight Zone* expert Jaime Fox, as well as Julia Gautho, Mariana Hernández, Nora Kennedy, Katie Kronbauer (eh?), Barbara Magaña, Jessica Pon and Rae-Anna Stz for helping with questions relating to the countries in World Showcase. Special thanks to the two best travel agents and Instagram content creators you're ever going to find: EJ Cruz @society_1955 and Steven Clark @dintroverts. I'm so thankful Steven was able to see an advance version of this book and give me some great tips! I always have to thank my dear friend Elizabeth "Bête-bête" Cross—who took me on my first visit to Walt Disney World in the 1990s—and my fun-loving Parks pals Stacie "The Dancing Queen" Smith and Debby "Dee Dee" Weinstein. My trusty assistant Dee Dee really gets the gold medal for being brave enough (or foolish enough?) to accompany me on my latest Research Expedition to Walt Disney World. Going to Florida in August is not for the faint of heart! Major appreciation goes to my wonderful publisher Orchard Hill Press. It's hard to believe they published the first Going To Guide almost TEN YEARS ago! I can't begin to express my thanks to my genius editor Hugh Allison. His attention to detail is unbelievable and I'm beyond grateful for his many brilliant ideas and contributions. Last but never least, I'd like to thank my family including my beloved parents, sloth-like (ha ha) niece Ivy, helpful husband, hilarious son Ed and sweet son Clark. I'm ever so grateful to you all. xoxo,

Shannon

Waiting Games!

If you've got some extra moments on your hands, play the games below. Time flies when you're having fun!

ALPHABET PAIRS
One player chooses a letter. For example, if they choose the letter M, they would start the game by saying a word that starts with A and a word that goes with it that starts with M, like "Action Movie." Now the next player says two words using B and M, like "Brave Merida." The game continues through the alphabet, leaving the letters X and Z out of the game. If a player is stumped, they are out. Whoever can say the last word combo wins.

FINISH THAT LYRIC
One player says the first part of a song lyric and the other players must compete to be the first to finish it. For example, the first person might say "Like everybody else…" And then one of the other players would say "…I've got a dream!" If the other players are stumped, the first player can sing the lyric, which may help the others to recognize it. Whoever guesses correctly gets to present the next lyric.

SILLY TALK
In this game, two players try to be the first to sneak a secret, silly phrase into their conversation together. Without the players hearing, the rest of the group comes up with a different sentence for each of them and whispers it to them. For example, one might be "I hope we get to see Goofy rollerskating in the air while we're here!" and the other could be "That's why I think popcorn should always be purple!" Once the players know their phrases, they start chatting. Either player can stop the chat if they think the other player has said their secret phrase. But if they guess wrong, they're out. If a player says their sentence without the other one noticing, and the conversation continues—they are the winner.

WHO AM I
One player per round is the guesser and the other players decide which character that person is. Now the guesser asks yes or no questions about themselves like "Am I a duck?" or "Do I have a bad temper?" until they can figure out who they are.

WORDS IN A MINUTE
This game is played as a group. Choose a common letter and see how many words you can all name in one minute that begin with it. Choose one person to time the round and another to keep track of how many words are said. Speaking one a time, the first player will say a word, then the next and so on. It may be easier to keep track of whose turn it is if you form a circle. If someone is stumped they can say "Skip me!" For more of a challenge, come up with a category first—like types of animals, candy or movie titles.

www.ingramcontent.com/pod-product-compliance
Lightning Source LLC
Chambersburg PA
CBHW040311240426
43666CB00022B/2927